D1191900

RECONSTRUCTING
THE RHYTHM OF
Beowulf

Robert Payson Creed

RECONSTRUCTING
THE RHYTHM OF
Beowulf

UNIVERSITY OF MISSOURI PRESS

COLUMBIA AND LONDON

Copyright © 1990 by
The Curators of the University of Missouri
University of Missouri Press, Columbia, Missouri 65211
Printed and bound in the United States of America
5 4 3 2 1   94 93 92 91 90

Library of Congress Cataloging-in-Publication Data
Creed, Robert P.
    Reconstructing the rhythm of Beowulf / Robert Payson Creed.
        p.   cm.
    ISBN 0–8262–0722–7 (alk. paper)
        1. Beowulf—Versification.   2. English language—Old English, ca.
    450–1100—Rhythm.   I. Title.
    PR1588.C7   1990
    829'.3—dc20   89–29252
                                                              CIP

⊗ This paper meets the requirements of the
American National Standard for Permanence of Paper
for Printed Library Materials, Z39.48, 1984.

Designer: Liz Fett
Typesetter: Graphic Composition, Inc.
Printer: Thomson-Shore, Inc.
Binder: Thomson-Shore, Inc.
Type face: Palatino

For Catherine Hilton
min rúnpita   7 *min rædbora*
eaxlʒestealla . . .

Contents

Acknowledgments

It is a pleasant task to thank the institutions that have supported the research and writing of this book. The John Simon Guggenheim Foundation supported what turned out to be the first of many years of work with a generous fellowship in 1962–1963. For several months in the middle of 1976 I held a fellowship at Edinburgh University's Institute for Advanced Study in the Humanities where I sketched what was to become Chapter 3. During the summer of 1978 I was the recipient of a Grant-in-Aid from the American Council of Learned Societies. Brown University granted me a sabbatical leave in 1962–1963; the University of Massachusetts/Amherst granted me a sabbatical in 1975–1976 and again in 1982–1983, when I completed an earlier version of the book. Finally, I am grateful to the institution of tenure, first granted to me by Brown, then by the State University of New York at Stony Brook, then by the University of Massachusetts. When Brown granted me tenure in 1961 I saw it as an opportunity to devote myself to a long-term project. Without such generous indications of trust from three universities I might have been tempted to give up long before complexity began to resolve itself into simplicity.

It is an even pleasanter but also a far more difficult task to thank the people who have helped me over the many years of the work. It is difficult because I am not sure that I can summon up the names of all the colleagues, students, friends, and associates who have argued (and sometimes agreed) with me, discussed their ideas with me or offered a platform from which I could present my ideas to a wider audience, listened to or read chapters or would-be chapters and even one of the three versions of the whole book. I will do my best. I apologize for any and all omissions. Not one is intentional.

I thank first of all the late Francis Peabody Magoun, Jr., and Jess B.

Bessinger, Jr., who taught me Old English, and John C. Pope for his *The Rhythm of Beowulf*. I thank my students—undergraduate as well as graduate—at Smith College, Brown University, Stony Brook, and the University of Massachusetts/Amherst; the names of some of them will appear in the following list of colleagues, students, friends, and associates (*not* mutually exclusive categories). These are some of those who have helped in one way or another, sometimes without being aware that they were contributing to a life's work: Warren D. Anderson, Karen Assunto, Emmon Bach, Cynthia Balcom, William Beattie, Michael Benskin, Jay Blair, Victor Bowman, Rupert Bruce-Mitford, Elliott van Kirk Dobbie, John H. Fisher, John Miles Foley, Nelson Francis, Don Freeman, Margaret Freeman, Don Fry, Barbara K. Halpern, William Hamrick, Jim Harper, Bob Hosmer, Kim Houston, Ted Irving, Neil Isaacs, Louis Leiter, David Lenson, Albert B. Lord, Charles Moran, Pierre Monnin, George Monteiro, Jane Morrissey, Tauno Mustanoja, Joseph Nagy, John Newfield, Wayne O'Neil, Les Perelman, Charles Potter, Robert Pratt, Burton Raffel, Neal Raisman, Aileen Raisman, David Rapkin, Mary Remnant, Alain Renoir, Rick Russom, Richard Senghas, Hedi Sioud, Margaret Swift, Wade Tarzia, Paul B. Taylor, Freeman Twaddell, Jimmy Thorne, D. J. Tittensor, Olaf von Felitzen, Louise Zak. . . . Joanne Pratt kept me honest when I was tempted to see in the facsimiles of Cotton Vitellius A. xv what I wanted to see.

I owe a great debt to Dorothy Eckert Grannis, who turned my procedures for lineating and half-lining into computer programs, thus providing a test for my hypothesis that John Mitchell Kemble had determined his verses by using a method. Sometime after I accepted her generous offer—an offer that tested the limits of Fortran in the late seventies—I realized that the study could be far more rigorous because of her brilliant programming.

There are some very special debts I have saved for this point. I am very grateful to Edward E. Creed, Blanche H. Creed, and Mary Louise Milam Creed, to Lisa and Rob Creed, and to Eliza Grannis.

I do not think I can adequately express my debt to John Mitchell Kemble. At the very least, I can perhaps remind readers of *Beowulf* that we all owe far more to his genius than most scholars have realized. Without his two editions of *Beowulf*, the struggle to produce a text that would gain wide acceptance would undoubtedly have taken longer. Kemble's monument is every edition of the poem made during the last century and a half.

Rick Boland guided the book to acceptance by the University of Missouri Press and has helped prepare the manuscript for publication. Jane Lago took on the huge job of copyediting the manuscript and seeing it through publication. I am deeply grateful to them and to Susan M. Denny, the Interim Director of the Press at the time the book was accepted.

The form of this book owes much to Dan Dixon, who advised me to cut drastically a gigantic earlier version. Readers should be as grateful as I am to Catherine Hilton for showing me at every point how to follow Dan's good advice.

Catherine has done far more. She has read or listened to every sentence of the present version of the work. She has made useful suggestions for many a sentence and sketched out ways to improve many parts. I take full responsibility for what remains but not all of the credit.

RECONSTRUCTING THE RHYTHM OF
Beowulf

Prologue

This study presents evidence that the prosody that can be reconstructed from the surviving text of *Beowulf* is one of the best prosodies that any society has ever devised. It may seem remarkable to modern readers that those who devised this prosody—speakers of early Germanic during the period from about 2000 B.C. to A.D. 600 —were unlettered. But what modern readers think of as a disadvantage was instead a tremendous advantage: the speakers who shaped the early Germanic oral tradition shaped it from resources that they understood better than we—sound-patterning and rhythm. These mnemonic devices made it possible for them to keep track of information without the aid of writing. At the same time they were also shaping something that bound them to each other and supported and sustained the whole community. What they did deserves to be ranked as one of the greatest achievements of prehistory.

It has not been possible to value Beowulfian prosody so highly until now. Its secrets have been locked up for nearly a thousand years, ever since the Old English language began to change into Middle English. For a few brief years the key was in the hands of John Mitchell Kemble, who, during the 1830s, used it to unlock the "verses" from the prose-seeming manuscript lines. But that key disappeared again when prosodists after him mistakenly took these verses as their proper data. What they failed to realize is that Kemble, whose verses form the basis of a well-founded consensus that has lasted for more than 150 years, extracted these verses from the manuscript text by attending to *prosodic* signals.

For example, Eduard Sievers analyzed this verse into two "feet," each of which, he insisted, has to contain a stressed syllable (marked /):

$$\bigg|_{\text{on}} \acute{\underset{\text{ʒear}}{}} \bigg| \acute{\underline{\underset{\text{daʒum}}{}}}$$

Yet this verse actually consists of two *measures*:

$$\bigg|_{\text{on}} \bigg|_{\text{ʒear}} \acute{\underset{}{}} \acute{\underline{\underset{\text{daʒum}}{}}}$$

It was from these two segments that Kemble had to reconstruct this halfline. Kemble could only extract the whole verse line of which this halfline forms the second "verse" by noting that *ʒear* completes the sound pattern begun by the *GAR* of the first verse. Yet Sievers and his followers have carried the day, and one prosodist after another looks no farther than the verse lines and halflines set out in modern editions of the great poem.

It would seem that someone would think of going back to the manuscript. Yet I confess it took me about a dozen years to realize that was what I had to do. And when, more than a dozen years ago, I began to try to figure out how to extract metrical units from manuscript lines, I faced formidable obstacles. What every other prosodist takes for granted, I had to question.

In my search for a solid foundation on which to build an acceptable prosody, I was forced to go back to what the scribes had written in the manuscript. They had, I hypothesized, recorded the *syllables* spoken by the poet. Once I satisfied myself that the scribes had carried out their task very ably, I had to ask what information each of these syllables carries. Then I had to devise and justify a new way of dealing with stress, with initial sound linkage ("alliteration"), with phrase and clause boundaries, and so on. Even after I had reconstructed and tested the method Kemble used to elicit verse lines from manuscript lines and halflines from verse lines, I faced an even more formidable obstacle: how to divide acceptably into measures certain verses that Sievers and others had had no trouble assigning to his "Type A."

The solution to this problem turned out to lie in comparing metrical units of the same kind, that is, comparing verse lines with verse lines, halflines with halflines, measures with measures. (In the halfline quoted above, *on* represents the verbal part of the first measure; *ʒeardaʒum* is the second measure.) But that method turned out to be far more powerful than I first imagined. In order to compare constituents with constituents—verse lines with verse lines, halflines with halflines, measures with measures—I had to build a grid. With the grid I found a way to verify a hypothesis that remains only a tantalizing insight in the work of my most important predecessor, John C. Pope. This is the hypothesis that certain parts of certain measures are created not by speech but by silence (more accurately, timed pauses) or by the sound of the accompanying instrument. The grid made it possible to demonstrate that every measure consists of two "Parts." In certain environments, one Part—and precisely one Part—may be empty of syllables and hence indicate the length of the pause.

Because Part 1 of most measures contains a stressed *syllable*, I could argue that Part 1 of every measure indicates a heavy downbeat. Part 2 completes the pulse by indicating the lighter upbeat.[1] That is the rhythm of *Beowulf*. It is the simplest of rhythms. Yet, because it governs Parts that can contain one syllable, or two syllables, or three syllables—or none—it is extraordinarily powerful. It can encode and transmit an almost limitless number of messages.

But there are limits, and it is these very limits that make the prosody such an astonishing achievement. Since every verse line is built around two syllables linked by their initial sound, and since the tradition recognized only nineteen different initial sounds, this sound-patterning sets certain limits on what the prosody can express. At the same time the syllables that create and control syntactic relationships, such as prepositions, case- and verb-endings, conjunctions, and so on make it possible to use the same sound-linked stressed syllables in different syntactic situations, to build different verse lines around them.

That is the secret of this great traditional prosody. For example, a poet who knew that DOOM (*dom*, the judgment of the tradition as to the value of what one DOES) should come before DEATH (*deaþ*) knew these sound-linked syllables (*dom/deaþ*) as a structure. I have elsewhere called these pairs "Ideal Structures," because they convey the ideals of the society.[2] Since he built several different verse lines around the structure DOOM/DEATH (five in *Beowulf*), it is clear that

---

1. In the exemplar halfline, Part 1 of the second measure is the stressed syllable ʒear, Part 2 of the first measure is *on*, and Part 1 of this first measure contains no syllable.
2. "*Beowulf* on the Brink: Information Theory as Key to the Origins of the Poem," in *Comparative Research on Oral Traditions: A Memorial for Milman Parry*, edited by John Miles Foley (Columbus, Ohio: Slavica Publishers, 1987), 139–60.

in some sense the *Beowulf*-poet understood that it is the structure that generates these different verse lines. And, since the etymologist can trace far back into the past the roots of the pair of words whose stem syllables form the structure, it is likely that speakers created this structure and others many generations before the prosody as we know it crystallized around them. So it appears that the prosody that survives in *Beowulf* took its shape over many, many generations, after prehistoric speakers of Germanic had found that sound-patterning, because of its memorability, preserves information.

But what is perhaps most beautiful about this prosody is the way in which it mimes the production of speech in the brain.[3] The syllables of the Ideal Structures—and, indeed, all semantically weighty syllables—seem to require for their production an intact Wernicke's area, located on the borders of the parietal and temporal lobes of the human cortex. The syllables that create syntactic relationships appear to be produced by an area in the prefrontal lobe, Broca's area. The poets of the Germanic tradition generally disposed Wernicke's syllables in Part 1 of the measure and Broca's syllables in Part 2. Did they do so because they had inherited a prosodic tradition that had, over the course of perhaps hundreds of generations, helped shape or tune human verbal memory?

More than a quarter of a century ago, when I began my study of Beowulfian prosody, I had no idea that this prosody would turn out to be something as wonderful as a time machine. In the following pages I show how this time machine works.

3. See my "A Student of Oral Traditions Looks at the Origins of Language," in *Studies in Language Origins*, ed. Jan Wind et al. (Amsterdam and Philadelphia: John Benjamins, 1989), 43–52.

Chapter 1

Two Hypotheses

INTRODUCTION

This study attempts to reconstruct the prosody of *Beowulf*. It begins where no other Beowulfian prosody begins—with the syllables
of the poem as they can be reproduced audibly or subvocally from the
signs written by the two scribes of the manuscript.[1] The study goes
farther than any other—to the smallest (not previously identified)
prosodic unit of the poem—and in an orderly way.

Beginning with the manuscript text of *Beowulf*, I first show that it
is possible to construct a working definition of the largest prosodic
unit of the poem, the verse line, and to test that definition by eliciting
verse lines systematically from the syllables as they are indicated in
the text.[2] Next, I show that the verse line divides into two *halflines* (the
so-called "verses"). Then I show that each halfline consists of what I

---

1. The text of the poem used throughout this study has been constructed from
three sources: (1) the photographic plates in *Beowulf . . . in Facsimile*, transliteration
and notes by Julius Zupitza; 2d ed., intro. by Norman Davis, Early English Text Society
(London: Oxford University Press, 1959); (2) photographic plates 1–90 only ("Thorkelin
A") in *The Thorkelin Transcripts of Beowulf in Facsimile*, ed. Kemp Malone, Early English
Manuscripts in Facsimile (Copenhagen: Rosenkilde and Bagger, 1951); (3) a few read-
ings from Humphrey Wanley's transcription of what are now verse lines 1–19 and 53–
73 in *Antiquae Literaturae Septentrionalis Liber Alter . . . Catalogus Historico-Criticus* (Oxford, 1705), 218–19; I have used the second and third sources only where material is
missing from or obscured in the plates of the 1959 edition. Material taken from the
second and third sources always appears in square brackets. The text I use is thus
extremely conservative.

2. Curiously, students of Old English prosody generally avoid attempting to define
the larger units of that poetry and focus instead on the "feet" or "measures" of the
verse. Geoffrey R. Russom's *Old English Meter and Linguistic Theory* (Cambridge: Cambridge University Press, 1987), is an exception; but even Russom is content to accept
the verses as set out in modern editions, verses that he says are indicated in part by
the punctuation of the scribes. Even if this were true in Cotton Vitellius A. xv, it would
still be necessary to define the units indicated by the punctuation.

first refer to as *halfline constituents* (abbreviated "HCs") but later designate as *measures*, of which there are usually two but occasionally three in a halfline. Finally, I analyze every measure into two *Fine Parts*. The first Part contains a stressed syllable about 80 percent of the time; the second Part far more often than not contains an unstressed syllable or syllables.

The disposition of the syllables into Fine Parts can be accounted for by a simple hypothesis: the two Fine Parts of the measure indicate a *rhythm*. The first Part usually contains the syllable or syllables that mark the heavier downbeat; the second Part contains the syllable or syllables that mark the lighter upbeat. The relationship between the two Parts of the measure indicates the dynamic of the prosody: syllables are clustered together in each Part of the measure to mark the two phases of a rhythm. Two, sometimes three, measures repeat this rhythm in each halfline.

The analysis of the measure into its constituents makes this study more than merely descriptive and static; it indicates at every level the relationships among hierarchically organized constituents. This study differs from previous studies of the prosody of *Beowulf* in another way. It is constructed from hypotheses and sets of hypotheses presented as such, then tested and either verified or discarded. My overarching hypothesis is this: *Beowulf* is unmistakably a poem, not simply "a tidied form of the spoken language, i.e., prose," in Marjorie Daunt's words.[3] That is, each level of the text—verse line, halfline, and so forth—is composed of constituents comparable to all other constituents of the same level. The entire study tests this hypothesis.

My approach will seem unusual because students of Beowulfian prosody are accustomed to dealing in "certainties" rather than hypotheses. Since certainties have a way of being based on assumptions, I have tried at every point to turn mere assumption into testable hypothesis. The assumption that underlies every other study of Beowulfian prosody is this: the prosodist performs his or her operations upon the so-called verses of the poem as they appear in acceptably edited texts. Thus the prosodist can consider each verse in isolation

3. Marjorie Daunt, "Old English Verse and English Speech Rhythm," *Transactions of the Philological Society (London)* (1946): 56–72, rpt. in *Essential Articles for the Study of Old English Poetry*, ed. J. B. Bessinger, Jr., and S. J. Kahrl (Hamden, Conn.: Archon Books, 1968), 289–304. The quotation appears on p. 300 in *Essential Articles*.

from its verse line, that is, apart from the verse with which it is paired by alliteration. As I show in the next section, this assumption has produced confusion.

By contrast, I hypothesize that the prosodist must begin with the syllables of the manuscript text and look for indications of relationships among these syllables. The first indication of a prosodic relationship is the existence of groups of syllables having the same initial sound (alliteration). It is only on the basis of this relationship that the prosodist can extract the verse line and then divide it into two half-lines, or "verses." The "verse" thus emerges as one half of the verse line—a "halfline" in my terminology. The verse cannot be extracted or defined in isolation from its verse line. That is, the verse is not prosodically neutral but is instead the product of the application of prosodic analysis to the next higher level, the verse line. Yet prosodists have heretofore tried to scan the verses of the poem without taking into account the relationship of the verse to the verse line and the derivation of the verse line from the whole text.

PREVIOUS ATTEMPTS TO SCAN *BEOWULF*

There have been many attempts to scan the verses of *Beowulf* and other Old English poems. In 1813, one of the early editors of the poem, John J. Conybeare, suggested that many verses consist of two *feet*, usually trochees.[4] As recently as 1987, Geoffrey Russom published his *Old English Meter and Linguistic Theory.*[5] Between these attempts there have been many more, but only three have so far gained wide acceptance.

The best-known scansion of *Beowulf* is that published in three parts by Eduard Sievers between 1885 and 1905.[6] Sievers found that most of the verses of the poem contain two stressed syllables. After studying the patterns formed by stressed and unstressed syllables in the verses, Sievers was able to divide almost every verse into two "feet" in such a way that every foot contains a stressed syllable. He

---

4. William D. Conybeare, ed., *Illustrations of Anglo-Saxon Poetry* . . . (London, 1826). See pp. v–lvi, esp. ix–xi.

5. See note 2, above.

6. Eduard Sievers, "Zur Rhythmik der germanischen Alliterationsverses," *Beiträge zur Geschichte der deutschen Sprache und Literatur* 10 (1885): 206–314 (I) and 451–545 (II). See also (III) Sievers, "Altgermanische Metrik," in *Grundriss der germanischen Philologie,* ed. Hermann Paul (Strassburg: Karl J. Trübner, 1905), 2:1–38.

found that nearly all the verses of the poem can be grouped into five patterns, or "Types" A through E, depending on the relative placement of the stressed and unstressed syllables.

Sievers's "Five Types" are still the best-known descriptions of Old English verses. His *Metrik* has attracted probably the largest number of disciples. The extent to which Sievers's work has been accepted is indicated not only by his influence on other prosodists but by this 1959 statement by the grammarian A. Campbell: "The evidence for the accentuation of native and foreign words . . . is largely metrical. For the determination of accent the metrical system of Sievers is sufficient."[7] Even the prosodist whose work differs most from his, John Pope, insists that Sievers's *Metrik* is still worthy of serious study.[8]

Sievers did indeed describe and categorize important features of the verses of *Beowulf*. Yet, despite his division of each verse into feet, his *Metrik* offers the speaker of the verse no guidance other than that he or she should stress certain syllables, something that does not require a metrical *system*. If Sievers offers any guidance to the grouping of syllables within the verse—which is, after all, what a *Metrik* should do—it is often to guide the reader to divide words and compounds in awkward ways, as even one of his most ardent supporters has pointed out.[9]

Another avowed follower of Sievers, Thomas Cable, has refined the five verse types into five patterns of "contours of ictus."[10] Unlike Sievers, Cable argues that no foot division within the verse is necessary. Such division would, in fact, get in the way of the "melody" of each verse, the pitches of which are indicated by the relative placement within the verse of "higher pitched" (stressed) and "lower pitched" (unstressed) syllables. Cable does try to offer guidance to the performer of the verse. But his guidance is based on the assumption that each verse is an indivisible unit. As I shall show, about 40 percent of the verses of *Beowulf* are clearly *not* indivisible. This fact suggests

7. A. Campbell, *Old English Grammar* (Oxford: Oxford University Press, 1959), 356.
8. John C. Pope, in his frequently reissued *Seven Old English Poems* (Indianapolis: Bobbs-Merrill, 1966, rpt. 1976), devotes pp. 109–16 to "The Sievers Types."
9. A. J. Bliss, *The Metre of Beowulf*, rev. ed. (Oxford: Blackwell, 1967). See his Table II, pp. 123–24, verse types numbered 1–5 and 8, in which Bliss explicitly rejects Sievers's foot divisions.
10. Thomas Cable, *The Meter and Melody of Beowulf* (Urbana: University of Illinois Press, 1974).

the possibility that every verse can be divided into at least two constituents.

In 1942 John Collins Pope published in a lengthy study titled *The Rhythm of Beowulf* what is perhaps the most interesting prosody of the poem.[11] Unlike Sievers, Pope tries to discover the rhythm that groups certain syllables together to form the two measures of the verse. Pope assigns a precise quantity to each syllable within the measure, using the musical notation of half notes, quarter notes, dotted quarters, triplets, and so on. Pope's analysis does indeed indicate a rhythm. His work shows that it is possible to move within carefully determined temporal patterns from one stressed syllable to the next. Pope's work thus represents the furthest extreme from Sievers's static description of stress patterns.

An important difference between Pope's division of verses into two measures and Sievers's division into two feet is that Pope's divisions tend to keep the two parts of a compound, or a word consisting of a stem and a formative, in the same prosodic unit, which he calls the "measure," whenever the compound or heavy simplex does not occupy the entire verse. In his insistence that every foot must contain a stressed syllable, Sievers is often led to distribute the first element of a compound or the first part of a simplex plus formative in the first foot and the rest of the word or compound in the second whether or not the simplex or compound is the only constituent of the verse.

But Pope's analysis of the rhythm of *Beowulf*, though it has had some success, has not ended the quest for Beowulfian prosody. There are two reasons for its failure to achieve a consensus among scholars. First, it does not adequately support the case for the measure divisions just discussed. Unlike Sievers's "sensible" basis for foot-division—every foot contains at least one stressed syllable—Pope divides many verses in such a way that one measure of a pair might contain not a single stressed syllable. His division raises the question, then, of what defines a measure. What is it in the manuscript text of the poem that allows the prosodist to divide some verses into unequal parts? As I shall show, this question can be answered, even though Pope fails to do so. Pope then compounds the problem of credibility by attempting to complete the lighter measure with a *rest* worth so

---

11. John Collins Pope, *The Rhythm of Beowulf* . . . (New Haven: Yale University Press, 1942).

many notes, a rest that, in this case, takes the place of a stressed syllable. If one is going to argue for rests in *Beowulf* it will be necessary to account for them more persuasively than by such circular reasoning. Again, I shall demonstrate that the precise location and value of each rest can be determined only by comparing measure with measure in the context of the halfline and verse line.

Second, Pope's *Rhythm* gives the reader the sense of being left somewhere in the middle of the analysis. Pope does not attempt to compare different kinds of measures; nor does he categorize them into types. Instead, he is content to sort the verses into 279 different subtypes. He attempts to generalize only by arranging all the verses of the poem according to Sievers's five verse types, even though he divides most of his "Type B and C" verses at very different points from Sievers. One must conclude that Pope considered his work done when he had merely located (though not demonstrated) a measure boundary or boundaries inside the verse. But the bewildering array of possible verse-types in his catalog does not constitute a prosody.

These are three of the major approaches to the prosody of *Beowulf* that compete with each other today. The existence of these and other approaches gives the impression that any reasonable analysis of the verses of the poem is as good as any other.

THE MAKING OF THE CONSENSUS ON VERSES

In contrast to the diversity of approaches to Beowulfian prosody stands the consensus on the verses themselves. What that consensus means is that scholars are in agreement on two points: (1) the poem can be divided into verses, and (2) all, or nearly all, verses are correctly indicated in recent editions of the poem. This consensus is just over 150 years old, since it can be dated to the publication of John Mitchell Kemble's two editions of the poem set out in verses in 1833 and 1835.[12]

Few scholars today realize the importance of Kemble's editions. Fr. Klaeber is the exception. Of the 1835 edition Klaeber writes that it is "scholarly; the first real edition."[13] Despite Klaeber's praise, Kemble's name has been all but forgotten by prosodists of *Beowulf*. Yet, ironi-

---

12. John M. Kemble, ed., *The Anglo-Saxon Poems of Beowulf, The Travellers Song and The Battle of Finnsburh* (London: Wm. Pickering, 1833; 2d ed., 1835).

13. Fr. Klaeber, ed., *Beowulf and the Fight at Finnsburg*, 3d ed. (Boston: D. C. Heath, 1950), cxxvii. Klaeber never saw the 1833 edition.

cally, the verses of *Beowulf* that he more than anyone else worked out survive almost to a verse in every recent edition of the poem. It is these verses that form the basis of every previous approach to the prosody of *Beowulf*. No matter how much each approach differs from the others, every prosodist during the last 150 years has attempted to scan the verses that Kemble largely worked out.

The fact that all prosodists share this common ground should lead one to survey that ground carefully. On the one hand, it may turn out that the verses themselves contain the clue to the puzzling fact that no prosody has even approached the consensus that Kemble's verse lineation has achieved for six generations. On the other hand, it may turn out that Kemble's verses are in some way at fault, despite their widespread and long-lasting acceptance. The verses may be improper units of the text, or they may have been improperly derived.

Even to suggest such possibilities is to raise troubling questions: is it possible to determine the correctness of the verses of *Beowulf*? By what criteria do we judge the acceptability of a verse? These questions have not been satisfactorily addressed during the 150 years of the consensus. Yet until they are answered the consensus will rest on an unexamined foundation.

Before I compare Kemble's work with that of his two major predecessors, however, it is necessary to determine the extent to which the scribes indicate the verses that have formed the basis of the consensus. The reader of the manuscript soon learns that he or she cannot depend on scribal conventions to distinguish one "verse" from another. Punctuation, such as the raised point, occurs infrequently; the scribes do not set off units smaller than the so-called "fitt" with capitals or spacing. If the poet did indeed compose in verses, those verses are not immediately obvious from an examination of the manuscript.

Since many of the now-accepted verses were not obvious to the first editor of the poem, the process of extracting acceptable verses from the manuscript took several generations. The Icelander Grimur J. Thorkelin, who had taken nearly thirty years to edit the manuscript he had had copied and had copied himself in the late 1780s, brought out in 1815 the first complete modern edition of the poem, the first attempt to set out the entire text in verses.[14] Klaeber understandably

---

14. G. J. Thorkelin, *De Danorum rebus gestis secul. III & IV. poema danicum anglosaxonica* (Copenhagen, 1815).

dismisses Thorkelin's work as "of interest chiefly as the 'editio princeps.'"[15]

While Thorkelin was seeing the 'editio princeps' through the press, the English scholar John J. Conybeare was preparing his *Illustrations of Anglo-Saxon Poetry*. That at least is what his brother William titled the collection of John's posthumous papers when he published them in 1826. The "illustration" of *Beowulf* amounts to one-quarter of the poem set out in verses.[16]

Seven years after the publication of the *Illustrations*, the twenty-six-year-old Kemble published the second complete edition of the poem set out in verses. In his preface he had unkind words for both Thorkelin and Conybeare, as well as other earlier scholars. Unfortunately, Kemble neither commented specifically on the verse lineation of the two earlier editions nor explained his own method of determining verses. Many of his verses differ from Thorkelin's and a few differ from Conybeare's. Kemble wrote in his preface as though he thought of himself as an editor who simply cleaned up the mistakes of his predecessors. Anglo-Saxonists since his day have taken him at his word. What is far more important, later editors have silently adopted almost every one of his verses in their editions.

There is something very puzzling about the ease with which Kemble's verse lineation was accepted. Both of his important predecessors make it clear that it is possible to go astray in attempting to elicit the verses of *Beowulf* from the manuscript text. Yet Kemble treats the job as something that requires only common sense or editorial acumen and makes no comment on his method. And no one after Kemble has asked any questions about his method. The verses of *Beowulf* that Kemble extracted from the text in the face of one inadequate and one incomplete attempt to set them out simply appear in all later editions of the poem. The question of verse lineation appears to have been closed.

There seems to be little point in trying to reopen it. Everyone who reads *Beowulf* in an edition such as Klaeber's quickly comes to accept the division of the text into lines (which are sometimes called "verse pairs" and which I call "verse lines"), with each verse line divided

15. Klaeber, *Beowulf*, cxxvii.
16. Conybeare, ed., *Illustrations of Anglo-Saxon Poetry*, 30–167. John Conybeare's text of a total of 1577 "verses" of *Beowulf* (788½ "verse pairs") appears on pp. 82–136.

into two verses. It is the rare reader of the poem who asks *why* the text has been set out in this way. It is difficult to believe that there can be any other way of dividing the text.

Yet it was possible for the early editors to disagree about the details of the division of the manuscript text into verses. Their disagreements must have seemed crucial, since the verse divisions of only one early editor survive in later editions. Although he gives no reason for dismissing Thorkelin's edition of *Beowulf*, it is likely that Klaeber did so partly because he preferred Kemble's verses to Thorkelin's. In any case, it is Kemble's verse that appears in Klaeber's edition—and in every recent edition of the poem—whenever Thorkelin and Kemble differ. It is Kemble's verse that survives on those rare occasions when his differs from Conybeare's.

It will be instructive to examine a particular example of the difference between Thorkelin and Conybeare on the one hand and Kemble on the other. I begin by quoting the source of these verses exactly as it appears in the manuscript. This is what the scribe has written on lines 4 and 5 of folio 137V (135v in Zupitza):

[þ]oht ofost is selest to ȝecýðanne
[h]panan eopre cýme sýndon· (137V04–5)[17]

At the top of p. 22 of his edition Thorkelin sets out the last six words of this passage as follows:

To gecydanne
Hwanon eowre
Cyme syndon.

The same passage appears halfway down p. 89 of Conybeare's *Illustrations of Anglo-Saxon Poetry* set out in the same way:

To ȝecýðanne
Hwanan eowre
Cyme syndon.

17. See above, note 1, for an explanation of the square brackets. I number manuscript lines according to the following system: the first three digits represent the number of the folio according to the "new official British Museum numbering, introduced in 1884" (Zupitza, *Beowulf . . . in Facsimile*, xvi–xvii); the capital R or V indicates the *side* of the folio (recto or verso); the last two digits, from 01 to 22, indicate the number of the manuscript line. The folio number that actually appears on the manuscript page and also on Zupitza's facing transliteration appears in parentheses in the text.

Kemble departs radically from the verse lineation of his two predecessors, dividing the same passage into only two verses. This is how he prints the passage in his 1835 edition, where it forms verses 511 and 512 on p. 19:

> to ge-cyðanne
> hwanan eowre cyme syndon.

Klaeber, along with every other recent editor, follows Kemble's verse division, rather than Conybeare's and Thorkelin's, of what is now printed as verse line 257.

Both in 1833 and in 1835 Kemble found reason to print as verse 512 the four words in eight syllables that his predecessors had printed as two verses. Every editor since Kemble has followed him. So far as I have been able to discover, neither Kemble nor any recent editor explains why he or she prefers the eight-syllable verse to the neater four-syllable verses of Thorkelin and Conybeare. Kemble's distribution must seem too obvious to call for explanation.

The difference between Kemble's verse lineation at this point and that of his predecessors is indeed obvious. In the passage of thirteen syllables that begins with *to*, Kemble finds material for only two verses because the passage contains only two alliterating syllables, *-cÿ-* and *cÿ-*. By dividing the passage beginning with *hpanan* into two "verses," Thorkelin and Conybeare place a "verse" containing no alliterating syllable—*Hwanan eowre*—between the two "verses" that contain the only alliterating syllables in the passage.

The analysis of the attempts to divide the passage that begins with *to* and ends with *sÿndon* exemplifies Kemble's way of eliciting verses. He agreed with his predecessors that the text invites division into verses. But he disagreed with them about the basis of verse division. Kemble's analysis of the passage in question reveals that he was consistent on the basis of his disagreement: for him a verse must contain a syllable that alliterates with a syllable in one of the flanking verses.

It is easy to test this formulation of Kemble's methods: one has only to look for alliterating syllables in every pair of his verses. What is less easy to figure out is why Kemble placed certain alliterating syllables where he did in the verse. Is there, for example, any reason for placing the first alliterating syllable of the pair *-cÿ-/cÿ-* inside the first verse of this set? The morphology of the word suggests one reason. The syllable *-cÿ-* is not the first syllable of the word *ȝecÿðanne*. It is possible that the poet would have distributed between two verses syllables belonging to the same word. But such a separation does not seem to be required, here or elsewhere in the poem. The syllable ʒe-seems to belong in the same verse with -cýðanne.

The syllable *to*, however, is a separate word. Why should the verse lineator place it in the same verse as the word that contains the alliterating syllable? This part of the answer is based on the syntax of the passage: *to* belongs with ʒecýðanne; together they form a phrase. Even Thorkelin and Conybeare knew that much and generally acted upon that knowledge. But those two editors forgot or ignored such knowledge when it came to the next passage, *hpanan eopre cýme sýndon.* Together *eopre* and *cýme* form a phrase, but only Kemble kept them together in the same verse.

If one looks more closely at this passage in its context it is possible to develop more precise formulations about Kemble's method of eliciting verses. Kemble may have accepted Thorkelin's and Conybeare's separation of *to* from *selest* (the word that precedes *to* in the manuscript) because *to* is a preposition and prepositions by definition should be preposed to their nouns. *To* also belongs to the grammatical category of "proclitics"—a word, syllable, or group of syllables that is syntactically linked to a word that follows. All three early editors probably separated *to* from *selest* because they understood that *to* is proclitic to ʒecýðanne and thus syntactically bound to the following word. It is at the same time much more loosely linked to what precedes it. A verse of *Beowulf* can, it appears, begin with a passage that is proclitic to a word that contains an alliterating syllable.

The three editors also agree that a verse may begin with another sort of nonalliterating syllable, in this case an adverb serving as a conjunction. All three seem to mark the importance of the clause boundary at *hpanan* by placing that word at the left margin. Then Kemble parts company with the other two. Thorkelin and Conybeare complete their next verse with the fourth syllable of this passage. Thorkelin might have justified his verse by observing that many verses in *Beowulf* consist of just four syllables and far fewer consist of eight syllables. Conybeare would probably have argued that *hpanan eopre* consists of two trochees. Neither argument could have persuaded Kemble. He might have observed that the words *hpanan* and *eopre* do not form a phrase while *eopre* and *cýme* do, but that would not have been his main argument for adding the first two words to *cýme sýndon* to form a rather long verse. The first two words contain no alliterating syllable, Kemble would have pointed out. So Kemble elicits his verse

512 as *hpanan eopre cyme syndon*. When we compare his lineation of this passage with that of his predecessors, we can formulate the matter in this way: Kemble synthesized verse 512 from two parts, a passage that contains no alliterating syllable and the immediately following passage that does.

If we set this passage in a slightly wider context by including the two preceding manuscript lines, we can then extrapolate Kemble's method of eliciting verses from manuscript lines.

> [fu]rþur feran nu ȝe feorbuend mere
> liðende mine ȝehẏra∂ anfealdne ȝe
> [þ]oht ofost is selest to ȝecẏ∂anne
> [h]panan eopre cẏme sẏndon· (137V02–5)

Kemble lineates as follows:

505	furþur feran.
	Nu ge feor-buend,
	mere-liðende,
	mine ge-hyra∂
	an-fealdne ge-þoht:
510	ofost is selest
	to ge-cy∂anne
	hwanan eowre cyme syndon.

Alliteration proved a sure and easy guide to five of the first six verses for all three early editors. These six verses have remained the same from Thorkelin's edition to the present.

If all the editor had to do was to place the first alliterating syllable at the left margin, the job would be easy. No editor has, of course, done that. Instead, editors have had to ask whether the first alliterating syllable *belongs* at the beginning of the verse.

How did Kemble determine that the first alliterating syllable of his verses 505 and 507–10 belongs at the head of each successive verse? The answer is, by asking whether anything in the immediately preceding passage is closely attached to the word that contains the alliterating syllable. It was probably easiest for him as for his predecessors to place *ofost* at the head of its verse, since the first syllable of that word not only alliterates but also marks a clause boundary. In a sense, as I shall argue in Chapter 3, *mere*- also heads its clause. But it seems that an alliterating syllable does not have to head a clause in order to head a verse. Neither [*fu*]*rþur* nor the first part of the compound adjective *anfealdne* does. Nor does *mine* necessarily head a clause. Thus Kemble determined that an alliterating syllable heads its verse whenever there is nothing in the immediately preceding passage that is closely attached to the word that contains the alliterating syllable.

We can now summarize Kemble's method of extracting verses from the text of the poem in the manuscript. In its general outlines and effects, his method turns out to be rather simple. First, he looked for each successive alliteration. In the passage near the top of folio 137V, he found first an F-alliteration ([*fu*]*r*-, *feor*-), then an M-alliteration (*mere*-, *mine*), then a *vocalic* alliteration (*an*-, *o*-), and then a C-alliteration (-*cÿ*-, *cÿ*-). As Kemble's handling of the C-alliteration demonstrates, these alliterations are the only basis on which the lineator can be sure that a new pair of verses is forming.

The first alliterating syllable of each successive alliteration thus became the benchmark from which Kemble determined the beginning of the first verse of each pair. When Kemble decided, as he did in the case of the last two verses of this passage, that the first alliterating syllable might not mark the beginning of the verse, he then went back into the preceding passage to look for a clause boundary before or a proclitic passage to the first alliterating syllable. He then began the verse with the first syllable of either the new clause or, as in his next-to-last verse, the proclitic.

Thus Kemble synthesized from two clearly defined segments every verse that he did not begin with an alliterating syllable. In such verses it is always the second segment, the one that begins with the alliterating syllable, that is located first, precisely because it carries the alliteration. The first segment is then retrieved from the passage that precedes the second (alliterating) segment.

To separate the second verse of each alliterating pair of verses from the first, Kemble worked from the *last* alliterating syllable. This syllable became his second benchmark in each alliteration. From that benchmark he repeated the operations he had used to find the beginning of the first verse of the pair. But this time he went back into the preceding passage only as far as the next syllable after the end of the word containing the next-to-last alliterating syllable.

It appears that Kemble, unlike his predecessors, developed and consistently applied to the syllables of the manuscript text a method for extracting verses. Even though this method has not until now been extrapolated from Kemble's lineation and properly tested, it nevertheless appears to have played a crucial role in the acceptance of the standard verse lineation. I contend that it is Kemble's *method* that underlies the 150-year consensus. It is time to turn that method into a set of testable hypotheses.

THE FIRST MAJOR HYPOTHESIS: LINEATION IMPLIES A METHOD

In the preceding section I analyzed one instance of the differences between Kemble's lineation and that of his predecessors. From that analysis I inferred that Kemble, unlike his predecessors, pursued a method. The next step is to turn Kemble's method into a hypothesis and test it. The importance of working in this way cannot be overestimated. If it can be demonstrated that Kemble worked methodically, that demonstration will help guarantee that the verses of the consensus are indeed verses, because it will have been shown that each was derived by applying the same method to the text.

In its strongest form, the first major hypothesis states that Kemble worked out all of the verses of the poem acceptably by applying a method to the text represented in the manuscript. A longer form of the hypothesis states that Kemble's method of eliciting verses requires, first, that each contain at least one syllable that alliterates with a syllable in one of the flanking verses; and, second, that each verse begin in one of three ways: (1) with the first (or only) alliterating syllable; or (2) with a clause boundary before or (3) a proclitic to the first alliterating syllable.

This hypothesis is based upon a simple definition of the verse line. On the basis of my extrapolation of Kemble's method, I define a verse line at this point as a sequence of words that begins either with the first alliterating syllable of an alliteration (two or more stressed syllables having the same initial sound that are in range of each other) or with a clause boundary before or proclitic to that first alliterating syllable; the verse line ends just before either the first syllable of the next alliteration or a clause boundary before or proclitic to that alliterating syllable.

So far I have applied my extrapolation of Kemble's method to an insignificant sample of the text. In the first half of this book, I apply the first major hypothesis to a far more substantial sample of *Beowulf*, a sample that represents about 13 percent of the text. The sample consists of two sections of the manuscript text. The first section begins with the first word of the text, *HPÆT* on folio 132R (129r), and continues through the last word on the first line of folio 139R (137r). The second sample begins with the first word on line 197Vo8 (193v) and continues through the last word on line 199V14 (195v).

In order to test my tentative definition of the verse line, I accepted the offer of a colleague, Dorothy Eckert Grannis, to translate my extrapolation of Kemble's general method into a computer program. Grannis's program operates on the lines of the text the two scribes wrote in the manuscript.

It is important that the reader understand the part the computer plays in this study. The computer demonstrates that verse lines and halflines can be elicited from the manuscript text systematically. It does so because Dorothy Grannis translated into computer programs my Procedures for Systematically Eliciting Verse Lines and Halflines from Manuscript Lines (see Appendix A). What at first appears to be a bizarre halfline will turn out to be the result of the rigorous application of a method. Thus the computer has served to keep the human lineator honest, to help me see what is really to be found in the syllables indicated in the manuscript text.

After determining in Chapter 2 that the two scribes of the manuscript have provided the modern reader with enough information to make possible an acceptable approximation of the text of the poem, I try in Chapter 3 to determine exactly what the lineator or computer needs to know in order to extract verses from manuscript lines. First of all it is necessary to know which syllables are stressed. I hypothesize that one does not need to know—and *cannot know* at this point in the analysis—whether the syllable bears a weakened degree of heavy stress, that is, intermediate or "half" stress. Hence a binary division into stressed (coded as "1") or unstressed (coded as "0") syllables is sufficient for lineation. Second, it is necessary to know exactly how alliteration operates to indicate verse lines (verse pairs). I hypothesize that alliteration operates over a certain range which can be calculated in terms of the number of intervening stressed syllables. Third, it is necessary to know whether or not the syllable is the first in its clause. In order to answer this apparently simple question in regard to the syllables of the manuscript (as opposed to the text as it appears in modern editions of the poem) it is necessary to construct a grammar of the poem from and around those syllables. The grammar occupies a sizable portion of Chapter 3.[18] The final section of Chapter 3 discusses proclitics since Kemble's lineation makes clear the necessity of locating any proclitic to the first or last alliterating syllable in a series of alliterations.

I have encoded these four kinds of information for each syllable in the sample passages, along with information about its length. The encoding is in the form of symbols that can be read by the computer. I give an example of a manuscript line encoded for the computer:

```
132V04  [þ]eon· him ða   scÿld ȝe   pat  to    ȝe   scæp hpil e
        1U/*    30-* 0U/* 2K/*  0G- 1W/* 40T-* 0G- 2K-+ 1H/ 0V-* Z
```

These symbols represent everything the computer is told about the text.[19]

Occasionally, scholars since Kemble have suggested that other methods might elicit acceptable verses. At the end of the first three sections of Chapter 3 I have included a "coda" in which I test whether it is possible to elicit correct verses consistently on any basis other than Kemble's general method. After Section 1, for example, I try to determine verse lines by counting first all stressed syllables and then certain kinds of stressed syllables in order to deal with the assumption that every verse must contain at least two stressed syllables. After Section 3, I first try to lineate by beginning each verse with a new clause boundary and then try to lineate by using only certain clause boundaries. All these attempts elicit some verses but only with very complicated sets of instructions. Only Kemble's general method, as Chapter 4 will demonstrate, elicits a high percentage of verse lines and halflines elegantly.

I begin Chapter 4 by setting out the steps for eliciting verse lines (verse pairs) from the manuscript text. These steps are simply rigorous formulations of Kemble's procedures. To keep clear the contrast between the rigorous procedures for programmed lineation on the one hand and Kemble's actual results on the other, I shall refer to computer-programmed verse lineation as *P-* (for "programmed") Linea-

---

18. The value of this grammar lies, I think, in the fact that it not only questions every assumption made by the modern editors of the poem but always provides answers, in some cases very interesting answers, to such questions as what constitutes a clause in the poem and whether clause boundaries are ever ambiguous.

19. For a full discussion of how syllables were encoded for computer programming, see Appendix C, "Encoding the Syllables of the Manuscript for Computer."

tion and Kemble's lineation as *C*- (for "conventional") Lineation. It will be useful, too, to divide the first major hypothesis into what I call a *weak* and a *strong* form. In the weak form the hypothesis states that it is possible to elicit verse lines and halflines from the manuscript text systematically. This form of the hypothesis can be tested by applying the procedures discussed in Chapter 4 to the manuscript text. The strong form of the hypothesis states that Kemble elicited all of the verses (halflines) of the consensus by the application of a method to the indications of the syllables in the manuscript text. The strong form of the hypothesis cannot be fully tested until Chapter 8.

After demonstrating that one can elicit verse lines systematically, I set out the procedures for detaching the second halfline of each verse line (the second verse of each alliterating pair) from the first. Again my formulations follow Kemble's practice but turn it into a rigorous program. My working definition of the halfline is this: the second half-line of the verse line is a word or sequence of words that begins either with the last alliterating syllable of the series or with a clause boundary before or proclitic to the last alliterating syllable. The ending of the second halfline is the same as the ending of the verse line (see above).

At the end of Chapter 4 I exhibit in a chart the results of the application of the computer program based on Kemble's general method to the syllables of the manuscript lines of the two-part sample. Kemble's general method, translated into a rigorous computer program, elicits 78.4 percent of the verses that Kemble himself elicited from the two sample manuscript passages in his second edition. This figure represents a statistically significant percentage, far above the 50 percent that might have been produced by chance from any set of procedures. Yet this percentage, high as it is, does not tell the whole story, which must wait until Chapter 8. Nonetheless, at the end of Chapter 4 the results of P-Lineation confirm that it is possible to elicit halflines systematically. Thus the weak form of the hypothesis has been verified.

THE SECOND MAJOR HYPOTHESIS: LINEATION IS THE KEY TO PROSODIC CONSTITUENTS

P-Lineation elicits nearly four-fifths of the halflines of the poem as accepted by scholars since Kemble's time. Other methods, such as stress-counting, are both less successful and less elegant.

The verification of the weak form of the first major hypothesis has this consequence: if one accepts the verses of the 150-year-old consensus, one must accept the method of lineation that elicited those verses. The method of lineating is based upon the first alliterating syllable in each series of alliterations. The method of half-lining is based upon the last alliterating syllable in each series. In order first to elicit the verse line and then to detach the second halfline, the computer program first locates the segment headed by the first alliterating syllable and then locates the segment headed by the last alliterating syllable. These segments become *interior* segments in 40 percent of the halflines. That is, they do not begin the halfline but instead are moved to a point inside the halfline. In these halflines the segment headed by the alliterating syllable marks the "stock" onto which the lineator grafts the nonalliterating segment. Thus, in the process of lineating methodically, the lineator joins together two segments each of which is necessarily smaller than the halfline. The lineator thus synthesizes about 40 percent of the verses/halflines from two clearly defined segments, each of which is de facto a *constituent* of the halfline. This fact suggests the following hypothesis: systematic lineation provides a key to the constituents of all verses/halflines. Chapter 6 shows how that key can be used to determine two constituents in every halfline of the poem. Chapters 6–8 thus present ways of testing the second major hypothesis.

This hypothesis brings together verse lineation and prosody. According to this hypothesis it should indeed be possible for a prosodist to scan the verses, but only by taking into account the way in which the verses/halflines have been elicited and in many cases synthesized by the lineator. That is what prosodists have so far missed.

The major approaches to Beowulfian prosody fail to take into account the synthesizing of 40 percent of the halflines. Cable's holistic approach finds no necessary point of division in any verse. Sievers's division of verses of his Types B and C places the benchmark alliterating syllable from which the lineator has to work not at the beginning of a "foot" but at the end. Even Pope fails to take account of the importance of the benchmark alliterating syllable to the lineator.

It is not enough to say that other prosodists are on shaky ground. One must point out the firm ground and test its firmness. Kemble's verses have long stood firm. Both his verses and his method of extracting them bring to prominence the smaller units that form the constituents of many of the verses. At the end of Chapter 5 I append what I call "Kemble's Legacy: A Matched Corpus of Verse Lines in

Beowulf." The Corpus consists of the two halflines (verses) of every verse line in the sample that matches Kemble's verse pairs. I leave for Chapter 8 consideration of verse lines/verse pairs in which one or both of the halflines does not match the verses of the consensus. The data that will be analyzed in the next two chapters are listed or presented in the three subcorpora of this Matched Corpus.

Two constituents of every synthetic halfline have become apparent during the process of half-lining. Verse 28a, for example, is made up of the two constituents *hi hyne* [*þ*]*a æt-* and *-bæron.*[20] Verse 28b is made up of the two constituents *to* and *brimes faroðe.* Verse 107a consists of *in* and *caines cynne,* and verse 107b of *þone* and *cpealm ʒepræc.* These are the segments that the verse lineator has extracted from the manuscript text separately and joined together to form each verse. These segments thus pose a problem for the prosodist: how to develop a prosody that takes into account the smaller constituents the lineator has used in the process of eliciting verses. A reformulation of the second major hypothesis is in order: a Beowulfian prosody can be constructed on the basis of the constituents the lineator has joined together to form the synthetic verses. That is the challenge I take up in Chapters 6 and 7.

The first step in developing such a prosody is to examine the constituents of synthetic verses. I begin by trying to determine which halfline/verse constituents are *single* and which segments represent more than one constituent of the halfline. It is easy to demonstrate that all of the nonalliterating segments are single, even those that consist of five or six syllables. Not even these polysyllable constituents contain a necessary point of division. Some of the alliterating segments, however, contain two or even three stressed syllables. I call these constituents "augmented." Later in Chapter 6 I propose a simple criterion for determining the singleness of augmented segments: if a segment smaller than a verse consists of all four of the following, that segment is made up of two constituents, not one, the second of which begins with segment (3): (1) A long stressed syllable (encoded for the computer as "1/"), followed by (2) an unstressed syllable (encoded for the computer as "0"), followed by (3) another long

---

20. I use "conventional" (or "C") numbers to refer to verse lines and verses. A conventional verse will always be followed by "a" for the first verse of a pair or "b" for the second. A verse line or halfline, which is always produced by the computer, will be identified as a "P" verse line or halfline. If a verse pair or verse is not designated "P," it represents a conventional verse line or verse.

stressed syllable, followed by (4) another unstressed syllable ("1/ o + 1/ o"). By this criterion verse 107a consists of three constituents: (1) *in*, (2) *caines*, (3) *cȳnne*. Almost any other segment smaller than a halfline, I hypothesize, represents a single halfline constituent. Verses 28a, 28b, and 107b consist of only two constituents, those indicated in the previous paragraph.

If such segments as *-bæron*, *cpealm ʒepræc*, and *brimes faroðe* represent single halfline constituents (which I designate "HCs"), then it will be possible to use such HCs as patterns or templates to determine the constituents of verses elicited intact by the lineator, that is, verses that begin with an alliterating syllable. Sievers and everyone after him assumed that the constituents—"feet" or "measures"—of verses that begin with alliterating syllables are obvious. Since, however, these verses are elicited intact by lineation and half-lining, the prosodist must locate the constituents of such verses without the help of lineation. By the end of Chapter 6, I have tentatively isolated the constituents of every verse/halfline in the Matched Corpus by using templates derived from the alliterating constituents of synthetic halflines.

The next step is to hypothesize and test the hypothesis that every verse line is comparable to every other verse line of the poem. There seems to be only one way to perform such a test. If every verse line is to be compared to every other verse line, and if the testing is not to be arbitrary, it will be necessary to align verse line with verse line—in other words, to build a grid. The first column of the grid will be made up of first HCs, the second of second HCs, the third column of the first HCs of second halflines, and the fourth column of the second HCs of those halflines. Units derived by the same procedures are now "stacked" in columns for comparison. So far as I have been able to discover, no other prosodist has used this simple and obvious way of comparing prosodic units assumed to be of the same order.

Before I begin stacking in Chapter 7 I deal with another problem. Some HCs are crowded with syllables, while some are relatively empty. "Crowding" occurs more often in the second HC of the halfline, but occurs also in the first HC. The first HC of 27a, for example, *[fe]lahror*, consists of three syllables, two of which are stressed. In these respects, though not in the length of the first stressed syllable, it is like the *second* HC of 107b, *cpealm ʒepræc*. But the greatest disparity occurs between, for example, *[fe]lahror* and the first HC of 28b, *to*.

The HCs *to* and *[fe]lahror* appear to be comparable in only one respect: each represents the entire first HC of its halfline. "Crowded"

HCs like *[fe]lahror* and *cpealm ʒepræc* are more obviously comparable. Each begins with the first alliterating syllable of its halfline, the syllable that most clearly marks the beginning of an HC. Each ends with a stressed syllable. This similarity suggests the hypothesis that these HCs might themselves consist of two constituents: (1) *[fe]la-* and (2) *-hror*, and (1) *cpealm ʒe-* and (2) *-præc*.

The apparent two-part structure of these HCs—the first being the first HC in its halfline, the second the second HC in its halfline—suggests the hypothesis that every HC, whether first or second, consists of two constituents. Unlike *[fe]lahror* and *cpealm ʒepræc*, however, most halfline constituents contain only a single stressed syllable. The second HC of verse 28a, *-bæron*, is an example. If *-bæron* consists of two parts, these are *-bæ-*, which is stressed and long, and *-ron*, which is unstressed and short. The unstressed short syllable occupies the same part of this HC as do the long stressed syllables *-hror* and *-præc* in their HCs. If it is possible to analyze every HC into two parts or constituents, the parts are going to be very different. Some second parts, like *-ron*, will be light; some, like *-hror-*, will be heavy. And some parts will be empty. If we hypothesize that every first HC is indeed comparable to every other first HC, then the difference between *[fe]lahror* in 27a and *to* in 28b not only suggests that nonsyllabic material completed the latter HC but also indicates the location and value of the nonsyllabic material relative to *to*.

In Chapter 7, then, I build the grid that makes possible the comparison of all prosodic units. I build it from the top down, that is, by matching verse lines at their beginnings and at the point at which the second halfline begins. Then I match the first HC of the first halfline with the first HC of the first halfline of other verse lines. It becomes obvious that one can build the grid only by dividing HCs into their two constituents according to clearly indicated criteria. The division of HCs into their constituents isolates "constituents" that are empty of syllables.

The fact that it is possible to build the grid to compare prosodic units does not, however, provide the strongest verification of the hypothesis that every HC consists of two constituents or parts. Verification of this hypothesis must await the arguments of Chapter 9. At that point I demonstrate that the two-part structure of the HC indicates the regularity that operates to control the disposition of syllables at this—the lowest—level.

There are indications of this regularity at a much higher level, in the fact that every verse line consists of exactly two halflines. The regularity is less evident within the halfline, since the halfline may consist—though in *Beowulf* it rarely does—of more than two HCs. With the paired constituents of the HC, however, which I call the two "Fine Parts," or, more simply, "Parts," we have reached the bedrock of the system. We have also reached the point at which the two constituents of the next higher constituent—the two Fine Parts of the HC—are radically different from each other: the first Fine Part cannot switch places with the second. In Chapter 9 I discuss the meaning of the irreversibility of the two Fine Parts of an HC.

In Chapter 8 I return to the verses—21.6 percent of the sample passages—that do not match computer-generated halflines. What is important to note is that the kinds of mismatching between verses and halflines can be categorized. Many mismatches are the result of an alliteration that consists of more than three syllables. Some mismatches are the result of my overscrupulousness in marking clause boundaries. Exactly twenty-one mismatches, or 2.4 percent, result from the fact that the text I analyze is very conservative and includes no emendations for missing or illegible passages. Mismatches caused either by a pattern of alliteration that continues on a fourth syllable or beyond, or by my overscrupulousness in marking clause boundaries, account for slightly less than 18 percent of the total. I show that it is possible to *plot* the categorically unmatched halflines so that they too fit the grid displayed in Chapter 7.

Even here Kemble's verse lineation offers guidance. Kemble generally based his lineation on the first and last alliterating syllables of each alliteration, but he also took other factors into consideration. If he found four or more alliterating syllables within range of each other, he usually looked for *two* pairs of benchmarks (and sometimes three pairs). At times he applied the principle that a verse will normally consist of only two constituents to complete a verse with a syllable that alliterates with a syllable in a following verse line (verse pair). Thus Kemble applied what I call the principle of "the two-HC norm." In Chapter 8 I plot on the grid a few examples of verse lines that do not match from both samples of the manuscript text.

If we add the nearly 18 percent of categorically explicable mismatches to the total percentage of matches, the percentage of matches and categorically explainable mismatches equals 96.3 percent. By the end of Chapter 8, then, it is possible to say that the strong form of the first major hypothesis has been verified: Kemble elicited *all* of the verses/halflines of the consensus by the application of a method. The second major hypothesis has also been demonstrated: Kemble's method of lineating, particularly his synthesizing of about 40 percent of his verses from an alliterating and a nonalliterating constituent, has provided the key to the constituents of all the verses. It is this key that was lost—ironically—immediately after Kemble used it to build the verses that form the basis of the six-generation consensus.

RECONSTRUCTING THE RHYTHM OF *BEOWULF*

Chapter 9 analyzes the significance of the two-part structure of halfline constituents. As I show in Chapter 7, each HC can be divided into exactly two Fine Parts. Eighty percent of the first Fine Parts contain a stressed syllable. Far more often than not, the second Fine Part contains an unstressed syllable. This is one indication of the radical difference between the first and second Fine Parts that I mentioned above.

What is the prosodist to make of this radical difference? The best hypothesis is that the overwhelming preponderance of heavily stressed syllables in the first Fine Part indicates a simple two-part rhythm: a relatively heavier downbeat (represented by the first Fine Part) begins a pulse completed by a relatively lighter upbeat (represented by the second Fine Part). Each two-part HC seems, then, to represent a quasi-musical *measure*. The onset of the measure is marked by a sense of greater emphasis created by a stressed syllable or a timed pause. The measure is completed by a passage of which the lighter emphasis prepares the hearer for the next downbeat (in the next HC). This is the rhythm that governs every syllable of the poem. Thus, John C. Pope's "theory" about the rhythm of *Beowulf* does indeed rest on something solid. But the structures that create this rhythm are both simpler and more complex than Pope indicated. They are more complex because each downbeat and each upbeat governs either one, two, or three syllables—or none. They are more complex because one syllable, two, or all three of the syllables may be short, and one—sometimes even two or three—may be stressed. The many possible combinations of these variables create enormous variety. Yet the simple rhythm—downbeat/upbeat—indicated by the radical difference between the two Fine Parts *controls* this variety. It is this simplicity that Pope failed to demonstrate by failing to compare the measures he generally located so precisely.

Enough information can be extracted from the signs the scribes wrote in Cotton Vitellius A. xv to reconstruct the rhythm of *Beowulf*. One must extract that information by asking the right questions in the right order. At the end of the process, each of the various hypotheses will have been tested. Thus verses can be extracted methodically from the manuscript text; some verses have been synthesized from two constituents; these constituents provide a clue to the structure of every verse; every halfline (or verse) constituent—which can now be called the measures of the verse—can be analyzed into two Fine Parts; two Fine Parts indicate a two-part rhythm. The rhythm, so firmly indicated by 80 percent of the measures, demands a "rest" whenever an empty Fine Part occurs. Thus it is the rhythm that distributes the syllables of the poem.

It is with an attempt to derive the syllables of the poet from the signs of the scribes that the detailed part of this study begins.

Chapter 2

From Sign to Syllable
The Poet's Syllables as the Data of the Prosodist

Since prosody charts temporal relationships between sounds, not spatial relationships between signs, the first step in reconstructing the prosody of *Beowulf* is to attempt to reconstruct the sounds of the poem. Partly because visual signs are pervasive in our society, and partly because our only path to *Beowulf*—or to any poem in an idiom no longer spoken—is through visual signs, we must take special care not to slide into the assumption that certain visual signs—writings— are themselves the objects of prosodic studies. Visual signs *represent* language. The process of deciphering the signs, and the use of the signs to guide the reconstruction of the sounds, produces the language that the prosodist analyzes.

The attempt to reconstruct the sounds of an idiom that is no longer spoken is daunting. In one sense, it is impossible. The nuances of the moment can never be recovered. Precise intonations are lost forever. But this is true of all language reconstructed from visual signs; it is true even of the language spoken by a familiar voice out of one's hearing. The prosodist of a dead language has to settle for something less than the richness and subtlety of language spoken by a native speaker in his or her community. But he does not settle for silence; to do his job he converts the signs—the cues provided by the writing system— into language that, more often than not, he alone may "hear" with his mind's ear.

The prosodist makes the language he analyzes his own. That is a very difficult task when nearly a millennium separates him from the last speaker of that language. But the task is not impossible. Modern English, after all, developed from Old English. And scholars during the last century and a half have done much to make it possible to translate the cues of Old English writers into an acceptable approximation of the spoken language they represent.

The task of the prosodist has been made easier by the two scribes of the manuscript. As I shall show in this chapter, the work of the scribes indicates that they were the heirs of a writing convention that had developed rather sophisticated methods for representing spoken language. Partly because our conventions for writing developed from those of the scribes, we can decipher what they wrote with some confidence. The scribes employed an alphabet largely adapted from Latin. The use of an alphabet rather than a syllabary or ideographic system made it possible for the scribes to analyze the syllable, the unit of spoken language, into smaller "features." The most prominent features are represented as *letters*. The scribes learned, as we have, how to assemble letters to represent many different syllables.

Letters are not sounds, although they can be used to indicate sounds. Some letters, "d" for example, cannot be produced in isolation. Indeed, every time we "speak a letter" we actually speak a syllable that *names* that letter. We must constantly remind ourselves that letters belong to one system, writing, while syllables belong to a very different system, spoken language. The two systems seem to overlap in that letters can be used to represent syllables. But the prosodist must never forget that he studies and employs letters only in order to try to reconstruct the syllables of the poet.

The prosodist attempts to reconstruct the syllables produced by the poet in order to deal with patterns created by their sounds and to determine their temporal relationships. Both from and *in* visual cues the prosodist constructs a formal account of the audible and temporal relationships between syllables. The prosodist of *Beowulf* must settle for an approximation of the sounds of the poem. But he should make every effort to work out an acceptable approximation, one that takes into account the best and the latest studies of the problem. Despite his efforts, he and his readers must accept the fact that the best approximation will be no more than an approximation.

In this chapter and the next I shall examine the visual cues the scribes set down in an effort to extract as much information from them as possible. The information is of two kinds, one more, the other less, obvious. In this chapter I discuss the more obvious kinds of information, what can, in effect, be "read off the page." In Chapter 3, I deal with a less obvious but very important kind of information that can be extracted from what the scribes wrote only if we construct and apply certain hypotheses to the language indicated by their signs. This kind of information has to do with such features as stress and such functions as heading a clause.

The question the prosodist of *Beowulf* has to keep constantly in mind is this: is it possible to reconstruct the syllables of the poet from the evidence provided by the scribes? To answer this question, the prosodist begins by analyzing the visual system, the notation of the scribes, for clues to the sound system it was designed to represent.

The visual system operates through a series of conventions. Anglo-Saxons borrowed from writers of Latin most of the now-familiar signs for letters, along with the convention of placing them horizontally to be read from left to right. The scribes also seem to have borrowed from writers of Latin some of the conventions for spacing letters. These conventions of the writing system have become familiar to us partly because of the work of early scribes.

Notations suggest syllables by using *graphs*, which occupy space. The graphs—the letters of the scribes—represent syllables by grouping letters along the space of the parchment. I call this dimension *extent*. By extent as applied to the signs of the manuscript I mean the left-to-right dimension of the written characters that represent (or single character that represents) a syllable. In reading silently or aloud from the manuscript, one translates this spatial dimension into a temporal one.

Every syllable contains a nucleus consisting of either a vowel (A) or a diphthong (B). The vowel or diphthong can either function as a complete syllable or be (1) preceded by one consonant, (2) preceded by two or more consonants, (3) followed by one consonant, (4) followed by two or more consonants, (5) both preceded and followed by a single consonant, (6) preceded by two consonants and followed by one, (7) preceded by one consonant and followed by two, or (8) both preceded and followed by two or more consonants. In Table 2.1, I give examples of all of these possibilities that indicate by signs the extent of the syllable. At one extreme, a single letter may represent a syllable, as in (A) in the table. At the other extreme, a syllable may require as many as six letters for its representation.

In each of the eighteen examples listed in Table 2.1, the boundaries of the syllable can be determined, even though some, like *in* (3A) at 132R02, may be written in the manuscript with no space separating them from the first letter of the next syllable: *inȝear*. The context makes it clear that *in* and *ȝear* were intended, not *inȝ* and *ear-*.

Table 2.1. Extent of Syllables

(A)	a	138R09
(B)	æʒ-	132R09
(1A)	ÞE	132R01
(1B)	fea-	132R07
(2A)	hpa	133R06
(2B)	hleo	141V06
(3A)	in	132R02
(3B)	eom	139R17
(4A)	Oft	132R04
(4B)	eorl	132R06
(5A)	þæs	132R15
(5B)	þeod-	132R02
(6A)	HÞÆT	132R01
(6B)	frean	132V05
(7A)	folc	164R20
(7B)	ʒeonʒ	132R12
(8A)	-hp̏lc	132R09
(8B)	-sceaft	132R07

The boundaries between word-interior syllables that begin with single consonants are not, however, always easy to determine. Yet both scribes suggest, by their handling of these syllables when they divide the word at the end of a manuscript line, that the consonant begins the following syllable:

pe/dera	136V17–18
pere/de	137R08–9

Scribal practice in regard to representing such syllables suggests two possibilities: (1) a sense that a vowel or diphthong before a single consonant is always "open"; (2) a sense that syllabic boundaries at such points are somewhat blurred. It will, nevertheless, always be possible to locate some sort of boundary between such syllables. I shall have more to say on this point a little later.

Some of the conventions of the scribes of Cotton Vitellius A. xv make it difficult at times for the modern reader of the manuscript to determine the extent of certain words. For example, both scribes at times either squeeze two words together or separate parts of the same word. In the passages I have sampled, the first scribe violates in these two ways our conventions for the spacing of words about 15 percent of the time, the second nearly 20 percent of the time. On the other hand, one can turn these percentages around to say that both scribes conform to our conventions for spacing words more than 80 percent of the time. More important for our purposes is the fact that both scribes, whenever they separate parts of words, do so at what we recognize as indications of syllable junctures. The following are examples from the first scribe: ȝe frunon (132R03), ȝeo ȝoð (133R19), hlifa de (133V12). From the second scribe I cite to pehton (197V10), hreð les (198V02), and ofer maðmum (198V03). A somewhat cursory search of the manuscript has failed to turn up a half or whole letter space on the same manuscript line at any point other than between what can be reconstructed—"read"—as two syllables.

There are, however, instances in which the first scribe, as he nears the end of the manuscript line, fails to break a word at a recognizable indication of syllable juncture. Table 2.2 lists all the instances I have noted in the manuscript. The eleven instances of unusual word division in more than five hundred instances of words broken at line ends comes to about 2 percent of the total. About 98 percent of the time, then, the scribes break words at line ends between syllables.

Table 2.2. Unusual Word Division

be/arn ("child")	143R15–16
scẏldi/nȝa	143R16–17
ȝre/ndel	148R13–14
beo/rhte	152V01–2
fer/hþe	158V10–11
hpea/rf	159R12–13
ear/m	162V19–20
hoc/ẏhtum	164V12–13
dry/hten	165V14–15
ȝehpe/arf	169V21–22
peo/[rþ]re	174V09–10

Both scribes generally follow certain conventions in dividing words that cannot be completed on the manuscript line. These conventions are as follows: first, if the word contains two interior consonants, the scribe will break the word between the consonants. I give one example from the first scribe and one from the second: bear/me (132V15–16), fol/dan (198R09–10). Second, if a word contains only a single interior consonant near the point of division, the scribe breaks the word so that the consonant begins the new line. In discussing above the boundaries between the syllables in the interior of words I cited two examples of this convention. I list further examples of this usage in the next paragraph. Both scribes divide compounds between the first and second element: *ʒuð/cÿninʒ* (136R17–18), *þeod/cÿninʒ* (198V15–16). Both scribes similarly divide a word made up of stem + formative between these: *ʒerum/licor* (135R04–5), *ealdor/leasne* (198V11–12). The latter practice must have been made easier by the fact that both scribes generally separate the two elements of a compound or the stem and formative even when these are written on the same manuscript line.

Table 2.3 lists all instances of word division near a single interior consonant on folios 132R–138V and then on folios 197V–199V14. (I do not list here instances such as *scede/landum*, 132R17–18, since the division is between the elements of a compound.) The examples in Table 2.3 suggest that scribal convention had, by circa 975, achieved a high degree of morphophonemic sophistication. Behind that sophistication, as I suggest in more detail elsewhere, lay a long tradition of care in the keeping of the syllables of Memorable Speech.[1]

One other matter should be taken up at this point. The manuscript contains a number of large and small capitals and some pointing and punctuation. In addition, there are forty Roman numerals, often flanked by single points, marking off large sections of the text. The capitals, Roman numerals, and punctuation heavier than a single point always occur at a boundary between clauses. The single points frequently occur in that position. These devices sometimes provide independent verification of verse boundaries. But the determination of verse boundaries does not, indeed cannot, depend on these devices, since few verses are marked by even one of them.

The most important indications of the phonetic qualities of the poet's syllables are the letters the scribes wrote. To approximate the sounds represented by the letters, the prosodist must make an important assumption, that is, that the same letter or the same combination of letters is intended to represent the same sound.

This assumption probably rests on rather firm ground with consonants and combinations of consonants, but it is on less firm ground with vowels and diphthongs. Such variations in the representation of

---

1. "*Beowulf* on the Brink: Information Theory as Key to the Origins of the Poem," in *Comparative Research on Oral Traditions: A Memorial for Milman Parry*, ed. John Miles Foley (Columbus, Ohio: Slavica Publishers, 1987), 139–60.

Table 2.3.   Word Division Near a Single Interior Consonant

GARDE/na	132R01–2
ʒe/[þ]eon	132V03–4
ʒestreo/num	132V18–19
pe/[s]ende	132V20–133R01
ʒefr[æ]/ʒe	133R09–10
ste/[de]	133V06–7
ni/ðe	133V14–15
b[e]/buʒeð	134R02–3
ʒe/feah	134R16–17
ʒi/[ʒantas]	134R20–134V01
scea/pedon	134V18–19
spe[oto]/lan	135R06–7
h[ẏ]/ne	135R07–8
ʒe/þolode	135R11–12
sinʒa/le	135R16–17
meto/de	135V09–10
ʒehe/ton	135V14–15
ʒ[e]/pendan	136R04–5
sinʒa/la	136R09–10
hiʒela/ces	136R13–14
scu/fon	136V10–11
fa/mi	136V12–13
pe/dera	136V17–18
pere/de	137R08–9
ʒe/medu	137R15–16
ʒe/[þ]oht	137V03–4
ʒæde/linʒū	197V10–11
bry/de	197V15–16
pre/cen	197V20–21
hiʒe/laces	198R11–12
ʒecea/. . . .	198V19–20
þu/send	199V07–8
be/punden	199V09–10

syllabic nuclei as that between *hi* (132V05), *hie* (132R14), and *hẏ* (138V10) may represent the original scribe's attempt to take account of varying pronunciations of what both he and we identify as "the same word."

Every syllable represented in the manuscript was spoken in accordance with a notion of *length*. By the length of a syllable I refer to the phonemic contrast between, for example, the first and fourth syllables of this passage at 193R07: *spelan 7 spella[n]*. This contrast may on occasion have been blurred in speech but could always have been sorted out by speaker and hearer. Whatever the actual length of time it may have taken to speak these two syllables on a given occasion, a native speaker would have understood the fourth syllable as "longer" than the first.

Again, Old English scholars have sorted out syllables that are long because they contain a long vowel or diphthong from identically spelled words that are short because they contain a short vowel or diphthong. Further, scholars have argued that a cluster of two or more consonants at the end of a syllable, when both consonants are in the same word, lengthens the preceding syllable. Accordingly, it is possible to mark every syllable either long or short with a reasonable degree of confidence.

One comment about scribal treatment of so-called "long" consonants is in order. I take *þrym*, for example, in 132R03 to represent a long syllable even though the vowel is short. With what seems to be a high degree of consistency, both scribes follow the practice of writing a single letter for the long consonant when it is word-final. When the same syllable is followed by another in the same word, scribal practice is to represent the long consonant by doubling the letter, as, for example, *þrymmum* (137R06).

Scribal practice, then, shows to an overwhelming degree an attempt to indicate the syllable. Indeed, judging by the higher percentage of attention to syllable boundaries (98 percent) than to word boundaries (82 percent), the scribes show an awareness that the "syllable" rather than the word is the important unit of information.

The reader of the manuscript can nearly always determine with confidence the boundaries between words. In order to do so, the reader has to apply semantic criteria to the writer's cues. The prosodist, who works with syllables, has to be concerned with the *position* of the syllable in its word. There are three possible positions that a syllable can occupy in a word: (1) word-initial, (2) word-interior, and (3) word-final. The adverb *a*, like any monosyllable, simultaneously occupies positions (1) and (3). Somewhat similarly, disyllabic simplexes (see below) occupy positions (1) and (3), though with different syllables; for example, *elle[n]* (132R03) is made up of (1) *el-* and (3) *-le[n]*. Trisyllabic simplexes like *ʒefrunon* (132R03) occupy all three positions with different syllables: (1) *ʒe-*, (2) *-fru-*, (3) *-non*. Polysyllabic simplexes contain at least two (2)s: *æþelinʒas* (132R03) contains (1) *æ-*, (2) *-þel-*, (2) *-inʒ-*, (3) *-as*.

Most words are simplexes, but a number are compounds. By *compounds* I mean words made up of two elements both of which can, at least potentially, function as independent words, as, for example, *GAR* + *DEna* in 132R01–2. I use the term *simplex* for all other words, such as, at one extreme, the adverb *a* (138R09) and, near the other, *feasceaft* (132R07). The latter is composed of the adjectival *fea* (which can and does often function independently) to which the formative *-sceaft* has been joined. A formative cannot function as an independent word.

I treat each element of a compound as a simplex: *GAR-* = (1) + (3); *-DEna* = (1) *DE-* + (3) *-na*. I identify in the compound *fæderæþelum* (152V14) two sets of syllables: (1) *fæ-* (3) *-der* and (1) *æ-* (2) *-þe-* (3) *-lum*.[2]

The prosodist must locate every word in relation to the phrase and clause in which it participates. This is, as I show in the next chapter, a somewhat harder task for the reader of the manuscript than locating word boundaries. The scribes rarely marked phrase boundaries and used punctuation and capitalization far more sparingly than modern editors do.

The preceding account of the habits and conventions of the scribes of Cotton Vitellius A. xv in their handling of the signs that can be translated into syllables suggests a high degree of consistency and therefore reliability. While we cannot be sure that, for example, each of the three instances of the similarly written phrase *þ pæs god cyninʒ* (132R11, 151V13, 186R07) sounded exactly the same to the ears of the scribes, we can be sure that the two scribes in each case represented what they would in all likelihood have identified as the same sequence of sounds. Such consistency in notating, while it by no means makes it possible for the reader to be sure that every subtlety of sound can be reconstructed, does make it possible for the prosodist to reconstruct in a consistent way an audible approximation of the data.

In the following chapter I discuss the ways in which one can determine certain phrase boundaries and all clause boundaries in the poem. The problem turns out to be far more complex and far more interesting than modern editorial conventions suggest. For the moment, the important point to be made is that almost any syllable that

---

2. See Appendix C for the method I used to encode the distinction between compounds and simplexes.

occupies position (1) in a word can also mark the beginning of a clause. Clause-heading, which is more important to the prosodist than the exact location of a word inside its phrase, can be dealt with as a characteristic of syllables.

The two scribes of the *Beowulf* manuscript seem to have employed sophisticated and highly developed procedures for translating spoken syllables into signs. We can undertake to reconstruct the rhythm of *Beowulf* with some confidence because the scribes did their work so well. The letters, spaces, and occasional punctuation by which the scribes notated the language of the poet have already yielded much information. They are capable of yielding even more when we begin applying to them more complex hypotheses.

Chapter 3

Recoverable Features and Functions of Syllables

INTRODUCTION

As I tried to show in the last chapter, the hypothesis that we can approximate the syllables of the poet from the signs of the scribes finds support in the care taken by the two scribes who wrote out the text of the poem. In this chapter I present and test hypotheses that have to do with certain less obvious features and functions of the syllables that we can, I believe, reconstruct with some confidence.

As speakers of the language that has developed from the poet's language, we assume that his language gave greater force to certain syllables in any utterance. That assumption cannot, of course, be tested directly. What can be tested is the hypothesis that the poet in his poetry made use of the contrast between syllables that seem to require emphasis and others that do not. It is possible to demonstrate that the poetic convention the *Beowulf*-poet employed built its prosody on the basis of that contrast.

The poet also employed a particular kind of sound-patterning in a particular way. He built each verse around at least one stressed syllable that shares what was perceived to be the same initial sound with at least one stressed syllable in a flanking verse. But the poet did not always begin his verse with the "alliterating" syllable. Sometimes he began with a clause boundary that falls on a syllable that does not alliterate. Sometimes he began a verse with a single nonalliterating syllable or a short group of syllables functioning as a proclitic to the first alliterating syllable.

Each of these statements is a hypothesis that must be tested. For most of these hypotheses, the testing will come when the hypotheses have been applied in the proper order to the syllables represented in the manuscript and have—or have not—made it possible to extract the verses of the poem.

STRESS
A Simple Binary Sorting

Prosodists who attempt to analyze the *verses* of the poem usually begin by marking certain syllables for heaviest stress, some for "half-stress" or even other degrees of intermediate stress, and the remainder for least stress. Because no prosodist has so far attempted to work directly on the syllables, words, and phrases of the manuscript text, no one has asked whether it is necessary or even possible to make such discriminations on these syllables. I do not think it is. If one is attempting to elicit the verses from the manuscript text, even a three-part discrimination of stress may be unnecessary. If, then, one can elicit verses using only a binary discrimination of stress/unstress, elegance demands that one do so. Finally, the application of a binary discrimination at this point has the added advantage of leaving the way open to determining intermediate levels of stress as a function of the *position* of certain heavily stressed syllables within the constituents of the verse lines as these emerge.

The proposal to begin prosodic analysis by sorting syllables according to a binary stress scale—heavy/light—is radical; it takes us at once to the roots of the problem of determining the minimal procedures necessary to elicit verse lines from manuscript lines. The knowledge that a syllable is capable of bearing heavy stress tells us whether it is likely to participate in what was accepted as alliteration (more properly, syllabic-initial sound-patterning) by the speakers and hearers of Old English poetry. Alliteration turns out to be crucial to eliciting verse lines.

It is very important at the outset to understand that stress is one thing and alliteration another. Stress is more basic than alliteration. Alliteration will on occasion, however, signal that a syllable that is usually lightly stressed has acquired heavy stress in a particular context. But the important point to remember is that the stress system of a language, on which the poetic tradition builds, is quite separate from the use of alliteration in the poetry. Since, then, stress is more basic than alliteration, it is necessary to begin a study of prosody by attempting to locate and mark all syllables that are capable of bearing stress heavier than that of, for example, case endings, and to do this independently of and prior to any consideration of alliteration.

An Inventory of Stressed Syllables

Which syllables did the poet stress? Earlier scholars, working partly from stress in Modern English and partly from alliteration in Old English verse, made up a three-part inventory to match their three-part scale. Nouns and adjectives had heaviest stress, verbs "half-stress," and "function words" least stress. I propose a simpler and more radical method: I mark for stress the stem syllables of every member of particular classes of words such as nouns or adjectives, or, when necessary, I make distinctions by definable subclasses.

I have tried the experiment, then, of simply marking for stress the stem syllable of every occurrence of the following eight classes of words: (1) nouns, (2) adjectives, (3) adverbs, (4) verbs (other than finite forms of the copula and *peorðan*), (5) infinitives, (6) present participles, (7) past participles, and (8) numbers. To this group I have added (9) pronouns other than personal, interrogative, possessive, and demonstrative. I have also marked for stress the stem syllables of the second elements of all compounds, except the compound *sippan*. Finally, I have marked for stress the first or only syllable of every formative except, of course, those whose surviving trace is nonsyllabic and those based on adjectival case endings. I discuss the problems of such formatives after taking up problems with pronouns. I have marked for *light* stress all other syllables, namely, the prefix *ȝe-* and all verbal prefixes; case and personal endings; the second (and rarer third) syllable(s) of di- and trisyllabic words that are neither compounds nor constructed with a formative; thematic vowels of verbs; conjunctions; personal, interrogative, possessive, and demonstrative pronouns; prepositions; and finite forms of the copula and *peorðan*.

If we take formatives as the tenth class of stressed items, all stressed items share the quality of semantic weight or richness. Most of the unstressed items are semantically light but functionally—syntactically—important. If, then, this discrimination provides a solid first step toward lineation, as I think it will be shown to do, it is an indication of the systematic way in which the Old English poet dealt with stress.

Stressed and Unstressed Pronouns

Indefinite pronouns and pronouns with a prefix (even *ȝe-*) containing or consisting of formatives all seem to be semantically richer than personal, interrogative, possessive, and demonstrative pronouns. It is possible, then, to do as I did in 1966, following D. Slay and his predecessors, and single out certain pronouns as exceptions to the rule that pronouns are unstressed.[1] On the other hand, one might cull out the four light subclasses and then assign all other pronouns to the stressed inventory. In the present study I have done the latter.

There is an advantage to the course I have followed here. *Self( )*, a difficult word to fit into a subclass but definitely a word bearing some semantic weight, now falls into the general class of stressed pronoun along with *sum* (indefinite), *ʒehpa* (indefinite with a prefix), and *æniʒ* (*an* + formative *-iʒ*). On the other hand, if the prosodist follows A. Campbell, for example, who turns out to be following Sievers's *Metrik*, and thus fails to mark these pronouns for stress, he will face problems in lineating any passage containing one of them.[2]

Compounds

Most compounds present no problem. Both elements are usually transparent: for example, in *hyʒelac*, *hyʒe-* appears to be the noun 'thought' and *-lac* the noun 'play'. Since both parts of the compound belong to the same class, and this class is in the stressed inventory, I have marked the first and third syllables of this example for stress.

But what about such a "worn" compound as *hlaford*? If *-ord*, the worn trace of the noun *peard*, is to be marked for stress, it will have to be marked for the same stress as the transparent first element *hlaf-*. One can put the matter another way. With a binary stress system *-ord* will be marked in the same way as a formative such as *-end*. Scholars have usually been willing to assign "half-stress" to such a worn syllable, but only when the syllable occurs in certain metrical environments. But this kind of determination is not available to the prosodic lineator, who must decide to mark stress on the second element of *hlaford* at this point or never.

The necessity of such an absolute decision is a matter of the order with which we must proceed. If we are to try to recover the stress

1. D. Slay, "Some Aspects of the Technique of Composition of Old English Verse," *Transactions of the Philological Society (London)* (1952): 1–14.

2. A. Campbell's discussion of stress has no independent value. In Chapter 1, I quote his remark that "for the determination of accent, the metrical system of Sievers is sufficient." The sentence that precedes this one in Campbell ends: "the evidence for the accentuation of native and foreign words . . . is largely metrical" (*Old English Grammar* [Oxford, 1959], 356). My attempt to assign stress to certain classes of words prior to locating them in verse lines and verses represents an effort to break out of this circularity.

system of the language as it was adopted and modified by the poets, we must begin our analysis by marking heavy stress on all the appropriate syllables. Some of these syllables will, because of their position in the verse line and verse, as that position becomes apparent, lose a degree, or possibly more than one degree, of stress. No syllable, except those usually lightly stressed syllables that are occasionally given rhetorical emphasis, can later be *raised* in stress. To raise any syllable to heavy or "half-stress" after taking the procedural step of marking stress on the syllables of the manuscript text is to be arbitrary and unsystematic. The assigning of either heavy or light stress must be completed before we continue.

Formatives

I have marked stress on all formatives partly on the basis of the evidence provided by *-lic-* in, for example, *earfoðlice* (133V15–16) and *cymlicor* (132V14). This formative and most others, like *-sceaft* and *-sum*, present no problems. Not so *-iȝ-*. Since it is a formative not derived from a case ending, I have, with some misgivings, marked it for stress whenever it is a syllable.

At 143R20 there is no difficulty in thus marking for stress the two syllables of *æniȝ*:

$$\text{u}\text{þe}\ \text{þ}\ \text{æni}\text{ȝ}\ \text{oðer man æfre}$$

At 142V09, however, all that is left of the *-iȝ-* is the consonant *ȝ*:

$$\text{on sefan minum ȝumena ænȝum hpæt}$$

To insist on marking stress on *-iȝ-* in the first occurrence seems, in the light of the second, to be inconsistent. Yet what is different about the formative in the two examples is that in the first the formative is a full syllable, while in the second it is a mere trace. I have, then, followed this rule: a formative that equals a syllable is to be marked for stress, unless of course the formative is derived from a case ending. A formative that survives only as a trace is not and cannot be marked for stress.

Problem Syllables

I have already indicated above some doubt about marking the syllabic *-iȝ-* for stress. I also have doubts about marking the superlative indicator *-est/-ost* for stress while not marking the comparative *-or/-er*. In my—admittedly weak—defense I argue that the superlative marker, unlike the comparative, was rarely reduced to a mere trace. Perhaps, then, I should have been more consistent and discriminated between syllabic *-or* and trace *-r-*, as I have done for *-iʒ/-ʒ-* above. The decision is not quite as easy in the former case as in the latter, since *-iʒ-* belongs to the class of formatives and both *-or* and *-est/-ost* are simply "markers."[3]

I have not marked for stress the syllable *-an*, either as an adverbial suffix—here a kind of formative meaning "from"—or as an infinitive marker. Again, I think I may have been guided—or misguided—by the ability of the marker to leave only a trace in such infinitives as *seon*.

Certain questions remain. At first I simply marked weak stress on every occurrence of *þa, þenden, þær*, and *hu*. Then I tried marking occurrences of these words for stress whenever Klaeber lists one of the first three as an adverb. This procedure works well enough for *þenden*, but not so well for the ubiquitous *þa* and the puzzling *þær*. Klaeber calls the latter a "demonstrative adverb," a designation that blurs a distinction I have so far relied on. I finally decided that *þær* is a true adverb (and therefore stressed) whenever it seems to be pointing to a particular place, and something weaker whenever it correlates with or implies some form of the copula or *peorðan*. I decided arbitrarily that *þa* is a "particle" and thus is in every instance to be marked light. Despite Klaeber's confusing "adv., . . . conj.," *hu* is, I think, always a light syllable.[4]

Decisions about these "problem syllables" represent the "fine tuning" of the stress system of the poem. Such decisions are not likely to matter much if the gross sorting has been done correctly.

First Coda: Attempts to Lineate (Stress)
Lineation Based on Four Stressed Syllables per Line

Since the line of Old English verse is sometimes defined as containing four stressed syllables, I make the first attempt to lineate by

---

3. The hypothesis that *-est/-ost* was stressed in the poetry seems to be falsified by the evidence discussed in Chapter 7.

4. Fr. Klaeber, ed., *Beowulf and the Fight at Finnsburg*, 3d ed. (Boston: D. C. Heath, 1950), 409–10. At his entry for *hu* (p. 361), Klaeber makes no attempt to separate adverbial from conjunctive uses of this particle.

counting stresses on syllables. If one simply counts four syllabic stresses and breaks the line after the syllable containing the fourth stress, the opening lines of the poem look like this:

Example A

HPÆT PE GARDEna· in ʒear 1

daʒum· þeodcýninʒ 2

a þrým ʒefrunon hu ða æþelinʒ 3

as elle[n] fremedon· Oft scýld . . . 4

I now attempt to lineate by counting four stressed syllables, as above, but this time ending the line with the last syllable of the word or compound containing the last stress:

Example B

HPÆT PE GARDEna· in ʒeardaʒum· 1

þeodcýninʒa þrým 2

ʒefrunon hu ða æþelinʒas elle[n] 3

fremedon· Oft scýld scefinʒ . . . 4

I now propose to ignore the stress assigned to the expletive *HPÆT* and the adverb *Oft*, as well as the stress assigned to the formatives. Lines in the passage now look like this:

Example C

HPÆT PE GARDEna· in ʒeardaʒum· 1

þeodcýninʒa þrým ʒefrunon 2

hu ða æþelinʒas elle[n] fremedon· Oft scýld . . . 3

Next, I try a variation on the last lineation. In this variation a formative counts as a stressed syllable only if it follows a disyllabic or polysyllabic stem:

Example D

$$\text{H}\text{Þ}\text{ÆT}\ \text{Þ}\text{E}\ \text{GARDEna}\cdot\ \text{in}\ \text{ʒeardaʒum}\cdot \qquad 1$$
$$\text{þeodcýninʒa}\ \text{þrým}\ \text{ʒefrunon} \qquad 2$$
$$\text{hu}\ \eth\text{a}\ \text{æþelinʒas}\ \text{elle[n]}\ \text{fremedon}\cdot \qquad 3$$
$$\text{Oft}\ \text{scýld}\ \text{scefinʒ}\ \text{sceaþe[na]}\ \text{þreatum} \qquad 4$$
$$\text{moneʒū}\ \text{mæʒþum}\ \text{meodosetla} \qquad 5$$
$$\text{ofteah}\ \text{eʒsode}\ \text{eorl}\ \text{sý\tilde{o}\tilde{o}an}\ \text{ærest}\ .\ .\ . \qquad 6$$

We can "adjust" line "5" by ignoring the stress on *-setla*, the second element of the compound *meodosetla*. But if we do so, we imperil the lineation of lines 1 and 2:

Example E

$$\text{H}\text{Þ}\text{ÆT}\ \text{Þ}\text{E}\ \text{GARDEna}\cdot\ \text{in}\ \text{ʒeardaʒum}\cdot\ \text{þeodcýninʒa}\ \text{þrým}\ .\ .\ . \qquad 1$$

From these attempts I conclude that acceptable verse lineation cannot be based solely on counting the number of syllabic stresses.

Lineation Based on a Count of Long Stressed Syllables

It is possible that lineation may be based on some distribution of long stressed syllables. In the opening lines of the poem the stressed syllables *GAR-*, *ʒear-*, *þeod-*, *-inʒ-*, *þrým*, *-fru-*, and *ell-* are long. If we distribute two of these long syllables to a verse line and then complete the line with the whole word or compound containing the second, then the fourth, then the sixth long stressed syllable, the lineation looks like this:

Example F

$$\begin{array}{cc} 1 & 2 \\ / & / \\ \underline{/}\ / & \underline{/}\ / \end{array}$$
$$\text{H}\text{Þ}\text{ÆT}\ \text{Þ}\text{E}\ \text{GÁRDEna}\cdot\ \text{in}\ \text{ʒéardaʒum}\cdot \qquad 1$$
$$\begin{array}{cc} 3 & 4 \\ \underline{/} & /\ \underline{/} \end{array}$$
$$\text{þéodcýninʒa}\ .\ .\ . \qquad 2$$

We can try defining the verse line as a sequence of at least four stressed syllables a minimum of two of which must be long. Now the lineation looks like this:

Example G

$$\text{1} \qquad \text{2}$$

HPÆT ÞE GÁRDEna· in ȝeardaȝum·   = 5   1

$$\text{3} \quad \text{4} \quad \text{5}$$

þeodcýninȝa þrým . . .   = 4   2

The next example of lineation adds to the conditions controlling Example G the conditions that long formatives do not count either as one of the long syllables or as one of the minimum of four syllables:

Example H

$$\text{1} \qquad \text{2}$$

HPÆT ÞE GÁRDEna· in ȝeardaȝum·   = 5   1

$$\text{3} \qquad\quad \text{4} \quad \text{5}$$

þeodcýninȝa þrým ȝefrunon   = 4 + (1)   2

$$\qquad\qquad \text{6} \qquad \text{7}$$

hu ða æþelinȝas elle[n] fremedon· Oft . . .   = 4 + (1)   3

I quickly add to the conditions for Example H that a long formative may count if it follows a disyllabic or polysyllabic—but not monosyllabic—stem:

Example I

$$\quad \text{6} \quad \text{7}$$

hu ða æþelinȝas elle[n] fremedon·   = 4   3

$$\text{8} \quad \text{9} \quad \text{10}$$

Oft scýld scefinȝ sceaþe[na] . . .   = 4 + (1)   4

Since it is apparent that *Oft* makes the unwanted fourth stress in "line 4," and since *HPÆT* is supernumerary in "line 1," I try the expedient of ignoring clause-heading adverbs:

Example J

$$\qquad \text{9} \quad \text{10} \qquad\qquad \text{11}$$

Oft scýld scefinȝ sceaþe[na] þreatum   = 4 + (2)   4

$$\qquad \text{12} \qquad\quad \text{13}$$

moneȝū mæȝþum meodosetla . . .   = 4   5

Example E makes it clear that we cannot add *ofteah* to "line 5" by ignoring the long stress on the second element of the compound *meodosetla*. But the same example also seems to hold open the possibility that verse lineation may count stresses on the second element of compounds but ignore the length of such stresses. I revise "line 5" accordingly and continue:

Example K

```
        12                13
 /       /        /   [ / ]  /                       = 5
moneʒū mæʒþum meodosetla ofteah                               5
 14     15         16          17
 /       /        / ( / )      /  ( / )              = 4 + (2)
eʒsode eorl sÿððan ærest   pear[ð] feasceaft . . .           6
```

We can try the expedient of allowing tensed forms of *pesan* and *peorðan* to bear stress whenever they occur immediately before the beginning of a new alliteration. I revise "line 6" accordingly and then continue:

Example L

```
 14     15         16      17
 /       /        / ( / )   /                        = 4 + (1)
eʒsode eorl sÿððan ærest   pear[ð]                           6
 18         19           20      21
 / ( / )    /            /       /                   = 4 + (1)
feasceaft  funden he þæs frofre ʒeba[d]                      7
 22         23      24
 /          /       /      [ / ]                     = 4
peox under polcnum peorðmÿndum . . .                         8
```

What seemed promising if complicated breaks down in the "eighth line."

To sum up: if we (1) assign at least two long stressed syllables to each verse line (F), and (2) insist that each verse line also contain at least four stressed syllables (G), and (3) do not count long formatives either as one of the two long stressed syllables or as one of the four stressed syllables (H), (4) unless the long formative follows a disyllabic or polysyllabic stem (I), and (5) ignore clause-heading adverbs (J), but (6) count the stress but not the length of the second elements of compounds (K), and (7) assign stress to a tensed form of *pesan* and *peorðan* whenever one of these forms falls just before a new alliteration (L), we can lineate the first seven lines of *Beowulf* in the conventional way. But the procedure breaks down with the "eighth line."

The procedure for lineating by counting stresses and/or long stresses not only breaks down early, it is ridiculously complicated. Logic suggests that we try lineating with the aid of alliteration.

A NEW THEORY OF ALLITERATION

I turn now from stress, which is fundamental to the language whether used in ordinary speech or in poetry, to syllabic-initial sound-patterning, alliteration for short, a feature of the language that has been seized upon by poets and turned into a poetic device. No student of *Beowulf* doubts that the poet employed alliteration in special ways. Yet no one has, I think, adequately analyzed the precise ways in which the poet and his fellows exploited this device.

I present my thinking and researches on alliteration in a series of hypotheses. But first I make one general comment, at the risk of emphasizing the obvious. The systematic use of alliteration by the *Beowulf*-poet and other Anglo-Saxon poets reminds us of something very basic in the character of the Old English language and its Germanic parent: alliteration is likely to be most effectively used in poetry composed in a language that employs stress as a significant means for indicating the importance of certain syllables.

Three Hypotheses Concerning Alliteration

The three hypotheses that follow are ordered. That is, the first hypothesis is the result of looking at every scribal indication of identity in the initial sound of syllables. The second hypothesis discriminates between alliteration on two different kinds of significant syllable. The third hypothesis determines the range within which dominant alliterations are effective.

Significant/Incidental Alliteration

First hypothesis: alliteration can be considered either significant or incidental.

Alliteration is a subtly pervasive feature of natural languages. In order to develop and exploit alliteration as a device, then, poets must devise ways to distinguish significant from nonsignificant alliteration.

In 132R06 the following alliterations occur (I mark alliteration with italics):

          /   /   /   / /
     ofteah eʒsode eorl sȳððan ærest pear[ð]

The alliteration that begins this manuscript line, that of the verbal prefix *of-*, occurs on an unstressed syllable. I argue that the poets did not attend to alliteration on unstressed syllables. The alliteration is there, and it may add a pleasing note, but it does not belong to the poetic system of alliteration. The alliteration of *eʒ-*, *eorl*, *ær-*, and *-est*, on the other hand, sounds louder in our ears because these syllables are stressed. We are, I think, meant to attend to the alliteration of these stressed syllables.

The first discrimination to be made, then, is between stressed and unstressed syllables having the "same" initial sound (as "sameness" appears to have been defined by that tradition). I hypothesize that only stressed syllables participate in the poetic systematization of alliteration. Alliteration that occurs on stressed syllables is *significant* alliteration. Alliteration that occurs on unstressed syllables is *incidental* alliteration.

Dominant/Subdominant Alliteration

Second hypothesis: not all alliterating stressed syllables participate in "dominant" alliteration, the most important kind of significant alliteration.

The alliteration of *-est* in 132R06 is the fourth alliteration of the series that begins with *eʒsode*. This fact is less important than the fact that to attend to the alliteration of formatives will complicate the systematic use of the device. I hypothesize, then, that poets did not regard the alliteration of formatives as participants in the most significant kind of alliteration, for which I shall use the musical term *dominant*. The alliteration of *-est* is undeniably there and contributes to the effect of the passage—more importantly, I think, than the alliteration of such an unstressed syllable as *of-*—but alliteration on formatives does not seem to play a part in the establishing of a verse line.

Manuscript lines 132R01–2 present a different problem. Both *GAR-DEna* and *ʒeardaʒum* contain two alliterations, that of *G* and that of *D*. The *G* pattern begins before the *D* pattern begins and ends before the *D* pattern ends. Not only because of the priority, as it were, of the *G* pattern but also because of the complexity of the "crossing" of the two patterns, I argue that the alliteration of the second elements of compounds is not dominant; that is, it does not play a role in establishing the verse line. Alliteration on the second element of compounds can be termed *subdominant*. Subdominant alliteration very often forms an important part of the sound-patterning within the line established by the dominants, but subdominants do not participate in setting the major "key" of the line, as it were.[5]

Dominant alliteration, then, can be said to involve only the stressed syllables of simplex words and first elements of compounds. Henceforth I shall refer to these syllables, when they alliterate, as *dominants*.

Range

Third hypothesis: dominant alliteration operates over a certain range.

Manuscript lines 132R03–4 contain two stressed, potentially dominant syllables with the initial sound *F*:

> /   /   / /   /
> þrym ȝefrunon hu ða æþelinȝas elle[n]
> /   /   / //   /
> fremedon· Oft scyld scefinȝ sceaþe[na]

Between the *F* in *ȝefrunon* and that in *fremedon*, however, lie the dominants *æ-* and *el-* that together establish vocalic alliteration. I argue that the interposing of an alliteration—that is, at least two stressed syllables that begin with the same sound—between two potentially alliterating syllables places the latter "out of range" of each other. Hence I have not marked as *dominant* the alliterating syllables *-frun-* and *frem-*.

On the other hand, alliteration may be established by two dominants over the interposition of several potential dominants. The range over which dominant alliteration can be effected seems to have been carefully calculated: if more than two stressed syllables occur between the dominants, no more than two of a maximum of three interposed stressed syllables may be potential dominants, that is, simplexes or first elements of compounds. The following passage illustrates what I argue is the maximum effective range of dominant alliteration in *Beowulf*:

---

5. I gratefully borrow the term *key* from my colleague and friend Jess B. Bessinger.

/   /   /   /   /
[m]id ýldum· þ hit pearð ealӡearo healær
/   /   /   /
na mæst scop him *h*eort naman se þe his
/   /   /   /   /
*þ*ordes ӡeþeald *þ*ide hæfde· He beot ne   (133V08–10)

In the rather long passage between the last instance of the vocalic dominant, *ealӡearo*, and the first *W* dominant, *þordes*, *H*-alliteration seems to emerge as the dominant. Yet the *H*-alliteration is carried only by *heal-* and *heort*. Between these two stressed syllables three stresses occur, on *-ærn-*, *mæst*, and *scop*. Since, however, *-ærn-* is the stressed syllable of the second element of a compound, only the potentially dominant simplexes *mæst* and *scop* count fully in the calculation of range.

In summary, then, dominant, or lineating, alliteration attends only to stressed simplexes and the first element of compounds. It attends to these syllables in order to establish the verse line, that is, to delineate. If such syllables are to delineate, they must be in range of each other. Range is calculated in terms only of stressed syllables, never unstressed. Maximum effective range between dominants appears to consist of no more than two potential dominants plus one subdominant. Any additional interposed stressed syllable places the two potentially alliterating syllables out of dominant range of each other.

The hypotheses discussed in this section cannot be completely tested until all the features and functions of syllables discussed in this chapter have been used in an attempt to elicit verses.

Second Coda: Attempts to Lineate (Alliteration)

An attempt to base verse lineation entirely on alliteration as defined above yields several possibilities. One we may call "early alliteration," the other, "late." By "early alliteration" I indicate that the verse line begins with the word or compound containing the first alliterating syllable of the series. By "late alliteration" I indicate that the line ends with the word or compound containing the last alliterating syllable of the series. I begin with a simple form of "late alliteration."

Example M

HÞÆT ÞE GARDEna· in ӡeardaӡum·	1
þeodcýninӡa þrým	2
ӡefrunon hu ða æþelinӡas elle[n] fremedon· *Oft*	3
scýld scefinӡ sceaþe[na] . . .	4

Andreas Heusler's approach to the meter of the poem suggests a way of dealing with such syllables as HƿÆT ƿE and ȝefrunon hu ða.[6] "Heuslerian lineation" treats such syllables as "interlinear" rather than as part of the verse line. From the point of view of meter, these syllables are treated as "anacrusis."

Example N

"Anacrusis"	"Verse Line"	
HƿÆT ƿE	GARDEna· in ȝeardaȝum·	1
	ƿeodcȳninȝa ƿrȳm	2
ȝefrunon hu ða	æƿelinȝas elle[n] fremedon· Oft	3
	scȳld scefinȝ sceaƿe[na]	4
ƿreatum	moneȝū mæȝƿum meodosetla	5
ofteah	eȝsode eorl sȳððan ærest	6

Heuslerian lineation has the virtue of consistency and simplicity. It has the defect of consigning to "anacrusis" not only such lengthy passages as ȝefrunon hu ða but such stressed words as ȝefrunon, ƿreatum, and ofteah. Even if one argues, as I do not, that the stress on verbs is less or less important than that on nouns, consigning the noun ƿreatum to anacrusis stretches anacrusis to the breaking point. Heusler's *Metrik* implies lineation like that in Example N.

"Early alliteration" provides a simpler way to build lines.

Example O

HƿÆT ƿE GARDEna· in ȝeardaȝum·	1
ƿeodcȳninȝa ƿrȳm ȝefrunon hu ða	2
æƿelinȝas elle[n] fremedon· Oft	3
scȳld scefinȝ sceaƿe[na] ƿreatum	4
moneȝū mæȝƿum meodosetla ofteah	5
eȝsode eorl sȳððan ærest pear[ð]	6
feasceaft funden he ƿæs frofre ȝeba[d]	7
peox under polcnum peorðmȳndum ƿah oð ƿ him . . .	8

Like Heuslerian lineation, this method is simple and consistent. But both methods obscure clause boundaries. The clause boundary in "line 2" falls just before the two final unstressed monosyllables, that in "line 3" just before the final *Oft*, that in "line 8" before the final three monosyllables. But I am getting ahead of myself. The possible role of clause boundaries in lineating is the subject of the next subsection.

---

6. Andreas Heusler, *Deutsche Versgeschichte*, Pauls Grundriss der Germanischen Philologie 8 (Berlin and Leipzig: W. de Gruyter, 1925–1929).

For the sake of completeness, I try lineating by combining the counting of stressed syllables, as in Example L, above, with alliteration. In this attempt all the words or compounds containing a syllable with the same alliteration will be placed on the same line. At the same time, every line will continue to the end of the word or compound containing the fourth stressed syllable, as stressed syllables are counted in Example L.

Example P

HƉÆT ƉE GARDEna· in ȝeardaȝum·	= 4 1
þeodcỳninȝa þrỳm ȝefrunon	= 4 2
hu ða æþelinȝas elle[n] fremedon·	= 4 3
Oft scỳld scefinȝ sceaþe[na] þreatum	= 4 4
moneȝū mæȝþum meodosetla . . .	= 4 5

In this example I have not considered *Oft* as alliterating since it is not counted as a stressed syllable. Even so, the lineation breaks down in the following line.

Alliteration considered by itself, as in Examples M, N, and O, has the great virtue of providing us with a far simpler basis for lineating than the various ways of counting stressed and/or long stressed syllables tried in the first coda.

CLAUSES AND CLAUSE BOUNDARIES IN *BEOWULF*
Introduction

The purpose of this section is to determine the part clause boundaries play in verse lineation. In order to locate clause boundaries it is of course first necessary to determine clauses. I have tried to do so with a listener rather than a reader in mind. What follows, then, is an attempt to formulate a grammar that takes into account the special problems likely to be faced by a listener. To take one example, a listener will, I think, hear the following passage in manuscript lines 132R17–18, *scỳldes eafera scedelandum in*—a passage that is isolated from both the clause that precedes it and the one that follows it—not "in apposition to" *beopulf þæs breme* in the preceding verse line but as a clause from which *þæs* has been deleted. It is true that the two noun phrases, *beopulf* in 132R16 and *scýldes . . . in*, are in apposition, but this fact tells us little about the dynamic of the listener.

It is because I am attempting to keep the listener in mind that I find particularly useful Berkley Peabody's distinction between "clause" and "sentence": "By 'clause' is intended a 'syntactically closed period,' a quantum of structure. By 'sentence' is intended 'a semantically closed period,' a quantum of sense."[7] Peabody's distinction can be used to discriminate a syntactic core, the minimal quantum of structure, from additions made to the core for semantic reasons. It is these syntactic cores that a careful listener must catch.

The syntactic core is, simply, a certain kind of relationship. In certain Indo-European languages the minimal relationship seems to be that of "subject" to "predicate," for example, *he . . . bæd* in manuscript line 132V07. The form of *he*—nominative, singular, masculine, third person—sets up the expectation that a verb in a certain form—third-person singular—will follow. To put it another way, *he* demands a verb in the third-person singular, whether that verb follows or precedes it. When a verb in the appropriate form occurs in the vicinity of *he*, the relationship is completed.

The Core Relationship

Noam Chomsky expresses this relationship with a tree diagram.[8]

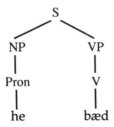

I borrow Chomsky's tree diagram but, following Peabody, substitute "C" (for "clause") for Chomsky's "S" (for "sentence") at the top of the

7. Berkley Peabody, *The Winged Word: A Study in the Technique of Ancient Greek Oral Composition as Seen Principally through Hesiod's Works and Days* (Albany: State University of New York Press, 1975), 118.
8. I first encountered Noam Chomsky's "tree diagrams" in his *Aspects of the Theory of Syntax* (Cambridge: MIT Press, 1965f.). I have found Adrian Akmajian and Frank Heny, *An Introduction to the Principles of Transformational Syntax* (Cambridge: MIT Press, 1975), useful in drawing my own trees. I hasten to add that neither Chomsky nor Akmajian and Heny should be blamed for strange growths in my nursery.

tree. What Chomsky's tree makes graphic is that the relationship between the noun phrase (NP) and the verb phrase (VP) is not linear but hierarchical. The relationship between the two is "dominated" by the concept "clause."

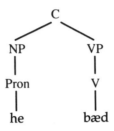

Certain kinds of words can be closely attached to this central and minimal quantum of structure. One kind of word is the adverbial particle *spa*. This close but less significant relationship can be diagramed in this way:

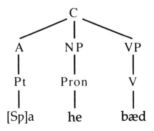

Particles like *spa* are not always expressed before the central relationship, as [*Sp*]*a* is in 132V07. Conjunctions, on the other hand, always indicate the beginning of a new syntactic relationship; for example: *oð þ . . . æʒhpýlc . . . scolde* (132R09–10). The conjunction *oð þ* will also be represented at the extreme left of the tree diagram:

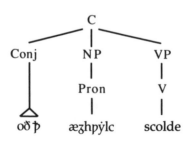

Like conjunctions, demonstratives, often in oblique cases, can introduce clauses in *Beowulf*, for example, *þone ʒod sende . . .* (132R12–13). Unlike conjunctions, such demonstratives will usually not occur at the extreme left of the tree diagram:

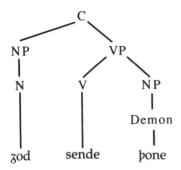

The accusative singular masculine *þone* expresses a relationship that is close to the central configuration, not peripheral as are conjunctions. But *þone*, because its function within the clause is clearly indicated by its form, can be moved to the beginning of its clause. A demonstrative in an oblique case can, then, mark the beginning of a clause.

Not every clause in *Beowulf* is introduced by either a conjunction or a demonstrative. In other words, the beginning of every clause is not so clearly signaled as are the beginnings of these clauses. What, then, does signal the beginning of each successive clause? To begin to answer this question, in Table 3.1 I list and then discuss ten of the simplest types of clauses in the order in which they occur in the early lines of the poem.

Table 3.1. A Short Inventory of Simple, Fully Expressed Clauses

1. hu ða æþelinʒas elle[n] fremedon·	132R03–4
2. he þæs frofre ʒeba[d]	132R07
3. þone ʒod sende folce to frofre	132R12–13
4. beopulf þæs breme	132R16
5. blæd pide spranʒ	132R17
6. þ hine on ylde eft ʒepuniʒen [pilʒ]esiþas	132V01–2
7. þonne piʒ cume	132V02
8. leode ʒelæsten	132V02
9. hi hyne [þ]a ætbæron to brimes faroþe	132V05–6
10. [Sp]a he selfa bæd	132V07

The clause numbered 8 expresses only the core relationship.[9]

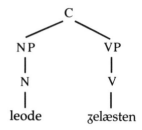

Number 7 expresses the core relationship after a conjunctive particle:

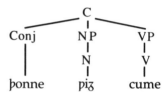

Number 5 expresses this core relationship along with a locative adverb:

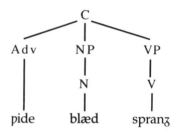

Number 4 replaces with an adjective the NP to the right of the V and under its domination:

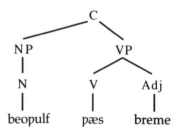

9. By "core" relationship I refer to the hierarchical "subject-predicate" relationship just discussed.

Number 10 has been partially diagramed above. A fuller diagram must take into account the stressed pronoun, *selfa*, an intensified repetition of the unstressed personal pronoun *he*:

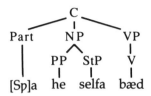

Number 1 expresses both the core relationship and the subordinate but still important "direct object" relationship after a conjunctive particle:

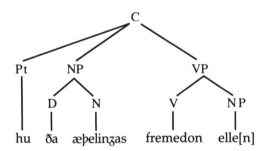

Number 6, despite its length, expresses only the core subject-verb relationship and the subordinate but important direct object relationship. It is introduced by *þ*, the abbreviation for *þæt*. Originally a form of the demonstrative, *þ* asserts itself as a conjunction partly by taking a position at the beginning of the clause. The two adverbial components, *on ylde* and *eft*, can be taken as a single unit from the point of view of structure:

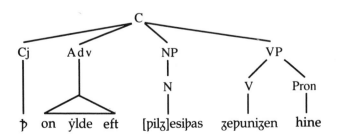

Number 2 expresses, along with the core relationship, both the direct object relationship and another that must be translated into Modern English by a prepositional phrase:

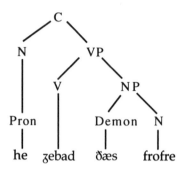

Number 3 has been partially diagramed above. A fuller diagram contains an indirect object and a prepositional phrase closely related to the latter:

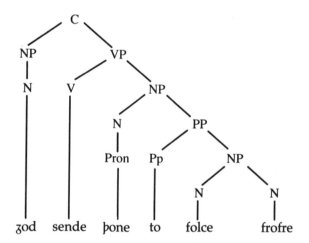

Number 9 contains the central relationship, a direct object, and a locative prepositional phrase. The particle [þ]a has been moved from the position of the conjunction to that of an adverb:

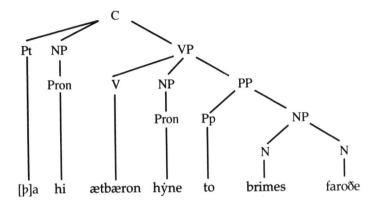

As the tree diagrams show, each of the ten clauses of this "short inventory" expresses fully the core relationship. The subject, the NP directly dominated by C, appears at the left or somewhat nearer left than center, and the predicate, the VP, appears farther to the right. For reasons that will become clear as I proceed, I refer to such clauses as "fully expressed," or "F-clauses."

Since the particular problem the lineator faces is locating the beginning of each successive clause, I tabulate the way in which each clause in the short inventory begins:

Two clauses (1 and 10) begin with a particle, *hu* and *[Sp]a*
Two clauses (2 and 9) begin with a personal pronoun, *he* and *hi*
One clause (3) begins with the demonstrative in an oblique case, *þone*
Two clauses (6 and 7) begin with a conjunction, *þ* and *þonne*
Three clauses (4, 5, and 8) begin with a noun, *beopulf*, *blæd*, and *leode*

Which of these five different kinds of word unequivocally signals the beginning of a clause? Despite numbers 4, 5, and 8, we can rule out nouns on the basis of numbers 1, 3, 6, and 7, in which a noun in the nominative case occurs after the beginning of the clause. Despite numbers 2 and 9, we can rule out the personal pronoun in the nominative case on the basis of number 10. Despite number 3, we can rule out a demonstrative in an oblique case on the basis of number 2. In each of these instances the short inventory makes it clear that a word of each class can, indeed does, introduce a clause. But it is equally clear that a noun or personal or demonstrative pronoun does not necessarily signal the beginning of a clause.

What about "particles," such as *hu* and *spa* in the inventory? The first, *hu*, unequivocally introduces a new clause at each of its fourteen occurrences in *Beowulf*. On the other hand, *spa* equivocates, as 157R06 shows: in *þa him spa ʒeþearfod* [*pæs*], *spa* functions as an adverb. Of the two particles that occur in the inventory, then, only one reliably signals the beginning of a clause.

One class remains, conjunctions, represented by *þ* and *þonne*. Like *spa*, *þonne* can on occasion function as an adverb, as 165V13–14 shows: *mæʒ þonne on þæm ʒolde onʒitan. þ*, too, equivocates, showing at times its origin as the neuter singular form of the demonstrative pronoun: *þ pæs ʒod cyninʒ* (132R11).

There are, indeed, unequivocal conjunctions, like *oð þ*, which occurs first at 132R09. If we study all the clauses, fully expressed or not, that occur between the beginning of the poem and our number 10, we find that only one clause is introduced by a pair of words that is always unequivocally a conjunction. We also find that only one more clause is introduced by the clause-heading particle *hu*. Clearly, the lineator cannot locate clause beginnings simply by looking for conjunctions and conjunctive particles.

What, then, can he rely on? The answer, I think, has to be a sense that a new core relationship is being set up.

Why cannot the lineator simply do what we have been doing so far? Why can't he work backward from the VP to the left-hand NP, from predicate to subject, and then simply mark the point at which the completed relationship begins? He can, of course, and often does exactly this. But what does he do when he comes to this phrase in 132R06: *eʒsode eorl?*

In this phrase, if we are not to take *eorl* as the subject, no subject occurs:

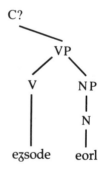

Only the VP of this truncated "clause" is expressed. Of course, we sense that the subject is a word that has already occurred: it is *scÿld* in 132R04.

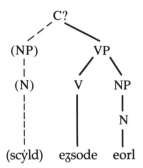

But *scÿld* has already completed one relationship: *scÿld . . . ofteah* (132R04–6). In fact, the crucial second member of the earlier relationship, the verb *ofteah*, occurs just before *eʒsode*. Immediately following the direct object of *eʒsode*, *eorl*, occurs the conjunction *syðða̋n*, an indication that yet another clause is beginning. *eʒsode eorl* is not a fully expressed clause, but it *is* isolated from the clauses that flank it.

The Isolation of "Clauses"

The phrase *eʒsode eorl*, if *eorl* is the direct object, does not make a complete clause. But in line 132R06 the phrase can be said to be isolated by *ofteah*, the verb that completes the core relationship with an earlier noun, and by the conjunction *syðða̋n* that follows the phrase. *eʒsode eorl*, then, must either be treated as a sort of coda or adjunct to the *scÿld . . . ofteah* clause, or in some way a clause by itself.

I prefer the latter possibility. Following Peabody's formulation, I take *eʒsode eorl* to belong to the same sentence as *scÿld . . . ofteah* but to a different clause. I argue for this analysis on the grounds that *eʒsode eorl* is isolated from the clauses that flank it.

The notion of isolation is, I think, of great importance to the study of the clauses of *Beowulf*. But before I go further, I sum up the ways in which a passage can be isolated:

(1) Any passage is isolated at its end by the beginning of the next clause. For example, the *ÞE . . . ʒefrunon* clause is clearly isolated by the conjunctive particle *hu* that belongs to and begins the following clause.

(2) A passage that occurs between the beginning of a following clause and the end of a fully expressed preceding clause is isolated. For example, *spæse ʒesiþas* (132V06) is isolated by the *[Sp]a* of the following clause and by the fact that the preceding clause contains the same constituent serving the same function as *ʒesiþas*, namely, the nominative plural personal pronoun *hi*.

(3) A slightly different criterion seems to apply to *scýldes eafera scedelandum in* (132R17–18). The passage is clearly isolated at its end by the *Spa* of the following clause. On the other hand, *eafera* in this passage refers to *beopulf* in 132R16. But the clause in which *beopulf* occurs is separated from the *eafera* passage by the F-clause *blæd pide spranʒ*, a clause to which nothing in the isolated passage is related. I conclude, then, that *scýldes . . . in* is isolated at its beginning by the interposition of an F-clause to which it has no syntactic relationship.

I argue that any passage that is isolated in the above ways functions as a clause in its context. It does so by seeming to borrow one or the other or even both of the constituents of the central relationship, that is, of the relationship of subject to predicate. The "clause" *eʒsode eorl* borrows its subject from the preceding clause, while *spæse ʒesiþas* borrows its verb from the preceding clause. From another point of view it is possible to argue that the poet has deleted the subject of *eʒsode* from the *eʒsode* clause and the predicate of *ʒesiþas* from that clause. This kind of deletion operates according to strict rules and can be tested, as I shall show later. But first I shall take up F-clauses that are somewhat more complex than those so far analyzed.

Fully Expressed Clauses

The importance of beginning with fully expressed clauses should by now be clear. The F-clauses form a skeleton, or at least a backbone, on which the poet can hang the clauses he does not fully express. But not all F-clauses are as simple as those in the short inventory. I begin with an example:

> Oft scýld scefinʒ sceaþe[na]
> þreatum moneʒū mæʒþum meodosetla
> ofteah . . .   (132R04–6)

Both subject and verb are expressed: *scýld* and *ofteah*. The problem lies in the doubling of the indirect objects of *ofteah*, *sceaþe[na] þreatum* and *moneʒū mæʒþum*. The two indirect objects cannot be "nested" since the second phrase seems to be a variation of the first. More important, the expression of the two indirect objects takes place before the occurrence of the second major constituent of the clause, the verb *ofteah*. In a sense, then, we cannot speak of a single clause but of at least two clauses telescoped together:

(1) scẏld ofteah meodosetla sceaþe[na] þreatum
(2) scẏld ofteah meodosetla moneʒū mæʒþum

I propose to call the *Oft . . . ofteah* passage a *splice*. I define a splice as a clause in which one of the constituents is repeated, usually with a variation in the expression, before the verb occurs or is completed. If the verb occurs or is completed before the variation takes place, then the passage is not a splice and may, indeed, be more than one clause. The late-occurring verb is, I believe, the hallmark of the splice.

In this passage the variation begins with *moneʒū*. Thus, whatever device we choose to mark a splice must be used at *moneʒū*. Since this is a question of punctuation, I leave the matter for later.

The second passage that seems to contain a splice occurs at 132R15–16:

him þæs liffrea þuldres pealdend
þoroldare forʒeaf

The verb *forʒeaf* occurs only after the left NP, *liffrea*, has been repeated and varied by *þuldres pealdend*. The clause is therefore a splice with *þuldres* marking the beginning of the variation.

Is the passage that begins the poem, *HÞÆT . . . fremedon*, a splice? The answer might seem to be yes, since this clause at first seems to fulfill the two conditions for a splice, that is, the passage contains two constituents of the same type and the verb occurs late. The two similar constituents are *GARDEna* and *þeodcẏninʒa*. Both are compound nouns inflected in the genitive plural. The difference between these two constituents and the two repeated constituents of the *Oft . . . ofteah* and *him . . . forʒeaf* clauses lies in the fact that *GARDEna* and *þeodcẏninʒa* do not necessarily have to replace each other. The first phrase can be taken as depending on the second: "*þrẏm* of great kings of spear-Danes." By contrast, there is no question about the repeated constituents in the two splices discussed earlier. *moneʒū mæʒþum* replaces, that is varies, *sceaþe[na] þreatum*. Even more clearly, the left NP *þuldres pealdend* varies *liffrea* in the second splice discussed. The often-mentioned device of variation in Old English poetry has its basis in such syntactic phenomena as the splice. The first passage in the poem, then, despite its length and apparent complexity, can simply be taken as a single clause. If it is taken as a splice, on the other hand, the two genitive plural constructions must be taken as independent of each other.

The analysis of splices would be incomplete without some account of more complex structures than those studied so far. The first such structure occurs at lines 132V12–13:

> þær þæs madma fela
> of feorpeȝum frætpa ȝelæded·

There can be little doubt that *þær* signals the beginning of a clause. The hearer or reader might at first take *fela* to complete a clause that indicates, somewhat vaguely, the wealth of Scyld's heirs. He or she can still fit *of feorpeȝum* into this clause: *þær þæs madma fela of feorpeȝum*. But the passage continues with *frætpa ȝelæded*. The last two words make it necessary to recall or return to *þæs* and *fela*, *þæs* in order to complete what now seems to be a preterit passive, *þæs . . . ȝelæded*, and *fela* because of the case of *frætpa*. One's sense of the syntax of the passage has been altered by the late occurrence of *ȝelæded*: the opening words no longer convey the vague sense that there was great wealth; instead, the opening words must now be taken as the beginning of a clause that states that great wealth was brought. The case of *frætpa* complicates matters further: the genitive plural makes it dependent upon *fela*, as is *madma*. Thus *frætpa* can be said to vary *madma*.

The more one studies this passage the more complicated it seems. It is possible to take the eight words as participating in six overlapping but different clauses:

> (1) þær þæs madma fela
> (2) þæs madma fela of feorpeȝum
> (3) þær þæs frætpa fela
> (4) frætpa fela þæs of feorpeȝum
> (5) þær þæs ȝelæded madma fela
> (6) þær þæs ȝelæded frætpa fela

For the purpose of lineating I regard the passage as a true splice in which the verb is completed late though begun early.

Many clauses in *Beowulf* give a somewhat similar impression of conflation and condensation. Just before this passage the following passage occurs:

aledon þa leofne
þeoden beaʒa brȳttan on bearm scipes
mærne be mæste (132V10–12)

There is no subject of *aledon* specified beyond the plural inflection of the verb. The first clause in the passage is, then, *(X) aledon þeoden*. The inflection of *brȳttan* seems to require that one recall *(X) aledon*. But the prepositional phrase following *brȳttan* seems to me to recall an earlier instance of a clause consisting of two linked nouns followed by a prepositional phrase: *scȳldes eafera scedelandum in* (132R17–18). I argue, then, that the *aledon* passage is not a splice. First and most important, the passage does not contain the hallmark of the splice, a late-occurring or late-completed verb. Second, it is possible to take *beaʒa brȳttan on bearm scipes* as a separate clause parallel in every way but the inflection of *brȳttan* to *scȳldes eafera scedelandum in*.

To sum up: a true splice is marked by a late-occurring or late-completed verb before which at least one constituent other than the verb phrase is repeated.

Infinitive Phrases

I begin with a lengthy fully expressed clause near the opening of the poem:

oð þ him æʒhpȳlc þara ȳmbsittendra
ofer hronrade hȳran scolde (132R09–10)

Despite the length of the left NP—*æʒhpȳlc* through either *ȳmbsittendra* or possibly *hronrade*—this clause is rather simple. But it neatly raises the question of the treatment of infinitives.

I treat every infinitive as a separate clause that is at times nested in the clause containing the main verb. The *oð þ* passage provides a good example of such nesting. A simplified analysis of the passage locates the following clauses:

(1) æʒhpȳlc hȳran
(2) æʒhpȳlc scolde

The apparently single clause can be split into two clauses each of which is based on a verb form. This splitting is the very opposite of the phenomenon I have described as splicing. Put simply, I take it to be the property of every verb form to generate its own clause.

Enough remains of the damaged clause beginning in 132R18 to make it possible to observe such splitting even here:

> Spa sceal..........ma ʒode
> ʒepýrcean

(1) (X) sceal
(2) (X) ʒepýrcean

There is a difference between these two examples, however. The first is nested; the second is not. What is left of the subject—if that is what *ma* represents—falls between the main verb, *sceal*, and the infinitive. *Spa sceal (X)* can therefore be taken as a separate clause from *(X) ʒode ʒepýrcean*, even though each clause shares the interposed subject. The same is true for the following passage:

> [l]ofdædū sceal in mæʒþa ʒehpære man ʒe
> [þ]eon·   (132V03–4)

(1) man sceal [l]ofdædū in mæʒþa ʒehpære
(2) man ʒe[þ]eon [l]ofdædū in mæʒþa ʒehpære

The passage following this one presents an interesting variation of it:

> him ða scýld ʒepat to ʒescæphpile
> [fe]lahror feran on frean pære   (132V04–5)

(1) scýld ʒepat
(2) [fe]lahror feran

In this passage both alliteration and the apparent functioning of *[fe]lahror* as a surrogate subject make it easy to detach the infinitive clause from the *ʒepat* clause. But *[fe]lahror* raises its own problems, which I take up in a section on adjectives.

Adjectives in Beowulf

Adjectives in *Beowulf* sometimes behave as they do in Modern English. For example:

þ pæs ʒod cýninʒ	(132R11)
beopulf pæs breme	(132R16)
ʒepýrcean fromum feohʒiftum	(132R19)

On the other hand, an adjective can appear in a clause containing neither a noun nor a pronoun:

> sýððan ærest pear[ð]
> feasceaft funden   (132R06–7)

How is the adjective functioning in such a clause? It is possible that the Anglo-Saxon poet and his audience understood the adjective as standing for an entire nested clause—"after (he who was) *feasceaft* first became found"—or that they sensed two separate clauses—"after (he) first became *feasceaft*, (he) became found." In the first interpretation the hearer has to supply three words; in the second, he has to supply the pronoun at two points.

A third possibility takes the adjective as a replacement for the missing subject: "after first *feasceaft* became found." I think there is good evidence that an adjective sometimes replaces a subject noun in *Beowulf*. For example:

> ðæm eafera pæs
> æfter cenned ʒeonʒ in ʒeardum   (132R11–12)

The last three words compose, I think, a separate truncated clause. The poet is not likely to have wanted *ʒeonʒ* to modify *eafera* in what I take to be the first clause. Such an interpretation would yield the following nonsense: "to him a young heir was afterward born in the enclosed-places." At birth an heir—or any other baby—is very young indeed. It makes more sense, then, to take *ʒeonʒ* as heading its own clause:

> (1) eafera pæs æfter cenned ðæm
> (2) (pæs) ʒeonʒ in ʒeardum

In another passage a compound adjective seems to me to head an infinitive clause. I quote the passage in its context:

> him ða scýld ʒepat to ʒescæphpile
> [fe]lahror feran on frean pære hi hýne
> [þ]a ætbæron   (132V04–6)

As I have argued in the section on infinitives, an infinitive functions in the same way as does a finite verb to complete the central relationship of a clause. Hence the passage seems to me to contain three clauses:

> (1) him ða scýld ʒepat to ʒescæphpile
> (2) [fe]lahror feran on frean pære
> (3) hi hýne [þ]a ætbæron

If we yield to the urge to turn the passage into prose, we can, of course, read something like this: "then [fe]*lahror* Scyld departed at shaped-time to fare into lord's keeping." Prose order here yields good sense. But it does so at the cost of wrenching [*fe*]*lahror* from its position as the initiator of an alliteration. In contrast, to take the passage as a series of clauses leaves each segment just as the poet composed it.

I argue that even an adjective marked with an oblique case inflection that links it with an earlier noun functions as the subject of a clause when the adjective is not adjacent to its noun:

> aledon þa leofne
> þeoden beaӡa brýttan on bearm scipes
> mærne be mæste   (132V10–11)

A prose-order translation might run like this: "(they) laid then beloved prince, well-known rings' distributor, in bosom of ship by mast." But again prose order wrenches *mærne* from its position at the head of an alliterating series. Further, there appears to be a splice in the repetition of the direct object of *aledon*. It turns out to be a false splice, however, since the verb occurs early in the passage. An alternative analysis leaves everything where it is:

> (1) aledon þa leofne þeoden
> (2) (aledon) beaӡa brýttan on bearm scipes
> (3) (aledon) mærne (brýttan) be mæste

Underlying the surface placement of the words in the passage is at least one other possibility:

> (1) aledon þa leofne þeoden
> (2) beaӡa brýtta . . . (þæs) on bearm scipes
> (3) mære (þæs) be mæste

This analysis takes the inflections on *brýttan* and *mærne* to be gestures—backward nods, as it were—used by the poet for a sort of syntactic account-keeping as he moves further away from the early-placed verb.

Not every adjective placed in a different alliterating series from its noun functions as do *ӡeonӡ* and *mærne*. The following passage makes this point:

> þa ӡýt hie him asetton seӡen [ӡe.]
> denne heah ofer heafod   (133R01–2)

Klaeber takes *heah* to be an adjective modifying *seӡen*. He does so by treating *seӡen* as masculine in regard to [*ӡe.*]*denne* and neuter in regard to *heah*.[10] If, for the moment, we follow Klaeber here and take *heah* as an adjective, it becomes clear that it does not head a separate clause because it produces an ungrammatical phrase:

heah (pæs) ofer heafod

There is an important distinction between *mærne be mæste* and *heah ofer heafod*. In the latter phrase *heah* and *ofer heafod* both have a spatial reference, but in the former only *be mæste* does. The *brÿtta* is *mære* no matter where he is.

But I think Klaeber is wrong in interpreting *heah ofer heafod* as he does: *heah* does not modify *seʒen*; it is part of a three-word adverbial phrase that indicates the placement of the sign in relation to the hero's body. But the passage can serve as a warning to beware of taking every adjective followed by a prepositional phrase as a separate clause.

The evidence suggests, then, that adjectives placed at some distance from the nouns they would probably modify in prose order, particularly adjectives that also alliterate differently from the noun, have a high degree of independence in *Beowulf*. The verse dialect of the poem frequently augments a short, "independent" adjective with a prepositional phrase the noun of which alliterates with the adjective. The whole phrase then often creates the sense of a clause in which the adjective functions as a subject from which the verb is deleted.

In accordance with the foregoing analysis, I have followed this procedure: I have taken an adjective that occurs after the core relationship (that is, subject and predicate) has been fully stated, or completed by implication, to be part of a different clause from the one containing the noun it modifies.

Clauses Showing Deletion
Introduction
There appear to be two different kinds of clause in the poem. The first kind contains both the left NP, the subject, and the VP, the predicate. In other words, both constituents of the core relationship are *expressed*. The other kind of clause is one that, isolated by flanking

---

10. Fr. Klaeber, ed., *Beowulf and the Fight at Finnsburg* (Boston, 1922f.), glossary entry *heah*, p. 352 (in 3d ed., 1936f.); fuller discussion in notes, p. 127.

clauses, does *not* express one or the other or both of the central constituents. I call these truncated clauses "deletion clauses."

Three types of deletion seem to provide a sufficient discrimination of these clauses: subject deletion, verb deletion, and deletion of both subject and verb, which I refer to as "double deletion." I take up each of these types in order.

Subject Deletion

If one accepts the argument that every verb implies a new clause, one is likely to take the words *eʒsode eorl*, sandwiched in line 132R06 between the verb *ofteah* and the conjunction *sȳððan*, as a clause. The usual understanding of this clause, diagramed earlier, requires the borrowing of a subject from an earlier clause, that based on *ofteah*. From another point of view *eʒsode eorl* is a clause from which the subject, *scȳld* or *he*, has been deleted.

The next word after *eorl* is *sȳððan*, here a conjunction and thus a signal that a new clause is beginning:

> sȳððan ærest pear[ð]
> feasceaft funden he þæs frofre ʒeba[d]   (132R06–7)

The end of the *sȳððan* passage is marked by the *he* that introduces the next clause and serves as subject to the next verb, *ʒeba[d]*. The five words between *eorl* and *he*, then, are isolated as though they formed a complete clause.

The earlier analysis of adjectives suggests that it is moot whether this clause should be included among those from which the subject has been deleted. The adjective *feasceaft* can be understood as a surrogate subject:

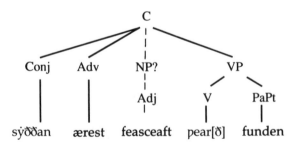

No matter how one takes *feasceaft*, *sȳððan* signals a new clause.

The entire manuscript line following *ʒeba[d]* consists of five words:

peox under polcnum peorðmẏndum þah   (132R08)

The two verbs, *peox* and *þah*, imply two clauses. The passage is properly isolated: *peox* is cut off from the previous clause by *ʒeba[d]*, *þah* from the following clause by the conjunctive phrase *oð þ* that begins the next manuscript line. Neither *peox* nor *þah* has an expressed subject, unless the inflection of each, first/third-person singular, preterit indicative, is subject enough. In any case, the ambiguities of the inflection—which person? which gender?—force the hearēr or reader to recall or examine the context in order to associate the appropriate subject or subjects with the two verbs. For this reason I take the *eʒsode* clause and the *peox* and *þah* clauses as showing deletion of their subject. From each clause the same subject has been deleted, *scẏld*, which occurred in line 132R04.

Immediately following the long clause that begins with *oð þ* in manuscript line 9 and ends with *scolde* in line 10 occurs a two-word passage, *ʒomban ʒẏldan*. The isolating of the passage is completed by *þ* in *þ pæs ʒod cẏninʒ*. Since the subject of *ʒẏldan* is *æʒhpẏlc . . .* , in the preceding clause, the two-word passage displays subject deletion. It is possible to take *ʒomban ʒẏldan*, then, as something "tacked onto" the previous fully expressed clause. But the very fact that a new infinitive has been tacked onto the complete *oð þ* clause tends to bear out the view expressed earlier that every infinitive as well as every verb generates its own clause.

The effect of subject deletion is obvious as soon as one makes the experiment of putting the deleted subject back into the clause:

> *scẏld eʒsode eorl
> *scẏld peox under polcnum
> *scẏld peorðmẏndum þah

And so on. The compression of these clauses is gone. More important, perhaps, *scẏld* would monotonously control the alliteration. On the other hand, *scẏld* need not always usurp the initial position:

> *eʒsode scẏld eorl
> *peox scẏld under polcnum
> *peorðmẏndum scẏld þah

The clauses still sound awkward, though all are possible realizations in which the problem of alliteration is handled somewhat better. We cannot, of course, speak yet of the way in which the verse line is affected by subject deletion. But clearly the sense of compression the poem often gives, of "loading every rift with ore," depends in part on subject deletion.

Verb Deletion

Earlier I proposed to apply the principle that every verb generates a new clause. The application of that principle seems to work well enough. Now we must deal with the opposite situation, that in which an isolated passage contains no verb. I begin with an example.

Between the clause *blæd þide spranȝ* and the capitalized *Spa* that heads the damaged clause toward the bottom of 132R these words occur:

> scȳldes eafera scede
> landum in   (132R17–18)

The four words are isolated by the flanking clauses. Yet there is no verb in the isolated passage. The words must, then, be attached in some way to a preceding clause.

The problem is that *blæd*, in the immediately preceding clause, is not an appropriate replacement for *eafera* in this. *beopulf*, however, in the clause just before the *blæd* clause, is indeed *scȳldes eafera*. The *blæd* clause might, then, be taken to be an interruption of or intrusion into a clause that begins with *beopulf* in manuscript line 16:

> beopulf þæs breme
> —blæd þide spranȝ—
> scȳldes eafera (þæs breme) scedelandum in·

This is the way Klaeber's punctuation interprets the passage.

A simpler way of dealing with the four words of the *scȳldes* passage is to assume the deletion of the single word *þæs*. The virtue of this reading is that the *blæd* clause no longer sounds like an intrusion:

> beopulf þæs breme
> blæd þide spranȝ
> scȳldes eafera (þæs) scedelandum in·

From the point of view of the lineator, it really matters little what we take to have been deleted from the *scȳldes* passage. That passage is isolated and should therefore be treated as a clause.

In the following passage the words *spæse ȝesiþas* have been isolated:

hi hȳne
[þ]a ætbæron to brimes faroðe spæse ȝesiþas
[Sp]a he selfa bæd   (132V05–7)

The phrase *spæse ȝesiþas* is isolated by the fact that the preceding clause contains the plural subject *hi* while the following verb, *bæd*, is singular. Although it might seem obvious that *ætbæron* has been deleted from the two-word passage—*spæse ȝesiþas ætbæron*—it is also possible to assume the deletion of the copula instead—*spæse (pæron) ȝesiþas*. The importance of this assumption will become clear later.

Is there any evidence for the deletion of a verb other than the copula (or possibly *peorðan*)? The simplest way of dealing with verb deletion would be, it might at first seem, to regard the verb of the preceding clause as what has been deleted. For example:

fæder ellor hpearf aldor of earde   (133R10)

The phrase *aldor of earde* is isolated: *hpearf* completes the clause beginning with *fæder*; the next manuscript line begins with the conjunctive phrase *oþ þ*. It seems strained to suggest that *pæs*, or perhaps *pearð*, rather than the obvious—and contiguous—*hpearf*, has been deleted from the *aldor* clause. In one sense the contiguous verb is indeed the one that has been deleted; in another sense the deleted verb is *always* the copula: *aldor (pæs) of earde*. I argue that "verb deletion" always creates a situation in which the appropriate form of the copula can be supplied with little if any loss of meaning. Verb deletion is deletion of the unstressed, finite forms of *pesan/peorðan*. For that reason it is possible to refer to verb deletion as "W-deletion."

Subject and Verb Deletion

If both the subject, the left NP, and also the verb do not occur in an isolated phrase, it would seem to make little sense to call so truncated a phrase a clause. I argue, however, that it makes good sense under certain conditions. Those conditions seem to me to operate on a phrase in the following passage:

Fand þa ðær
[i]nne æþelinȝa ȝedriht spefan æfter
[sȳ]mble sorȝe ne cuðon ponsceaft pera
[p]iht unhælo ȝrim 7 ȝrædiȝ ȝearo sona
pæs   (134V06–10)

Since the subject of *Fand* is many lines back, the passage begins with a clause showing subject deletion. In the next clause, *ȝedriht* is clearly the subject of the infinitive *spefan*. In the next clause, which consists of the three words *sorʒe ne cuðon*, there appears to be subject deletion again. Toward the end of the passage, *piht* is the subject of *pæs*, which words mark the boundaries of a fully expressed clause. This analysis leaves *ponsceaft pera* in line 8 unaccounted for.

Clearly, *ponsceaft pera* varies *sorʒe* in the preceding clause: the phrase is "in apposition with" *sorʒe*. The editor puts a comma after *cuðon* and indicates that *ponsceaft*, like *sorʒe*, is in the accusative case. This is surely a sensible way of dealing with *ponsceaft pera*.

It is not the only way. The phrase is isolated between *cuðon* and *piht*, each of which belongs to a different clause. The passage would make sense without this two-word phrase. The words *ponsceaft pera* fulfill the criteria for isolating a passage and thus have a certain independence in the larger passage. They are, I argue, a clause from which both the subject NP and the verb have been deleted:

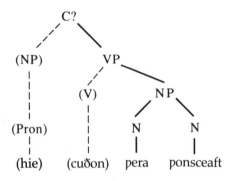

If the phrase were indeed omitted, there would be no alliteration for *piht* in the next clause. The chief function of the phrase is, I think, to provide that alliteration. There are many such "alliteration-bridge clauses" in *Beowulf*.

It is possible to devise a test to determine whether we are dealing with a "double deletion" clause. First, the words to be tested must be isolated, as I have shown *ponsceaft pera* to be. Second, they must fit into this test-frame:

$$
\left. \begin{array}{l} \text{se} \\ \text{seo} \\ \text{þæt} \end{array} \right\} \quad \text{is/pæs} \underline{\quad X \quad} /
$$

þa syndon/pæron _____ X _____

A word in the accusative case, as *ponsceaft* is taken to be, cannot fit into this test-frame. But we do not need to take *ponsceaft* as accusative; the form is ambiguous. It is possible to understand the passage somewhat like this: *sorʒe ne cuðon, þæt is ponsceaft pera.*

There are isolated phrases or even single words that are not ambiguously marked as is *ponsceaft.* Such a word is *þeodʒestreonum* in the following passage:

> Nalæs
> hi hine læssan lacum teodan þeodʒestreo
> num þon [þa dyd]on   (132V17–19)

The clause that begins with *Nalæs* is complete with *teodan.* In line 19 *þon* introduces another clause. Thus *þeodʒestreonum*, which varies *lacum* in the *Nalæs* clause, is isolated. I have been arguing that every isolated passage can be interpreted as a clause. If the argument is sound, it will have to deal with a compound noun inflected in the dative plural that seems to be the sole constituent of a "clause."

The dative plural ending of *þeodʒestreonum* seems to argue that the compound is simply in apposition with the noun *lacum.* On the other hand, *þeodʒestreonum* serves as a bridge between the *Nalæs* clause and the *þon* clause. Its dative ending can be interpreted as a backward nod to the previous clause, as I have argued in the section on adjectives, above. Thus I take *þeodʒestreonum* to be a clause in which the ending deftly evokes the rest of the *Nalæs* clause: *Nalæs hi hine læssan þeodʒestreonum teodan.*

Very neatly, *þeodʒestreonum* illustrates the phenomenon of the copying of a constituent to serve as an alliteration-bridge to what the poet wishes to say next. The copying of the ending serves two functions here: the first is to link the word to the appropriate referent and also to provide an unstressed syllable. We can, from one point of view, regard the compound as "in apposition with" *lacum* in the F-clause. From another point of view—closer, I think, to the poet's—we can regard the compound as an "aside"—**lac pæron þeodʒestreon.*

Treating *þeodʒestreonum* as an "aside" suggests that the way to fit it into the test-frame is to disregard the dative ending. That is, in effect, what I have done with what is usually taken to be the "zero accusative" ending of *ponsceaft.* Without the ending, *þeodʒestreonum* offers the poet the possibility of this clause: **þa pæron þeodʒestreon.*

A somewhat different kind of double-deletion clause occurs in the following passage:

þ hit pearð ealȝearo healær
na mæst scop him heort naman   (133Vo8–9)

In the two-word passage beginning with *healærna*, *mæst* varies *ealȝearo* in the preceding clause. Since the copied constituent here is in the nominative, there is no problem with a case-ending that has to be disregarded. Indeed, the larger passage presents us with a close approximation of the test-frame:

                    ealȝearo
            hit pearð
                    mæst

Test-Frames for Deletion

In the last section I proposed a test-frame for isolated passages from which both subject and verb seem to have been deleted. I propose now a test-frame into which any isolated passage without a verb must be inserted before being tested in the "double-deletion" test-frame. Because of this priority, I number this frame "1" and the double-deletion test-frame "2." This first frame might be derived from a clause in 132R16, *beopulf þæs breme*:

(1) ____X____ pæs/pæron____Y____

(2)
    se   ⎫
    seo ⎬ pæs ___X___ /
    þæt ⎭

    þa   pæron ___X___

Any passage to be tested must be tried in (1) before being tried in (2). A passage that fits the first frame shows verb deletion. A passage that fits the second frame shows deletion of both subject and verb, "double deletion." The keyword of the passage to be tested must be stripped of an oblique case-ending, if it has one, and equipped with a nominative ending, unless the nominative ending is "zero."

I have devised the two frames in order to distinguish with some rigor between these two kinds of deletion where either kind might at first seem possible. The need for rigor becomes apparent when we examine such a clause as *spæse ȝesiþas*, here quoted again in its context:

                hi hẏne
        [þ]a ætbæron to brimes faroðe spæse ȝesiþas
        [Sp]a he . . .   (132Vo5–7)

We have already noted that *spæse ʒesiþas* is isolated. At first it is tempting to take the *spæse* clause as showing double deletion: **hi hȳne þa ætbæron to brimes faroðe hi pæron spæse ʒesiþas*. On the elegant grounds that any isolated clause that can fit the first test frame must not be fitted to the second, however, I insert the passage into (1):

(1) *spæse pæron ʒesiþas*

There is a reasonable degree of fit; hence, the passage shows verb deletion rather than double deletion.

The first clause discussed in the section on verb deletion fits the first test-frame even more closely:

(1) *aldor pæs/pearð of earde*   (133R10)

What makes it possible to fit the *scȳldes* clause beginning in 132R17 into the verb-deletion test-frame is not the first noun, but the third noun plus its post-posed preposition. If the passage isolated only the first two words, *scȳldes eafera*, the isolated clause would not fit the first frame: **scȳldes (pæs) eafera*. A single noun, or a single adjective, then, or two nouns, if one is in the genitive case, probably should not be forced into the verb-deletion test-frame. A compound noun and a compound adjective, each of which is isolated by its environment, will make the point more clearly. Since the compounds are not far apart, I quote the entire context:

Nalæs
hi hine læssan lacum teodan þeodʒestreo
num þon [þa dyd]on þe hine æt frumsceafte
forð onsendon ænne ofer ȳðe umborpe
[s]ende þa ʒȳt hie him asetton   (132V17–133R01)

Both *þeodʒestreonum* and *umborpesende* are isolated; *þeodʒestreonum* varies *lacum*; *umborpesende* varies *ænne*. Neither can be fitted into the first frame:

(1) **þeod pæron ʒestreon*
(1) **umbor pæs pesende*

Each fits only the double-deletion test-frame:

(2) *þa pæron þeodʒestreon*
(2) *se pæs umborpesende*

How Many Kinds of Deletion Are Necessary?

The variation of any constituent is evident, and the lack of the subject constituent or the verb can be detected. But the supposed lack of the direct object of a usually transitive verb can only be surmised. The poet may be bending normal usage in the clause *leof landfruma lanȝe ahte* (132Vo8–9). On the other hand, he may have known of an intransitive use of *agan;* we can only surmise. What we cannot do is insist that the poet has deleted a direct object. I argue, therefore, that no deletion other than the three just discussed can be considered. The three are left NP or subject deletion; verb deletion; and double deletion, that is, the deletion of both left NP and V.

Difficult or Ambiguous Clause Boundaries
Discontinuous Clauses

The following passage well illustrates the sense of compression *Beowulf* often gives:

> fæder ellor hpearf aldor of earde
> oþ þ him eft onpoc heah healfdene heold
> þenden lifde ȝamol 7 ȝuðreoup ȝlæde scýl
> dinȝas   (133R10–13)

Five, possibly six, clauses make up the three-line passage:

(1) fæder ellor hpearf
(2) aldor (pæs) of earde (Verb Deletion)
(3) oþ þ him eft onpoc heah healfdene
(4) (he) heold . . . ȝlæde scýldinȝas
(5A) þenden (he?) lifde (Subject Deletion?)
(5B) (he pearð?) ȝamol 7 ȝuðreoup (Subject and Verb Deletion?)

The fourth clause seems to show subject deletion. What I shall first focus on, however, is the fact that the direct object of *heold* is separated from that verb by the clause or clauses marked 5A and 5B, which also shows or show deletion. Number 5A is clearly marked by *þenden,* functioning here as a conjunction. For the moment, I leave aside the possible relationship of 5A and 5B.

From the inflections it is possible to take *ȝlæde scýldinȝas* as nominative—*ȝlæde (pæron) scýldinȝas*—but to do so would be to deny *heold* its usual transitive character. The transitive bond seems strong enough to operate across an entire clause (or two clauses) consisting of five words. The parts of clause 4 may, then, be discontinuous.

"Sharing" Clauses

Clauses consisting of discontinuous constituents seem to be relatively rare in *Beowulf*. Somewhat less rare is the relationship between the last word in 3, above, and the first word in 4: *healfdene* and *heold*. The name is clearly needed to complete clause 3; yet it is this very word that has been "deleted" from the clause built around the next word, *heold*. A kind of *sharing* seems to be going on between clause 3 and clause 4: *healfdene*, the subject of each clause, is neatly placed at the point of juncture.

The question for the lineator is simple: where to place the clause boundary marker. I have placed it between *healfdene* and *heold*, though with some misgivings. The marker interrupts the flow from *healfdene onpoc* to *healfdene heold*. But, since *heold* takes us from Halfdene's birth to his reign and clearly belongs to a different clause from *onpoc*, I think the placement of the marker has some justification. Nevertheless, the boundary between clauses 3 and 4 is ambiguous.

In the section on adjectives above I argue that an adjective seems at times to replace a noun in a previous clause. That may be what is going on in 5A and 5B—*þenden ȝamol 7 ȝuðreoup lifde*—although it is probably unusual for a *pair* of epithets to fulfill this function. In any case, I have not marked a clause boundary between *lifde* and *ȝamol*.

I have not used any mark between *ȝuðreoup* and *ȝlæde*, even though there is no doubt that each word belongs to a different clause. To do so would be to suggest that *ȝlæde* introduces a new clause, since the only clause boundary marker I use marks the beginning boundary. In most cases the use of a single marker causes no problems.

Blends

The most complicated interplay between clauses occurs when a clause based on an infinitive is blended into a clause based on a finite verb. As I have argued in the section on infinitives, every infinitive generates its own clause. In many cases the boundary between the finite verb clause and the infinitive clause is clear:

[Ge]pat ða neosian sȳþðan niht becom (134V04)

(1) [Ge]pat ða (Subject Deletion)
(2) neosian (" ")
(3) sȳþðan niht becom

In this passage there is no blending of infinitive clause into finite verb clause.

Such is not the case with the following passage:

oð þ him æȝhpylc þara ẏmbsittendra
ofer hronrade hẏran scolde ȝomban   (132R09–10)

(1) oð þ æȝhpylc þara ẏmbsittendra (ofer hronrade?) scolde
(2) him æȝhpylc þara ẏmbsittendra ofer hronrade hẏran

The overlap between these two clauses consists of three to five words. Further, an important word in the infinitive clause, *him*, falls just after the conjunction that introduces the finite verb clause. The blending of the two clauses is complex. Since as a lineator I am concerned with clause beginnings, I have marked a clause boundary at the obvious point, before *oð þ*, and also at the not-so-obvious point where another clause seems to begin inside the first, that is, before *him*.

Although I have always tried to place the clause boundary marker before the first syllable that seems to me to belong to the second clause but not the first, it will at times be possible for others to quarrel with my judgment in this matter.

"Intruders" and "Semantic Isolation"

The phenomenon of clause blending might seem to confront the lineator with his or her most difficult problem. That honor, I think, belongs instead to certain "intruders" into discontinuous clauses. We confront that situation in the opening lines of the poem:

HPÆT PE GARDE
na· in ȝeardaȝum· þeodcẏninȝa
þrẏm ȝefrunon hu ða . . .   (132R01–3)

It is possible to understand the *PE . . . ȝefrunon* passage in two ways, first, as a single clause (which I abbreviate here to simplify):

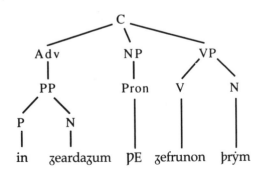

On the other hand, the phrase *in ȝeardaȝum* need not refer only to *our* having heard in the past; it seems at the same time to indicate that the *þrym* was performed in the past:

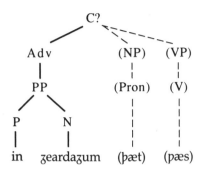

As a listener to the poem I delight in this ambiguity; as a lineator, on the other hand, I have had to make a choice. It seems to me that the second reading—"that was in the past"—deserves to be highlighted. Accordingly, I have marked a clause boundary before *in*.

If the phrase *in ȝeardaȝum* is a clause, it is severely truncated. Yet it fits the "double-deletion" test-frame. It should not, however, have been inserted into that frame until it passed the prior test of isolation. But *in ȝeardaȝum* is not isolated in any of the three ways discussed in the earlier section on isolation. It lies squarely between the subject NP and the V, between *ÞE* and *ȝefrunon*. If the phrase is to be regarded as isolated, it must be isolated in a way different from the ways discussed so far.

The three kinds of isolation discussed earlier are all, in a sense, "mechanical." The poet completes one clause, moves on to the next— the truncated clause—and then on to the next. Each boundary is clear. There is, however, no clear boundary between *in ȝeardaȝum* and either *GARDEna* or *þeodcȳninȝa*. Yet it is hard not to hear the prepositional phrase as referring, at least ambiguously, to the "pastness" of *þrym*. In a sense, then, the phrase is "semantically isolated."

If "semantic isolation" exists at all, it does not seem to occur very often. Indeed, I think we should invoke the notion of semantic rather than mechanical isolation as a late, if not last, resort. If the passage to be tested stubbornly refuses to yield important meanings after it has been tried in all possible Chomskyan trees, then it is semantically isolated.

Third Coda: Attempts to Lineate (Clause Boundaries)

If we try to lineate by placing on the same verse line every syllable belonging to the same clause, we are immediately faced with the problem of what to do about the clause *in ʒeardaʒum*. I have argued above that this phrase functions as a clause in its context. The problem, however, lies not with this phrase but with the fact that the phrase, functioning as a clause, interrupts another clause, *ÞE . . . ʒefrunon*. If we decide to include an interrupting clause on the same verse line with the interrupted clause, the first verse line of the poem looks like this:

Example Q

(1a) HÞÆT ÞE GARDEna· (2) in ʒeardaʒum· (1b) þeodcýninʒa þrým ʒefrunon

The line is unusually long. Further, it contains two different alliterations, the first on *G*, the second on *TH*. It seems sensible, then, to break the verse line whenever a new alliteration begins within the clause. If we try this expedient, the first fourteen "lines" of the poem look like this:

Example R

(1a) HÞÆT ÞE GARDEna· (2) in ʒeardaʒum		1
(1b) þeodcýninʒa þrým ʒefrunon		2
(3) hu ða æþelinʒas *e*lle[n] fremedon·		3
(4a) Oft *sc*ýld *sc*efinʒ *sc*eaþe[na] þreatum		4
(4b) *m*oneʒū *m*æʒþum *m*eodosetla ofteah		5
(5) *e*ʒsode *eo*rl		6
(6) sýððan ærest pear[ð]		7
*f*easceaft *f*unden		8
(7) he þæs *f*rofre ʒeba[d]		9
(8) *p*eox under *p*olcnum		10
(9) *p*eorðmýndum þah		11
(10) oð þ . . . æʒhpýlc . . . scolde		12
(11) him æʒhpýlc þara ýmbsittendra ofer		13
*h*ronrade *h*ýran scolde . . .		14

Since alliteration keeps clause (2) on the same line with the beginning of clause (1), we should follow this logic and place the first part of clause (6) on the same line with the clause containing the stressed syllables with which its stressed syllable, *ærest*, alliterates, that is clause (5). The same logic indicates that clause (7) be moved onto the same line with the second part of clause (6). Alliteration also aligns clauses (8) and (9).

Working in this way with clauses and alliteration, we can set up the first verse "lines" of the poem like this:

Example S

(1a) HPÆT PE GARDEna· (2) in ʒeardaʒum·	1
(1b) þeodcýninʒa þrým ʒefrunon	2
(3) hu ða æþelinʒas elle[n] fremedon·	3
(4a) Oft scýld scefinʒ sceaþe[na] þreatum	4
(4b) moneʒū mæʒþum meodosetla ofteah	5
(5) eʒsode eorl (6) sýððan ærest pear[ð]	6
feasceaft funden (7) he þæs frofre ʒeba[d]	7
(8) þeox under polcnum (9) þeorðmýndum þah	8
(10) oð þ . . . æʒhpýlc . . . scolde	9?
(11) him æʒhpýlc þara ýmbsittendra ofer	10?
hronrade hýran . . .	11?

Verse lines 1–8 now match conventional editorial lineation, but "lines" 9–11 still present problems. I have argued above that clauses like (10) and (11) are blends whenever the shared constituent, in this case *æʒhpýlc*, is not adjacent to both verb forms. Blends can almost always be separated at the point at which the first syllable of the first word belonging to the second but not the first blended clause occurs. That syllable—and word—in this case is *him*. Accordingly I have marked a clause boundary before *him*. Two clause boundaries, then, fall between the syllable that ends the last clause, *þah*, and the first alliterating syllable of clause (10), *æʒhpýlc*. It seems sensible to choose the first clause boundary as the point at which to begin the line. Otherwise the first clause boundary will be obscured at the end of the previous line. Whether this expedient can be generalized with acceptable results remains to be tested.

The second problem posed by the blended clauses (10) and (11) has to do with the interrupting of the *æʒhpýlc . . . scolde* clause by the *æʒhpýlc . . . hýran* clause. My solution to a similar problem involving clauses (1) and (2) was to be guided by alliteration. If we try that solution here, along with the solution suggested in the previous paragraph, lines "9" and "10" now look like this:

Example T

(10a) oð þ (11) him æʒhpýlc þara ýmbsittendra ofer	9
hronrade hýran (10b) scolde . . .	10

The beginning of "line 9" now matches conventional lineation, as does everything up to the last word in that line.

The last word, the preposition *ofer*, is out of place. It does not belong with the compound noun in the genitive case that precedes it. It does belong with the compound noun in the accusative case that follows it. Since the preposition is thus preposed, it cannot participate in the vocalic alliteration of "line 9." It is part of the phrase *ofer hronrade*; yet *hronrade*, since it begins a new alliteration, belongs in "line 10." The preposition *ofer* is left stranded in "line 9."

I try the expedient of beginning a new line with *ofer* on the ground that a preposition preposed to a noun belongs on the same line with its noun. "Line 10" now looks like this:

ofer *h*ronrade *h*ẏran scolde   10

If we generalize this expedient so that we begin a new line with any new preposition preposed to its noun, we must backtrack to "line 8" and the preposition *under*. I revise lines "8" and "9" in accordance with this expedient:

*p*eox   8
under *p*olcnum *p*eorðmẏndum þah   9

"Line 8" now looks very strange indeed. It appears that we cannot arrive at acceptable verse lineation every time simply by the expedient of beginning a new line with every new preposed preposition. Yet this expedient worked with *ofer hronrade hẏran scolde*. The conditions under which this expedient works are the subject of the next section.

PROCLITICS AND VERSE LINES

As we saw in the previous section, the preposition *ofer* (132R10) seems to play a role in verse lineation while the preposition *under* (132R08) does not. The difference between these two prepositions lies solely in their placement in relation to alliteration. In 132R10 *ofer* precedes both instances of the *H*-alliteration begun by the noun *hronrade*. On the other hand, *under* in 132R08 occurs between the first and second (but not last) instances of *W*-alliteration, that is, between *peox* and *polcnum peorðmẏndum*.

Prepositions are one kind of constituent that, joining closely with a word or words that follow, create a tightly linked phrase. There are other such constituents. Nonclausal *and* is one. Possessive and de-

monstrative pronouns are two others. Is there, then, a class of "proclitics" that behaves as a group in relation to lineation?

Neither the word nor the concept of the proclitic is new to Old
English studies. A. Campbell designates "demonstratives, posses-
sives, prepositions" as "proclitic words," and "adjectives of indefinite
quantity" as "proclitics." Campbell also notes, "Proclitic words receive a full stress if they are removed from the natural position immediately before the governed word."[11] Campbell is right when he
designates the three subclasses as "proclitic words"; he is right, too,
on the effect of shifting these kinds of words in the verse. But he is, I
think, on very shaky ground when he extends, as he seems to be
doing, the notion of the proclitic to prose as well as poetry and when
he includes adjectives of indefinite quantity as proclitics.

I propose to designate as proclitics only the classes and subclasses
of constituents listed later in this paragraph and to deal with the functioning of proclitics only in verse. I define a proclitic as an unstressed
syllable or closely linked group of syllables, whether bound or free,
that normally indicates its grammatical association by its placement
before a stressed syllable. Types of proclitics are (1) unstressed prefixes, (2) prepositions (both terms indicating the normal position of
the syllables so designated), (3) nonclausal *and/ond/*7, *ȝe*, (4) demonstrative pronouns, and (5) possessive pronouns.

Any member of these groups or classes, when that member is preposed to a word containing the first alliterating syllable of a series,
functions as a *verse line proclitic*. By this I mean that the proclitic rather
than the word containing the alliterating syllable will begin the verse
line. The lineator needs to be concerned not with every proclitic but
only with those that precede the first alliterating syllable. My proposed treatment of proclitics differs, thus, from my treatment of
stress, alliteration, and clause boundaries, above. I have marked
every stressed syllable, every alliteration within a certain range, and
every clause boundary. There is, however, some common ground between proclitics and clause boundaries in that only certain instances
of each play a role in verse lineation.

One point suggested by the second part of Campbell's remarks
about proclitics, their ability to gain stress by shifting, needs to be
considered. This phenomenon is directly related to lineation, as we

11. Campbell, *Old English Grammar*, 36.

shall see, because any stressed syllable can participate in alliteration and thus play a significant role in determining the verse line. Not every kind of proclitic can, however, be shifted. Prefixes cannot, and, although nonclausal *and* is free, it does not seem to be shifted in *Beowulf*. I take up the three kinds of proclitics that can be and are shifted in the poem.

Prepositions

> læʒ madma mæniʒo þa him mid scol
> don on flodes æht feor ʒepitan· Nalæs   (132V16–17)

The preposition *mid* can have no direct syntactic link with the stressed syllable that immediately follows it, *scol-* of the verb *scoldon*. Nor can *mid* have any syntactic link with the word that follows *scoldon*, the preposition *on*. The word with which *mid* is associated must, then, be the personal pronoun that precedes it, *him*. If we assume that *mid* has acquired stress by being postposed to its pronoun, stressed *mid* will then be in range of the alliterating syllables of *madma* and *mæniʒo*.

The stress of a shifted preposition like *mid* seems to have been designed to signal that the hearer should expect an unusual placement of phrase constituents in relation to each other. Stress may also signal that the preposition is functioning adverbially, that is, in a way similar to a member of one of the classes in the stressed inventory. But I would argue against referring to shifted prepositions as quasi-adverbs or adverbial prepositions on the grounds that there is no necessity to invent such a subcategory. The constituent class "preposition" and the operation "shifting" are sufficient to deal with the matter.

Demonstrative Pronouns

> spa ðeh ʒomela scilfinʒ ac forʒeald hra[ðe]
> pȳrsan prixle pælhelm þone sȳððan ðeo[d]
> cȳninʒ þȳder oncirde· Ne meahte se snella   (198R04–6)

The demonstrative *þone* cannot modify the conjunction *sȳððan* or any word that follows *sȳððan* since this conjunction introduces a new clause. Thus, *þone* must modify the masculine noun that precedes it, *pælhelm*. I assume that *þone* has acquired stress and mark it accordingly.

Since stressed *þone* comes in range of *ðeod-*, it poses an interesting question: can a demonstrative pronoun that has acquired stress by its placement after the noun it modifies then participate in dominant alliteration with a following noun? I argue that it cannot, on the grounds that the demonstrative has acquired stress through its relationship to the preceding noun. Its stress is dependent upon its position within the phrase *pælhelm þone*. To argue that *þone* and *ðeod-* can set up a dominant (as opposed to a subdominant) pattern is perhaps to undermine the integrity of the phrase. I have therefore marked *þone* for stress but not for alliteration, thus treating demonstratives differently from prepositions (see above) and possessive pronouns (see below).

Possessive Pronouns

[fu]rþur feran nu ʒe feorbuend mere
liðende mine ʒehýrað anfealdne ʒe
[þ]oht ofost is selest to ʒecýðanne   (137V02–4)

The possessive pronoun *mine* is either postposed to the noun *mereliðende*, with which it agrees in form, or preposed to but separated by the verb *ʒehýrað* from the noun *anfealdne*, with which it makes somewhat better sense. Accordingly, Kemble's emendation of the manuscript *mine* to *min[n]e* has been adopted by most editors since 1835. Whether one takes *mine* with *mereliðende* or with *anfealdne*, there is clear evidence of displacement.

If *mine* has acquired stress by such displacement, as I assume it has, then it is within range of *mereliðende*. It thus establishes a new alliteration between the *F*-alliteration of 137V02 and the vocalic alliteration of *anfealdne* and *ofost* in 137V03–4.

SUMMARY: FEATURES AND FUNCTIONS OF SYLLABLES AND VERSE LINEATION

I restate my first major hypothesis: it will be possible to elicit acceptable verse lines systematically from the syllables of the text of *Beowulf* as these are represented in the manuscript by attending only to the features and functions of syllables discussed in this chapter. The next chapter will discuss the testing of this form of the first major hypothesis by the application of simple procedures to the encoded syllables of a significant sample of the manuscript text.

Chapter 4

Systematic Lineation and Half-Lining
Testing the First Major Hypothesis

THE EMERGENCE OF THE VERSE LINE

In this chapter I shall test the hypothesis that the verses of the consensus can be elicited from the manuscript text by the application of what I call Kemble's general method. As I indicated in Chapter 1, the verses of the consensus can only be defined in terms of the relationship of one verse of a pair to the other verse of that pair. This means that the lineator or computer must begin by extracting pairs of verses, that is, the verse line. Only after extracting the whole verse line can the lineator then divide the verse line into its two constituents, the halflines—the so-called "verses." The verse line is a sequence of words that begins either with the first alliterating syllable of an alliteration or with a clause boundary before or proclitic to that first alliterating syllable. An alliteration consists of at least two stressed syllables having the same initial sound that are in range of each other, as defined in Chapter 3. The beginning of the first halfline (verse) of the verse line is the same as the beginning of the verse line. The end of the second halfline (verse) of the verse line is the same as the end of the verse line. The beginning of the second halfline of the verse line must be defined in terms of the last alliterating syllable of the alliteration: the second halfline of a verse line is a word or sequence of words that begins either with the last alliterating syllable of the alliteration or with a clause boundary before or proclitic to the last alliterating syllable.

Since I apply Kemble's general method more rigorously than Kemble did—so rigorously that it can be turned into a computer program—it will be useful, as I have explained in Chapter 1, to split the hypothesis into a weak and a strong form. The weak form states that it is possible to elicit verse lines and halflines from the manuscript text systematically. The strong form states that Kemble elicited all of the verses (halflines) of the consensus by the application of a method. The weak form of the first major hypothesis can be verified or falsified by the application of the tests discussed in this chapter. The testing of the strong form cannot be complete until Chapter 8.

The computer program operates on the syllables of the poem as they are represented in the manuscript text. For computer analysis, I divided the text of the poem into segments exactly as the scribes did, that is, into manuscript lines each of which is identified as such. The designation of each segment begins with the folio number and an indication that the folio is either right page (R for *recto*) or left (V for *verso*), followed by the line number on the page. I do not indicate the syllable that I think heads any verse. That is for the computer to determine.

The computer program that Dorothy Eckert Grannis devised on the basis of my extrapolation of Kemble's general method is easy to characterize. The computer is programmed to search for each cluster of alliterating syllables. When the computer discovers the second of two syllables that alliterate, it moves back to the first alliterating syllable. From there it continues to move back to search for the first clause boundary that occurs after the end of the word that contains the last alliterating syllable of the previous series. If a clause boundary occurs in the area between alliterations, the computer places the syllable that heads the clause at the left margin. If no clause boundary occurs in this area, the computer then searches for the first syllable of a proclitic to the first alliterating syllable of the new series. If the computer finds such a proclitic, it places that proclitic at the left margin. If it finds neither proclitic nor clause boundary between the two alliterations, it places the first alliterating syllable of the new alliteration at the left margin. In this way the computer indicates the beginning of successive verse lines.

The computer programmed to operate according to these procedures is responsible for placing at the left margin every syllable that occurs in that position in the chart that ends this chapter. This set of procedures is thus responsible for eliciting the verse lines (pairs of alliterating verses) of the poem. In order to determine verse lines, then, it is necessary to apply procedures based on the analyses of the features and functions of syllables discussed in the previous chapter. These procedures are as follows.

First, I have determined whether a syllable is either a formative or the stem of a word that belongs to one of the nine other classes that take stress. I have then marked the syllable for stress by placing a "1" before it.

Second, I have determined which stressed syllables beginning with the same sound lie within range of each other. I have then marked these syllables by changing the "1" to a "2."

Third, I have determined and marked with a "3" the first syllable of every clause.

Fourth, I have located and marked with a "4" the first or only syllable belonging to the first or only proclitic to the first alliteration of each series *unless* the first proclitic falls between a clause boundary, as determined in step three, and the first alliteration.

The text on which the computer program operates is the extremely conservative text discussed in the first note in Chapter 1. I give an example of one manuscript page from each sample of the text I have encoded for computer analysis. The first sample begins with *HPÆT* at the top of folio 132R (129r) and ends with the raised point after *healdan* at the end of the first manuscript line in folio 139R (137r). Folio 132V (129v) illustrates this sample. The second sample begins with *Pæs*, the first word on line 8 of folio 197V (193v) and ends with the "colon" and "dash" after *ðuhte*, the last word in manuscript line 14 on folio 199V (195v). I have chosen folio 199R (195r) to illustrate this sample of the text.

The computer operates not on the written or printed syllables, but on syllables I have encoded in accordance with the simple code discussed in Appendix C. The program determines the first syllable of each verse line in the following way: the first syllable of the verse line is the first *alliterating* syllable unless (1) that syllable is preceded by one or more clause boundaries that fall after the end of the word containing the last alliterating syllable of the old alliteration and before the first alliterating syllable of the new, or (2) that syllable is preceded by one or more proclitics. If (1) occurs, the first syllable of the verse line will be the one that marks the first clause boundary between alliterations. If (2) occurs, the first syllable of the verse line will be the first syllable of the first proclitic.

THE EMERGENCE OF THE HALFLINE

The computer has also been programmed to divide the verse line into two halflines, the two "verses" of the alliterating "verse pair." The set of procedures that locate the beginning of the second halfline operates upon the already determined verse line. The computer now searches the area between the last and the next-to-last alliterating syllables of the verse line for clause boundaries or proclitics in much the same way as it searched the area between successive sets of alliterations for syllables having these syntactic functions. If it locates a clause boundary between the next-to-last and last alliterating syllables, it places the syllable that marks that clause boundary at the head of the second halfline. If it finds no clause boundary in this area, it searches for an already identified proclitic to the last alliterating syllable. If it finds such a proclitic, it places it at the head of the second halfline. If it finds neither clause boundary nor proclitic, the computer places the last alliterating syllable of the series at the head of the second halfline.

In the chart that follows this chapter, the beginning of the second halfline of each verse line is indicated by a break equal to three letter spaces. As the chart shows, the computer must be programmed first to extract verse lines from manuscript lines and then to divide the verse line into two halflines. The computer demonstrates, then, that the verse line and its constituent halflines can be elicited *systematically*. The beginnings of most of the systematically determined verse lines match the beginnings of the first verses of the verse pairs in editions published during the last 150 years. The beginnings of most of the systematically determined second halflines match the beginnings of the second verses of verse pairs in these editions. Every one of these editions is based directly or indirectly on Kemble's editions of 1833 and 1835.

Kemble accepted or worked out a total of 636 verses in the first five sections of the poem comprising the unnumbered first section and the sections numbered ".1." through ".1111." From the syllables in these same sections of the manuscript, computer-programmed lineation—henceforth "P-Lineation"—elicits 305 verse lines and then divides them into a total of 610 halflines. P halflines match 509 C (for "conventional") verses; most of the matches are exact. The match thus amounts to 80 percent.

Kemble accepted or worked out 224 verses in the section numbered ".xli." From the syllables in this section of the manuscript, P-Lineation elicits 109 verse lines that divide into a total of 218 halflines. P halflines match 165 C verses. This match amounts to 73.7 percent.

Combining the two passages gives a total of 860 C verses and a total of 828 P halflines. The total of matched verses/halflines is 674,

The verso of the first folio that contains the text of Beowulf (132V/129v). By permission of the British Library.

The recto of folio 199R/195r. By permission of the British Library.

giving a combined percentage of 78.4 percent. If we take into account the fact that the 21.6 percent total of mismatches includes twenty-one (about 2.4 percent) caused by missing or illegible passages in the manuscript, the mismatches decrease to 19 percent. Ten more mismatches, or slightly more than 1 percent, are caused by Kemble's selection of certain normally unstressed syllables for unusual emphasis, that is, rhetorical stress. The remaining mismatches are caused by alliterations that continue beyond three instances or by unusually placed clause boundaries. Mismatches of these kinds amount to slightly less than 18 percent.

P-Lineation "tracks" Kemble's verse lineation about four-fifths of the time. The only other method of eliciting verses from the manuscript text that can be elegantly described, lineating by placing the first alliterating syllable at the head of the verse, tracks Kemble's method only three-fifths of the time. P-Lineation can thus be said to reproduce Kemble's general method of lineating. The procedures of P-Lineation were, in general, Kemble's guiding principles. The fact that these principles underlie Kemble's lineation led to the acceptance of Kemble's verse lineation and thus to the 150-year-old consensus on Beowulfian prosody.

Kemble did not, then, need to leave a record of his procedures for lineating. P-Lineation both reconstructs his general method and indicates when that method fails to achieve acceptable results. P-Lineation thus provides a precise way of reckoning Kemble's adherence to his general method. The hypothesis that Kemble extracted verses from the manuscript by following a method is partially demonstrated.

MAJOR AND MINOR HYPOTHESES REGARDING LINEATION

The weak form of the first of the two major hypotheses, namely that it is possible to lineate systematically, has been demonstrated. So have several subordinate hypotheses. First, the application of the two hypotheses about stress has proved sufficient to extract a significant percentage of acceptable verse lines and halflines. One of these hypotheses states that only two degrees of stress, 0 or unstress and 1 or stress, are needed to lineate. The second hypothesis regarding stress states that the stem syllables of certain *classes* of words receive stress. The hypothesis that alliteration is the basis of the verse line has also been demonstrated. The computer works back from the first alliterating syllable in each new alliteration to determine whether a segment must be added before the segment that begins with the first alliterating syllable. The computer locates the midpoint of the verse line by working back in a similar way from the last alliterating syllable. The hypothesis that dominant, or lineating, alliteration operates over a certain range has been partially demonstrated. In Chapter 8 I shall discuss apparent exceptions to this hypothesis. Finally, systematic lineation has demonstrated that a clause boundary before, or a proclitic to, the first (or last) alliterating syllable marks an acceptable beginning of both the verse line and its second halfline.

The working definitions of the verse line and the halfline presented in the first paragraph of this chapter have demonstrated their value. The halfline is a symmetrical constituent of the verse line as the verse line is an asymmetrical constituent of the poetic text as a whole.

Kemble created the 150-year-old consensus on Beowulfian prosody because he worked methodically. What Kemble discovered in the manuscript text may be called the prosodic basis of verse lineation. Kemble thus laid a firm foundation for Beowulfian prosody, even though he did not carry his researches further than the extraction of verses. The negative form of the second major hypothesis, which states that prosodists since Kemble have not paid proper attention to the process of lineating, must now be put into positive form and tested. That will be the work of the following chapters.

VERSE LINES AND HALFLINES DETERMINED BY PROGRAMMED LINEATION

The results of computer lineation appear in the chart that follows. Every verse line and halfline in the chart is the work of the computer. To make the charts I simply replaced the groups of coded symbols that stand for the syllables in the printout with the letters of the words of the text as these appear in the manuscript or, when they do not appear or are now illegible, in the first Thorkelin transcript, Thorkelin A.

For convenience I have done what the computer does not do, that is, I have provided running verse line numbers for the computer-elicited verse lines. For comparison with standard texts, I have placed in parentheses in the right margin line numbers from modern editions such as that of Klaeber.

The first halfline of each verse line begins at the left margin; the second halfline usually follows on the same printed line. The second halfline is always separated from the end of the first halfline by three letter spaces. If a verse line continues beyond one line of type and the continuation begins two letter spaces from the margin, there is no break in the halfline begun on the preceding printed line.

Illegible areas of the manuscript are, where they can be measured, indicated by a row of points. Each point represents roughly one letter space in the manuscript.

HÞÆT ÞE GARDEna·   in ȝeardaȝum·
þeodcẏninȝa   þrẏm ȝefrunon
hu ða æþelinȝas elle[n] fremedon·   Oft
scẏld scefinȝ   sceaþe[na] þreatum
5   moneȝū mæȝþum   meodosetla ofteah   (5)
eȝsode eorl   sẏððan ærest pear[ð]
feasceaft funden   he þæs frofre ȝeba[d]
þeox under polcnum   þeorðmẏndum þah
oð þ him æȝhpẏlc   þara ẏmbsittendra
10   ofer hronrade   hẏran scolde   (10)
ȝomban ȝẏldan   þ þæs ȝod cẏninȝ·
ðæm eafera þæs   æfter cenned
ȝeonȝ in ȝeardum   þone ȝod sende
folce to frofre   fẏrenðearfe onȝeat
15   þ hie ær druȝon   aldor..ase.   (15)
lanȝe hpile   him þæs liffrea
puldres pealdend   poroldare forȝeaf·
beopulf þæs breme   blæd pide spranȝ
scẏldes eafera scedelandum in·   Spa sceal..........ma
20   ȝode ȝepẏrcean fromum feohȝiftum   on fæder....[r]me   (21)
þ hine on ẏlde   eft
ȝepuniȝen [pilȝ]esiþas   þonne piȝ cume·
leode ȝelæsten   [l]ofdædū
sceal in mæȝþa ȝehpære   man ȝe[þe]on·
25   him ða scẏld ȝepat   to ȝescæphpile   (26)
[fe]lahror feran   on frean pære
hi hẏne [þ]a ætbæron   to brimes faroðe
spæse ȝesiþas   [Sp]a he selfa bæd
þenden pordum peold   [p]ine scẏldinȝa
30   leof landfruma   lanȝe ahte   (31)
þær æt hẏðe stod   hrinȝedstefna

isiʒ 7 útfus   æþelinʒes fær·
aledon þa   leofne þeoden
beaʒa brýttan   on bearm scipes
35   mærne be mæste   þær pæs madma   (36)
fela of feorpeʒum   frætpa ʒelæded·
Ne hýrde ic cýmlicor   ceol ʒeʒýrpan
hildepæpnum   7 heaðopædum
billum 7 býrnum   him on bearme læʒ
40   madma mæniʒo   þa him mid scoldon   (41)
on flodes æht   feor ʒepitan·
Nalæs hi hine læssan   lacum teodan
þeodʒestreonum þon [þa dyd]on þe hine æt
frumsceafte   forð onse[nd]on
ænne ofer ýðe   umborpe[s]ende
45   þa ʒýt hie him asetton   seʒen [ʒe.]denne   (47)
heah ofer heafod   leton holm ber[an]
ʒeafon on ʒarsecʒ   him pæs ʒeomor sefa
murnende mod   men ne cunnon·
secʒan t[o] soðe   selerædenne
50   hæleð under heofen[ū]   hpa þæm hlæste onfenʒ·   (52)

·1·

ÐA pæs on burʒum   beopulf scýldinʒa
leo[f] leodcýninʒ   lonʒe þraʒe
folcum ʒefr[æ]ʒe   fæder
ellor hpearf aldor of earde   oþ þ him eft onpoc
55   heah healfdene   heold   (57)
þenden lifde ʒamol 7 ʒuðreoup   ʒlæde scýldinʒas
ðæm feoper bearn   forðʒerimed
in porold pocun   peoroda ræspa
heoroʒar 7 hroðʒar 7 halʒa til hýrde ic þ elan cpen·
heaðoscilfinʒas healsʒebedda þa pæs hroðʒare   heresped
ʒýfen
60   piʒes peorðmýnd   þ him his pinemaʒas   (65)
ʒeorne hýrdon   oðð þ seo ʒeoʒoð ʒepeox
maʒodriht micel   hī on mod bearn
þ healreced   hatan polde·
[medoæ]rn micel   men ʒepýrcean
65   þone y[ldo bea]rn æfre ʒefrunon· 7 þær on innan eall
[ʒe]dælan ʒeonʒum 7   ealdum   (72)

spẏlc him ȝod [se]alde buton folcscare 7 feorum
ȝumena·   [ð]a ic pide ȝefræȝn peorc ȝebannan
maniȝre [m]æȝþe   ȝeond þisne middanȝeard
folcste[de] frætpan   him on fẏrste ȝelomp
ædre [m]id ẏldum·   þ hit pearð ealȝearo
70 healærna mæst   scop him heort naman   (78)
se þe his pordes ȝepeald   pide hæfde·
He beot ne aleh   beaȝas dælde
sinc æt sẏmle   sele
hlifade· heah 7 hornȝeap   heaðopẏlma bad
75 laðan liȝes   ne pæs hit lenȝe þa ȝen   (83)
þ se secȝhete   aþum sperian
æfter pælniðe   pæcnan scolde·
ða se ellenȝæst   earfoðlice
þraȝe ȝeþolode   se þe in þẏstrū bad
80 þ he doȝora ȝehpam   dream   (88)
ȝehẏrde· hludne in healle   þær pæs hearpan
speȝ sputol sanȝ scopes   sæȝde
se þe cuþe frumsceaft fira   feorran reccan . . ,
[cpæð] þ se ælmihtiȝa   eorðan
85 [þorh..] plitebeorhtne panȝ   spa pæter b[e]buȝeð   (93)
ȝesette siȝehreþiȝ   sunn[an] 7 monan
leoman to leohte   landb[uen]dum
7 ȝefrætpade   foldan sceata[s]
leomum 7 leafum   lif eac ȝesceop
90 cẏ[n]na ȝehpẏlcum   þara ðe cpice hpẏrf[aþ.]   (98)
Spa ða drihtȝuman   dreamum lif[don]
eadiȝlice   oð ðæt án onȝan
fẏrene fr[e]man   feond on helle
pæs se ȝrimma ȝæ[st]   ȝrendel haten
95 mære mearcstapa   se þe moras heold   (103)
fen 7 fæsten   fifelcẏnnes eard
ponsæli per   peardode hpile
siþðan him scẏppen^d   forscrifen hæfde
in caines cẏnne   þone cpealm ȝepræc
100 ece drihten   þæs þe he abel sloȝ·   (108)
Ne ȝefeah he þære fæhðe   ac he hine feor forpræc
metod for þẏ mane   mancynne fram
þanon untẏdras ealle onpocon eotenas 7 ẏlfe   7 orcneas

spÿlce ӡi[ӡantas]   þa [þi]ð ӡode punnon
105 lanӡ[e þraӡe   he] him ðæs lean forӡeald.   (114)

·11·

[Ge]þat ða neosian   sÿþðan niht becom
[h]ean huses   hu hit hrinӡdene
æfter [be]orþeӡe   ӡebun hæfdon.
Fand þa ðær [i]nne   æþelinӡa ӡedriht
110 spefan æfter [sÿ]mble   sorӡe ne cuðon   (119)
ponsceaft pera   [p]iht unhælo
ӡrim 7 ӡrædiӡ   ӡearo sona pæs
reoc 7 reþe   7 on ræste ӡenam
þritiӡ [þ]eӡna   þanon eft ӡepát
115 huðe hremiӡ   to ham faran   (124)
mid þære pælfÿlle   pica neosan·
ða pæs on uhtan   mid ærdæӡe
ӡrendles ӡuðcræft   ӡumum undÿrne
þa pæs æfter piste   póp up ahafen
120 micel morӡenspeӡ   mære þeoden   (129)
æþelinӡ ærӡod   unbliðe sæt
þolode ðrÿðspÿð   þeӡnsorӡe dreah
sÿðþan hie þæs laðan   last sceapedon
perӡan ӡastes   pæs þ ӡepin to stranӡ
125 lað 7 lonӡsum   næs hit lenӡra [fÿrs]t   (134)
ac ÿm[b] ane niht   e[ft ӡefremede]
morðbeala mare   7 no mearn
for[e] fæhðe 7 fÿrene   pæs to fæst on þam
þ[a] pæs eaðfÿnde   þe him elles hpær
130 ӡeru[m]licor   ræste   (139)
bed æfter burum   ða hi[m] ӡebeacnod pæs
ӡesæӡd soðlice   spe[oto]lan tacne
healðeӡnes hete   heold [hÿ]ne sÿðþan
fÿr 7 fæstor   se þæm feo[nde] ætpand·
135 Spa rixode   7 pið rihte pan   (144)
ana pið eallum   oð þ idel stod
husa seles[t]   pæs seo hpil micel
·xii· pintra tid   torn ӡeþolode
pine scÿldenda   peana ӡehpelcne
140 sidra sorӡa   (149)
forðam pearð ÿlda bearnum   undÿrne cuð

ʒȳddū ʒeomore þætte ʒrendel þan
hƿile ƿið hroþʒar heteniðas pæʒ
fȳrene 7 fæhðe fela missera
145 sinʒale sæce sibbe ne þolde (154)
ƿið manna hƿone mæʒenes deniʒa
feorhbealo feorran fea þinʒian
ne þær nꜳniʒ þitena þenan þorfte
beorhtre bote to banū folmū.
150 [..æʒlæca eht]ende pæs (159)
[de]orc [deaþscua du]ʒuþ[e 7] ʒeoʒoþe
seomade 7 sȳrede [sin]nihte heold
mistiʒe moras men ne [cu]nnon
hƿȳder helrunan hƿȳrftum [sc]riþað
155 spa fela fȳrena feond mancȳn[ne]s (164)
atol anʒenʒea oft ʒefremede·
[h]eardra hȳnða heorot eardode
sinc[fa]ʒe sel speartum
nihtum no he
160 þone [ʒ]ifstol ʒretan (168)
moste maþðum for meto[d]e ne his mȳne
ƿisse þ pæs præc micel [þ]ine scȳldinʒa
modes brecða moniʒ oft ʒesæt
rice to rune ræd eahtedon
165 hƿæt spiðferhðum selest pære (173)
ƿið færʒrȳrū to ʒefremmanne·
Hƿilum hie ʒeheton æt hrærʒtrafum
ƿiʒpeorþunʒa [þ]ordum bædon
þ him ʒastbona ʒeoce ʒefremede·
170 ƿið þeodþreaum spȳlc pæs þeap hȳra. (178)
hæþenra hȳht helle
ʒemundon in modsefan metod hie ne cuþon
dæda demend ne þiston hie drihten ʒod·
[ne hie h]uru [h]eof[ena h]elm herian [ne] cuðon
175 þuldres þaldend þa bið þæm (183)
ðe sceal þurh sliðne nið saþle bescufa[n]
in fȳres fæþm frofre ne
þenan þihte ʒ[e]þendan þel bið þæm
þe mot æfter deaðdæʒe drihten secean·
180 7 to fæder fæþmum freoðo þilnian· (188)

·111·

Spa ða mælceare   maʒa healfdenes
sinʒala seað   ne mihte snotor hæleð
pean onpendan   þæs þ ʒepin to spýð
laþ 7 lonʒsum   þe on ða leode becom
185 nýdpracu niþʒrim   nihtbealpa mæst   (193)
þ fram ham ʒefræʒn   hiʒelaces þeʒn
ʒod mid ʒeatum   ʒrendles dæda
se þæs moncýnnes   mæʒenes strenʒest on þæm dæʒe þýsses
     lifes
æþele 7 eacen   het him ýðlidan
190 ʒodne ʒeʒýrpan   cpæð he ʒuðcýninʒ   (199)
ofer spanrade   secean polde
mærne þeoden   þa him þæs manna þearf
ðone siðfæt him   snotere ceorlas
lýthpon loʒon·   [þeah h]e him [l]eof [þære]
195 h[pet]ton [h]iʒ[e þofne   hæ]l sceapedon hæfde   (205)
se ʒoda   ʒeata le[od]a
[ce]mpan ʒecorone   þara þe he cenoste
                 na
findan mihte   ·xv·
sum sundpudu sohte   secʒ pisade
200 laʒucræftiʒ mon   landʒemýrcu   (209)
fýrst forð ʒepát   flota þæs on ýðum·
bát under beorʒe   beornas ʒearpe
on stefn stiʒon   streamas pundon
sund pið sande   secʒas
205 bæron on bearm nacan   beorhte frætpe   (214)
ʒuðsearo ʒeatolic   ʒuman ut scufon
peras on pilsið pudu bundenne· ʒepat þa ofer
     pæʒholm   pinde
ʒefysed flota famiheals   fuʒle ʒelicost
oð þ ýmb antid   oþres doʒores
210 pundenstefna   ʒepaden hæfde   (220)
þ ða liðende   land ʒesapon
brimclifu blican   beorʒas steape.
side sænæssas   þa þæs sund liden
eoletes æt ende   þanon up hraðe
215 pedera leode   on panʒ stiʒon·   (225)
sæpudu sældon   syrcan hrýsedon·
ʒuðʒepædo   ʒode þancedon

þæs þe him ýþlade   eaðe purdon·

[þa] of pealle ȝesea[h]   peard scildinȝa

220   se [þe holm]clifu   healdan scolde   (230)

beran ofer bolcan   beorhte randas

fýrdsearu fuslicu   hine fýrpýt bræc

modȝehýȝdum   hpæt þa men pæron·

Gepat him þa to paroðe   picȝe ri[dan]

225   þeȝn hroðȝares   þrýmmum cpehte   (235)

mæȝe[n]þudu mundum   meþelpordum fræȝn·

hpæt sýndon ȝe searohæbbendra býrnum per[e]de   þe þus

    brontne ceol

ofer laȝustræte   lædan

cpomon hider   ofer holmas

230   le pæs endesæta   æȝpearde heold   (241)

þe on land dena   laðra næniȝ

mid scipherȝe   sceðþan ne meahte

no her cuðlicor   cuman

onȝunnon· lindhæbbende   ne ȝe leafnes pord

235   ȝuðfremmendra   ȝearpe ne pisson   (246)

maȝa ȝemedu   næfre ic maran ȝeseah

eorla ofer   eorþan

þonne is eoper sum secȝ on searpum   nis þ seldȝuma

pæpnum ȝepeorðad   næfre him his plite leoȝe

240   ænlic   ansýn   (251)

nu ic eoper sceal frumcýn þitan   ær ȝe fyr [heon]an

leassceaperas   on land [dena

fu]rþur feran   nu ȝe feorbuend

mereliðende   mine ȝehýrað

245   anfealdne ȝe[þ]oht   ofost is selest   (256)

to ȝecýðanne   [h]panan eopre cýme sýndon·

        ·1111·

[H]im se ýldesta   7sparode

perodes pisa   pordhord onleac

pe sýnt ȝumcýnnes   ȝeata leode

250   7 hiȝelaces   heorðȝeneatas·   (261)

pæs min fæder   folcum ȝecýþed

æþele ordfruma   ecȝþeop haten·

ȝebad pintra porn   ær he on peȝ hpurfe·

ȝamol of ȝeardum   hine ȝearpe ȝeman

255   pitena pelhpẏlc   pide ʒeond eorþan·   (266)
        pe þurh holdne hiʒe hlaford þinne   sunu healfdenes secean
        cpomon
        leodʒebẏrʒean   pes þu us larena ʒod·
        habbað pe to þæm mæran   micel ærende
        deniʒa frean·   ne sceal þær dẏrne sum
260   pesan þæs ic pene   þu pæst   (272)
        ʒif hit is spa pe soþlice   [se]cʒan hẏrdon
        Þ mid scẏldinʒum   sc[eaðona] ic nat hpẏlc.
        deoʒol dædhata   deorcu[m] nihtum
        eapeð þurh eʒsan   uncuðne ni[ð]
265   hẏnðu 7 hrafẏl   ic þæs hroðʒar mæʒ   (277)
        þur[h] rumne sefan   ræd ʒelæran·
        hu he fro[d. 7] ʒod   feond oferspẏðeþ
        ʒyf him edpend[an]   æfre scolde.
        bealupa bisiʒu   bot eft
270   cuman 7 þa cearpẏlmas   colran purðaþ   (282)
        oððe a sẏþðan   earfoðþraʒe
        þreanẏd þolað   þenden þær punað
        on heahstede   husa selest·
        peard maþelode   þær on picʒe sæt
275   ombeht unforht   æʒhpæþres   (287)
        sceal scearp scẏldpiʒa   ʒescad
        pitan porda 7 porca   se þe pel þenceð
        ic Þ ʒehẏre   þæt þis is hold
        peorod frean scẏldinʒa ʒepitaþ forð beran pæpen 7
        ʒepædu   ic eop pisiʒe
280   spẏlce ic maʒuþeʒnas   mine   (293)
        hate   pið feonda ʒehpone flotan eoperne
        niptẏrpẏdne   nacan on sande
        arum healdan   oþðæt eft bẏreð
        ofer laʒustrea[mas   l]eofne mannan
285   pudu punden[hals   to] pedermearce   (298)
        ʒodfremmendra   [sp]ẏlcum ʒifeþe bið
        Þ þone hilderæs   [há]l ʒediʒeð·
        ʒepiton him þa feran   flota [st]ille bád
        seomode on sole   sidfæþmed [sci]p
290   on ancre fæst   eoforlic scionon   (303)
        [o]fer hleorberan   ʒehroden ʒolde

fah [7] fȳrheard   ferhþearde heold
ȝuþmod ȝrummon   ȝuman onetton
siȝon æt   somne

295   oþ þ hȳ æltimbred· ȝeatolic 7 ȝoldfah   onȝȳton mihton· (308)
þ pæs foremærost   foldbuendum
receda under roderum   on þæm se rica bad·
lixte se leoma   ofer landa fela·
him þa hildedeor of modiȝra torht ȝetæhte   þæt hie him to
mihton

300   ȝeȝnum ȝanȝan   ȝuðbeorna sum   (314)
picȝ ȝepende   pord æfter cpæð·
mæl is me to feran   fæder
alpalda   mid arstafum eopic ȝehealde·
siða ȝesunde   ic to sæ

305   pille pið [prað] perod   pearde healdan·   (319)
(xli·)
Þæs sio spatspaðu   spona 7 ȝeata
pælræs peora   pide ȝesȳne
hu ða folc mid hī   fæhðe
topehton·   ȝepat him ða

A5   se ȝoda   mid his ȝædelinȝū   (2949)
frod felaȝeomor   fæsten secean
eorl onȝenþio   ufor oncirde
hæfde hiȝelaces   [hild]e ȝefrunen
plonces piȝcræft   piðres [ne] trupode

A10   þ he sæmannū   onsacan mihte   (2954)
[h]eaðoliðendū   hord forstandan
bearn 7 brȳde   beah
eft þonan· eald under eorðpeall.   þa pæs æht boden
speona leodū   seȝn hiȝelace.

A15   freoðoponȝ þone   ford ofereodon   (2959)
sȳððan hreðlinȝas   to haȝan þrunȝon
þær pearð on[ȝ]enðioþ   ecȝū speordū
blondenfexa   on bid precen
þ se þeodcȳninȝ   ðafian sceolde

A20   eafores anne dom   hȳne ȳrrinȝa   (2964)
pulf ponr[e]d[inȝ]   pæpne ȝeræhte
þ hī for spenȝe   spat ædr[ū] spronȝ
forð under fexe   næs he forht spa ðeh
ȝomela scilfinȝ   ac forȝeald hr[aðe]

A25   pẏrsan prixle   pælhlem þone   (2969)
       sẏððan ðe[od]cẏninʒ   þẏder oncirde.
       Ne meahte se snella   sunu ponredes
       ealdū ceorle hondslẏht ʒiofan ac he hī on heafde   helm ær
         ʒescer
       þ he blode fah   buʒan sceolde
A30   feoll on foldan   næs he fæʒe þa ʒit   (2975)
       ac he hẏne ʒepẏrpte   þeah ðe hī pund
       hrine let se hearda   hiʒelaces þeʒn
       brade mece   þa his broðor læ[ʒ]
       eald speord eotonisc   entiscne helm
A35   brec[an] ofer bordpeal   ða ʒebeah cẏninʒ   (2980)
       folces hẏrd[e] pæs   in feorh dropen.
       ða pæron moniʒe   þe h.. mæʒ priðon
       ricone arærdon   ða hī ʒerẏmed pearð
       þ hie pælstope   pealdan moston
A40   þende[n] reafode   rince   (2985)
       oðerne nam on onʒenðio   irenbẏrnan
       heard spẏrd hilted 7 his helm somod hares hẏrste   hiʒelace
         bær
       h.... frætpū fenʒ   7 hī fæʒre ʒehet
       leana.... leodū   7 ʒelæsta spa
A45   ʒeald þone ʒuðræs   ʒeat[a dry]hten   (2991)
       hreðles eafora þa he to hā becóm ..fore 7 pulfe mid
         ofermaðmum sealde [h]iora ʒehpæðrū   hund þusenda
       landes 7 locenra beaʒa   ne ðorfte hī ða lean oðpitan
       mon on middanʒearde   sẏðða hie ða mærða ʒesloʒon.
       7 ða iofore forʒeaf   anʒan dohtor
A50   hampeorðunʒe   hẏldo to pedde   (2998)
       þ ẏs sio fæhðo   7 se feondscipe
       pælnið   pera
       ðæs ðe ic hafo þe us seceað to   speona leoda
       sẏððan hie ʒefricʒeað   frean
A55   userne ealdor[l]easne   þone ðe ær   (3003)
       ʒeheold pið hettendū hord [7 r]ice æfter hæleða hrẏre   hpate
         scildinʒas
       folcred fremede.   oððe furður ʒen
       eorlscipe efnde   me is ofost betost
       þ þe þeodcẏninʒ   þær sceapian
A60   7 þone ʒebrinʒan   þe us beaʒas ʒeaf   (3009)

on adfære   ne scel anes hpæt
meltan mid þā modiȝan   ac þær is [m]aðma hord
ȝold unrime   ȝrīme ȝecea....
7 nu æt siðestan   sẏlfes feore
A65   beaȝas ......te þa sceall brond   (3014)
fretan æled þeccean   nalles eorl peȝan
maððū to ȝemẏndum   ne mæȝð scẏne
habban on healse   hrinȝpeorðunȝe
ac sceal ȝeomormod   ȝolde bereaf[od]
A70   oft nalles æne   elland tredan   (3019)
nu se herepisa   hleahtor aleȝde
ȝamen 7 ȝleodream   forðon sceall ȝar
pesan moniȝ morȝenceald   mundū bepunden
hæfen on handa   nalles hearpan speȝ
A75   piȝend peccean   ac se ponna hrefn   (3024)
fús ofer fæȝū   fela reordian
earne secȝan   hu hī æt æte speop
þende[n] he við pulf   pæl reafode.
spa se secȝ hpata   secȝȝende pæs
A80   laðra spella   he ne leaȝ fel[a]   (3029)
pẏrda ne porda.   peorod
eall aras eodon u[n]bliðe   under earna næs
pollenteare   pundu[.] sceapian
fundon ða on sande   sapulleasne
A85   hlimbed healdan   þone þe hī hrinȝas ȝeaf   (3034)
ærran mælū   þa pæs endedæȝ
ȝodū ȝeȝonȝen   þ se ȝuðcẏninȝ
pedra þeoden   pundordeað[e]
spealt ær hi þær ȝeseȝan   sẏllicran
A90   piht pẏrm on ponȝe   piðerræhtes þær   (3039)
laðn.. licȝean   pæs se leȝdraca
ȝrimlic ȝrẏ....   [ȝ]ledū bespæled
se pæs fiftiȝes fotȝemear[ces]   ..nȝ
on leȝere   lẏftpẏnne
A95   heold nihtes   hpilū   (3044)
nẏðer eft ȝepat dennes niosian   pæs ða deaðe fæst
hæfde eorðscrafa   ende ȝenẏttod
him biȝ stodan   bunan 7 orcas
discas laȝon   7 dẏre spẏrd
A100   omiȝe þurhetone   spa hie við eorðan fæðm   (3049)

þusend ƿintra   þær
eardodon. þōn þæs þ ẏrfe eacencræftiȝ   iumonna
ȝold   ȝaldre beƿunden
þ ðam hrinȝsele   hrinan ne moste

A105 ȝumena æniȝ   nefne ȝod
sẏlfa siȝora soðcẏninȝ   sealde   (3054)
þā ðe he ƿolde he is manna [ȝe]hẏld   hord
openian   efne spa hƿẏlcū
manna   spa hī ȝemet ðuhte :-   xlii·

Chapter 5

The Second Major Hypothesis

As a consequence of accepting Kemble's lineation, as scholars have done for 150 years, one must accept the basis of that lineation. Kemble based his extraction of verses on alliteration. As his handling of verse line 257 demonstrates, he insisted that every verse, no matter how long, must contain an alliterating syllable.

In treating alliteration as ornament, prosodists since Kemble's day have missed the crucial fact that Kemble built each of the verses of the consensus around a constituent headed by an alliterating syllable. Thus the first alliterating syllable of every halfline marks the beginning of a constituent of the halfline.

The constituent marked by the first alliterating syllable is not always the first constituent of the halfline. But it is always the point from which the other constituent(s) must be determined. P-Lineation demonstrates that Kemble worked from the first and last alliterating syllables in each series, which, for convenience, I shall call *base 1* and *base 2*. This means that, in order to construct about two-fifths of his verses, Kemble had to assemble segments smaller than the verse. When the editor or the computer program locates the first alliterating syllable of a new series, he, she, or it must then go back into the preceding text to locate a clause boundary or a proclitic to that syllable. Whenever a clause boundary occurs in this area, or there is a proclitic to the first alliterating syllable, the clause boundary or the proclitic heads a segment that must be added to the segment beginning with the alliterating syllable. If neither clause boundary nor proclitic occurs, the first alliterating syllable heads the first segment of the verse line. My second major hypothesis, then, is this: it is possible to construct a prosody based on the constituents on which verse lineation and half-lining depend.

It will be easier to follow the argument from an analysis of a brief sample of the manuscript text of the poem. I quote lines 5 to 9 on folio 132V (129v):

> [fe]lahror feran on frean pære hi hẏne
> [þ]a ætbæron to brimes faroðe spæse ʒesiþas
> [Sp]a he selfa bæd þenden pordum peold
> [p]ine scẏldinʒa leof landfruma lanʒe
> ahte þær æt hẏðe stod hrinʒedstefna isiʒ   (132V05–9)

The lineator, human or computer, begins by lining up successive base 1s at the left margin. Since from the excerpt one cannot determine whether [fe] is the first F-alliteration, I start with the first alliteration that clearly begins and ends within the passage. I continue with each alliteration in the passage, placing the successive base 1s at the left margin:

> **BASE 1**
>
> bæron to brimes faroðe
> spæse ʒesiþas [Sp]a he selfa bæd þenden
> pordum peold [p]ine scẏldinʒa
> leof landfruma lanʒe ahte þær æt
> hẏðe stod hrinʒedstefna isiʒ

With the moving of each base 1 to the left margin, I have completed the first sorting of the text.

Now the lineator has to move back from each base 1 to determine whether a clause boundary occurs after the end of the word that contains the last alliterating syllable of the *previous* alliteration. There is a clause boundary at *hi* that occurs after the completion of the F-alliteration. The clause boundary after the completion of the B-alliteration coincides with base 1 *S*. There is a clause boundary at *þenden* after the completion of the S-alliteration that does *not* coincide with base 1 *W*. The clause boundary after the completion of the W-alliteration coincides with base 1 *L*, but the clause boundary at *þær* does not coincide with base 1 *H*. I move each clause boundary that does not coincide with a base 1 to the left of the first alliterating syllable in the clause:

> hi hẏne [þ]a ætbæron to brimes faroðe
> þenden pordum peold [p]ine scẏldinʒa
> þær æt hẏðe stod hrinʒedstefna isiʒ

Next, I look for a proclitic to each base 1. But since a clause boundary takes precedence over a proclitic, and since a clause boundary occurs either before or simultaneously with each base 1, I find no proclitic in the exemplar passage that belongs at the left margin. At this point, then, I have located the beginning of each verse line in the passage:

> hi hýne [þ]a ætbæron to brimes faroðe
> spæse ʒesiþas [Sp]a he selfa bæd
> þenden þordum þeold [p]ine scýldinʒa
> leof landfruma lanʒe ahte
> þær æt hýðe stod hrinʒedstefna isiʒ

Next, I locate each successive base 2 and move it and the segment it heads to the left margin:

> **BASE 2**
>
> brimes faroðe
> selfa bæd
> [p]ine scýldinʒa
> lanʒe ahte
> hrinʒedstefna isiʒ

I then follow the same process I followed for each base 1; that is, I move back from each base 2 to locate a clause boundary that occurs between the next-to-last and last alliterating syllables. If I find a clause boundary in this position, I displace base 2 with the clause boundary. I quote here the single instance in which a clause boundary occurs in this position:

> [Sp]a he selfa bæd

Finally, I look for a proclitic to each base 2. I find only one in the exemplar passage, *to*, a preposition that governs *faroðe*. But *faroðe* is preceded by another noun, this one in the genitive case, that modifies it and happens to contain base 2. The two nouns form a tightly knit unit governed by the preposed preposition *to*. I move the proclitic *to* to the left margin, thereby completing the process of eliciting the half-lines in the five verse lines:

> to brimes faroðe
> [Sp]a he selfa bæd
> [p]ine scýldinʒa
> lanʒe ahte
> hrinʒedstefna isiʒ

I have elicited five verse lines consisting of ten halflines. In the process of doing so I have isolated fifteen segments:

(1) hi hӯne [þ]a æt
(2) bæron
(3) to
(4) brimes faroðe
(5) spæse ӡesiþas
(6) [Sp]a he
(7) selfa bæd
(8) þenden
(9) pordum peold
(10) [p]ine scӯldinӡa
(11) leof landfruma
(12) lanӡe ahte
(13) þær æt
(14) hӯðe stod
(15) hrinӡedstefna isiӡ

Some of these segments are halflines: numbers 5, 10–12, and 15, the last with a tail that disappears as soon as it becomes clear that *isiӡ* represents base 1 of the next alliterating series. Ten of these segments are smaller than the halfline: numbers 1–4, 6–9, and 13–14. Each of these smaller segments has played its role in determining the halfline of which it is a part. None of these segments has been determined arbitrarily: each either begins with an alliterating syllable from which I have calculated the beginning of the halfline or is a clausal or proclitic segment determined in relation to the alliterating syllable.

The smaller segments demonstrate that Kemble's text is not what it appears to be—a series of indivisible verses. Instead, Kemble's text consists both of verses he extracted intact and of verses he extracted in parts and then assembled or synthesized. Kemble joined the appropriate parts into whole verses and thus created the impression that each verse is a simple whole. In one sense that is true; in perhaps a more important sense it is not. Many of Kemble's verses are synthetic.

Some recent prosodists appear to suggest that every verse of *Beowulf* is a seamless whole. Thomas Cable, in particular, argues that we can only scan each halfline according to its "contours of ictus."[1] But Cable's "holistic" assumption, though it might seem to take account of such halflines as *spæse ӡesiþas*, is falsified by the fact that the halfline that is paired with it, [*Sp*]*a he selfa bæd*, has been elicited in two segments.

1. Thomas Cable, *The Meter and Melody of Beowulf* (Urbana: University of Illinois Press, 1974), 88.

Other prosodists may be termed "dividers." Eduard Sievers is perhaps the best known of this group. He assumes that every halfline consists of at least two segments. Lineation shows that many half-lines—about 40 percent—do indeed consist of two segments. There is, thus, in Kemble's work some justification for Sievers's assumption. When, however, we compare Sievers's segmentation of the halflines in the exemplar passage with the segmentation the lineator depends on, the two prosodists, Sievers and the lineator, part company. Sievers divides these ten halflines in the following way:[2]

x| ˊ x x x | ˊ. x hi |hyne þa ætl\bæron	Type A 288/289
x ˊ x || ˊx x to brimes\faroðe	Type C 244/248
ˊ x x| ˊ x swæse ge\siþas	Type A (271–2)/276
x x ˊ | x ˊ swa he sel\fa bæd	Type B 236/242
x x ˊ | x ˊ þenden wor\dum weold	Type B (291)/294
ˊ x | ˊ ˋ x wine | Scyldinga	Type D 252/261
ˊ || ˊ ˋ x le of\landfruma	Type D 300/307
ˊ x | ˊ x lange | ahte	Type A 222/235
x x ˊ| x ˊ þær æt hy\ðe stod	Type B (291)/294
ˊ x | ˊ x hringed\stefna	Type A 222/235

2. See Eduard Sievers, "Zur Rhythmik der germanischen Alliterationsverses," *Beiträge zur Geschichte der deutschen Sprache und Literatur* 10 (1885): 206–314. The number before the slash is the page on which Sievers quotes the verse. If he does not quote the particular verse, the page on which he discusses verses of the same pattern appears in parentheses. The number after the slash indicates the page on which Sievers summarizes in schematic form the various realizations of the Type. My quotations of Sievers's patterns in the form of acutes, graves, *x*, macrons, and bars are based on his schematic summaries.

Sievers's segmentation of halflines is based on the assumption that the halflines consist of two "feet," each of which contains or consists of a stressed syllable. Sievers has imposed his notion of the "foot" built around a stressed syllable on these halflines in ignorance of the fact that some of the halflines already represent the synthesis of two prosodically determined segments.

No one has so far tried to build a prosody on the foundation that Kemble laid. That is what I shall try to do in the remaining chapters. The place to begin is with certain verses in "Kemble's legacy." That legacy at first appears to consist of a series of whole verses, the more than 6,300 verses of *Beowulf* he published in each of his two editions of the poem. But my extrapolation of the method by which Kemble determined these verses indicates that the appearance is in many cases deceptive. About 40 percent of Kemble's verses have been synthesized from two parts, the first a nonalliterating segment, the second an alliterating segment. That is the basis on which I shall try to construct a prosody. The second segment of *hi hyne [þ]a ætbæron, -bæron*, is the *first* segment to emerge from the manuscript text. Kemble had to go back from this first alliterating syllable and extract the first segment of the verse from the syllables that lie between the end of the word that contains the last syllable of the previous alliteration and the beginning of the *B*-alliteration. This is the clue that Kemble's work offers the prosodist. This is the clue no prosodist so far has used.

Only about 40 percent of the halflines of the poem, however, have had to be synthesized in this way. The fact that some halflines have had to be synthesized suggests that the poet may have constructed *every* halfline from smaller parts. But how do we determine the smaller parts of the halflines that the lineator has elicited intact from the manuscript text? If it is possible to find a way to answer that question, it will be possible to complete the work that Kemble began and to complete it on the foundation he laid.

The answer may lie in the fact that the second segment of *hi hyne [þ]a ætbæron*, that is, *-bæron*, matches, in the length and the stress pattern of its two syllables and in the fact that it alliterates, *-siþas* in one of the intact halflines of the exemplar passage. Further, *-bæron* matches in all these ways *lanȝe* in a later intact halfline in the passage. If we place *-bæron* "over" *-siþas*, it sets off the segment *spæse ȝe-*. If we place it over *lanȝe*, it sets off the segment *ahte*. The base 1 segment

-bæron, from which the lineator builds the verse beginning with *hi*, thus serves as a pattern or "template" for locating possible points of segmentation in unsegmented halflines.

If the prosodist is to use such inner base segments in this way, the first step must be to list all of Kemble's inner base 1 and base 2 segments. I do so in a section appended to this chapter. In the next chapter, I shall begin by testing the following hypothesis: there are two and only two constituents of every synthetic halfline in *Beowulf*. Each second alliterating constituent of verse lines that begin with a nonalliterating constituent can serve as a pattern or template for determining the constituents of halflines elicited intact.

KEMBLE'S LEGACY: A MATCHED CORPUS OF VERSE LINES IN *BEOWULF*

In the following pages I set out a small part of Kemble's legacy. A complete account of his legacy would contain every verse in his second (1835) edition of *Beowulf*. An accurate account of his legacy would show about 60 percent of his verses intact and about 40 percent segmented. My account is accurate but incomplete.

Each intact verse/halfline begins with either "base 1" or "base 2," that is, the first (base 1) or last (base 2) alliterating syllable of each successive series of alliterations in the poem. Each segmented verse/halfline begins with a nonalliterating syllable. The first segment consists of all the syllables up to but not including either base 1 or base 2. The second segment begins with the interior (or "inner") base and includes every syllable to the end of the verse/halfline.

In the following accurate but incomplete account of his legacy, I display Kemble's segmented verses in their segmentation. The corpus does not contain all of the matched C (conventional) verses/P halflines of the two samples. It contains only *paired* C verses that match *whole* P verse lines. For example, although P halfline 4b, *sceaþe[na] þreatum*, matches C verse 4b, neither P4a/C4a nor P4b/C4b is included.

I have divided the corpus of matched C verse pairs/whole P verse lines into three subcorpora on the basis of their segmentation. The first subcorpus consists of verse lines that have been elicited from the manuscript text in only two parts: the first halfline of a verse line and the second halfline of the same verse line.

The second subcorpus consists of verse lines that can only be elicited from the manuscript text in three parts: one part is an intact halfline; the other two parts consist of the two segments of a halfline with an *inner* base, whether 1 or 2. The nonalliterating segment begins either at the beginning of the line or at the midpoint of the line—the first syllable of the second halfline—marked "M." The base segment always begins with the first (or only) alliterating syllable of the half-line.

The third subcorpus consists of a small number of verse lines in the Matched Corpus that can only be elicited from the syllables of the manuscript in four parts. Both base 1 and base 2 head *inner* segments. The first nonalliterating segment follows the verse line number; the second nonalliterating segment follows the "M."

Line numbers in the three subcorpora do not equal Kemble's verse numbers. Here, and throughout the rest of this volume, "C" stands for "conventional" verse line number. Kemble's two editions are hard to find, but Klaeber's third edition is likely to be on every scholar's and most students' shelves. Most numerations since 1857 are close enough to Klaeber's to make it easy to locate a passage on the basis of the following C numbers.

These segments, then, accurately represent a portion of the legacy of the prosodist John Mitchell Kemble.

Subcorpus I: Matched Two-Segment Lines

To save space, I list the matched two-segment lines of Subcorpus I here. I use the conventional ("C") line numbers familiar to users of such editions as Klaeber's or Dobbie's. The reader can refer to the chart at the end of the previous chapter, using the line numbers in the right margin.

Subcorpus I: 2, 5, 8, 14, 17, 18, 31, 33, 46, 50, 51, 54, 69, 95, 97, 101, 104, 105, 110, 119, 120, 121, 123, 127, 129, 130, 131, 142, 147, 148, 152, 153, 154, 156, 160, 161, 162, 163, 165, 166, 171, 172, 176, 193, 195, 209, 210, 211, 215, 222, 226, 227, 231, 235, 236, 246, 255, 256, 259, 263, 266, 275, 276, 295, 302, 305, 306, 314, 315; 2947, 2950, 2951, 2952, 2953, 2955, 2958, 2959, 2965, 2969, 2979, 2991, 2998, 3017, 3019, 3025, 3032.

Subcorpus II: Matched Three-Segment Lines

C6		eʒsode eorl	10		ofer
	M	sýððan			hronrade
		ærest pear[ð]		M	hýran scolde
7		feasceaft funden	11		ʒomban ʒýldan
	M	he þæs		M	Þ pæs
		frofre ʒeba[d]			ʒod cýninʒ·

12		ðæm	43		Nalæs hi hine
		eafera pæs			læssan
	M	æfter cenned		M	lacum teodan
13		ȝeonȝ in ȝeardum	47		þa ȝýt hie him a
	M	þone			setton
		ȝod sende		M	seȝen [ȝe.]denne
15		Þ hie	48		heah ofer heafod
		ær druȝon		M	leton
	M	aldor..ase·			holm ber[an]
16		lanȝe hƿile	49		ȝeafon on ȝarsecȝ
	M	him þæs		M	him pæs
		liffrea			ȝeomor sefa
27		[fe]lahror feran	52		hæleð under heofen[ū]
	M	on		M	hƿa þæm
		frean pære			hlæste onfenȝ·
29		spæse ȝesiþas	53		ÐA pæs on
	M	[Sp]a he			burȝum
		selfa bæd		M	beopulf scýldinȝa
30		þenden	59		ðæm
		ƿordum ƿeold			feoper bearn
	M	[ƿ]ine scýldinȝa		M	forðȝerimed
32		þær æt	60		in
		hýðe stod			ƿorold ƿocun
	M	hrinȝedstefna		M	ƿeoroda ræspa
34		a	65		piȝes peorðmýnd
		ledon þa		M	Þ him his
	M	leofne þeoden			pinemaȝas
35		beaȝa brýttan	66		ȝeorne hýrdon
	M	on		M	oðð Þ seo
		bearm scipes			ȝeoȝoð ȝepeox
38		Ne hýrde ic	67		maȝodriht micel
		cýmlicor		M	hī on
	M	ceol ȝeȝýrpan			mod bearn
39		hildepæpnum	68		Þ
	M	7			healreced
		heaðopædum		M	hatan polde·
40		billum 7 býrnum	75		maniȝre [m]æȝþe
	M	him on		M	ȝeond þisne
		bearme læȝ			middanȝeard
41		madma mæniȝo	76		folcste[de] frætpan
	M	þa him		M	him on
		mid scoldon			fýrste ȝelomp
42		on	77		ædre [m]id ýldum·
		flodes æht		M	Þ hit pearð
	M	feor ȝepitan·			ealȝearo

78		healærna mæst	114		lanȝ[e þraȝe
	M	scop him		M	he] him ðæs
		heort naman			lean forȝeald.
79		se þe his	116		[h]ean huses
		þordes ȝepeald		M	hu hit
	M	þide hæfde·			hrinȝdene
80		He	118		Fand þa ðær
		beot ne aleh			[i]nne
	M	beaȝas dælde		M	æþelinȝa ȝedriht
83		laðan liȝes	122		reoc 7 reþe
	M	ne þæs hit		M	7 on
		lenȝe þa ȝen			ræste ȝenam
85		æfter	124		huðe hremiȝ
		þælniðe		M	to
	M	þæcnan scolde·			ham faran
86		ða se	125		mid þære
		ellenȝæst			þælfýlle
	M	earfoðlice		M	þica neosan·
87		þraȝe ȝeþolode	128		þa þæs æfter
	M	se þe in			þiste
		þýstrū bad		M	þóp up ahafen
94		ȝe	132		sýðþan hie þæs
		sette siȝehreþiȝ			laðan
	M	sunn[an] 7 monan		M	last sceapedon
96		7 ȝe	133		perȝan ȝastes
		frætpade		M	þæs þ ȝe
	M	foldan sceata[s]			þin to stranȝ
98		cý[n]na ȝehpýlcum	134		lað 7 lonȝsum
	M	þara ðe		M	næs hit
		cþice hpýrf[aþ.]			lenȝra [fýrs]t
99		Spa ða	135		ac ým[b]
		drihtȝuman			ane niht
	M	dreamum lif[don]		M	e[ft ȝefremede]
100		eadiȝlice	140		bed æfter burum
	M	oð ðæt		M	ða hi[m] ȝe
		án onȝan			beacnod þæs
102		þæs se	141		ȝe
		ȝrimma ȝæ[st]			sæȝd soðlice
	M	ȝrendel haten		M	spe[oto]lan tacne
103		mære mearcstapa	143		fýr 7 fæstor
	M	se þe		M	se þæm
		moras heold			feo[nde] ætþand·
108		ece drihten	145		ana þið eallum
	M	þæs þe he		M	oð þ
		abel sloȝ·			idel stod

146		husa seles[t]	192		laþ 7 lonʒsum
	M	þæs seo		M	þe on ða
		hpil micel			leode becom
151		ʒýddū ʒeomore	194		þ fram
	M	þætte			ham ʒefræʒn
		ʒrendel pan		M	hiʒelaces þeʒn
155		þið	198		æþele 7 eacen
		manna hpone		M	het him
	M	mæʒenes deniʒa			ýðlidan
157		ne þær næniʒ	199		ʒodne ʒeʒýrpan
		þitena		M	cpæð he
	M	þenan þorfte			ʒuðcýninʒ
158		beorhtre bote	200		ofer
	M	to			spanrade
		banū folmū.		M	secean polde
164		spa	201		mærne þeoden
		fela fýrena		M	þa him pæs
	M	feond mancýn[ne]s			manna þearf
173		hpæt	202		ðone
		spiðferhðum			siðfæt him
	M	selest pære		M	snotere ceorlas
175		Hpilum hie ʒeheton	203		lýthpon loʒon·
	M	æt		M	[þeah h]e him
		hrærʒtrafum			[l]eof [pære]
177		þ him	206		[ce]mpan ʒecorone
		ʒastbona		M	þara þe he
	M	ʒeoce ʒefremede·			cenoste
181		dæda demend	212		on
	M	ne piston hie			stefn stiʒon
		drihten ʒod·		M	streamas pundon
182		[ne hie	219		oð þ ýmb
		h]uru [h]eof[ena h]elm			antid
	M	herian [ne] cuþon		M	oþres doʒores
188		7 to	220		pundenstefna
		fæder fæþmum		M	ʒe
	M	freoðo pilnian·			paden hæfde
189		Spa ða	221		þ ða
		mælceare			liðende
	M	maʒa healfdenes		M	land ʒesapon
190		sinʒala seað	223		side sænæssas
	M	ne mihte		M	þa pæs
		snotor hæleð			sund liden
191		þean onpendan	224		eoletes æt ende
	M	pæs þ ʒe		M	þanon
		þin to spýð			up hraðe

225 þedera leode
M on
 þanʒ stiʒon·

228 þæs þe him
 ýþlade
M eaðe purdon·

229 [þa] of
 pealle ʒesea[h]
M peard scildinʒa

230 se [þe
 holm]clifu
M healdan scolde

232 fýrdsearu fuslicu
M hine
 fýrpýt bræc

233 modʒehýʒdum
M hpæt þa
 men pæron·

234 Ge
 þat him þa to paroðe
M picʒe ri[dan]

242 þe on
 land dena
M laðra næniʒ

243 mid
 scipherʒe
M sceðþan ne meahte

247 maʒa ʒemedu
M næfre ic
 maran ʒeseah

250 þæpnum ʒepeorðad
M næfre him his
 plite leoʒe

253 leassceaperas
M on
 land [dena]

254 [fu]rþur feran
M nu ʒe
 feorbuend

258 [H]im se
 ýldesta
M 7sparode

260 þe sýnt
 ʒumcýnnes
M ʒeata leode

261 7
 hiʒelaces
M heorðʒeneatas·

262 þæs min
 fæder
M folcum ʒecýþed

265 ʒamol of ʒeardum
M hine
 ʒearpe ʒeman

269 leodʒebýrʒean
M pes þu us
 larena ʒod·

270 habbað þe to þæm
 mæran
M micel ærende

271 deniʒa frean·
M ne sceal þær
 dýrne sum

274 þ mid
 scýldinʒum
M sc[eaðona] ic nat hpýlc

277 hýnðu 7 hrafýl
M ic þæs
 hroðʒar mæʒ

278 þur[h]
 rumne sefan
M ræd ʒelæran·

279 hu he
 fro[d. 7] ʒod
M feond oferspýðeþ

280 ʒyf him
 edpend[an]
M æfre scolde.

283 oððe
 a sýþðan
M earfoðþraʒe

284 þreanýd þolað
M þenden
 þær punað

285 on
 heahstede
M husa selest·

286 peard maþelode
M ðær on
 picʒe sæt

296		arum healdan	2966		þ hī for
	M	oþðæt			spenᵹe
		eft býreð		M	spat ædr[ū] spronᵹ
297		ofer	2967		forð under fexe
		laᵹustrea[mas		M	næs he
	M	l]eofne mannan			forht spa ðeh
298		þudu punden[hals	2968		ᵹomela scilfinᵹ
	M	to]		M	ac for
		þedermearce			ᵹeald hr[aðe]
299		ᵹodfremmendra	2970		sýððan
	M	[sp]ýlcum			ðe[od]cýninᵹ
		ᵹifeþe bið		M	þýder oncirde.
300		þ þone	2971		Ne meahte se
		hilderæs			snella
	M	[há]l ᵹediᵹeð·		M	sunu ponredes
301		ᵹepiton him þa	2974		þ he
		feran			blode fah
	M	flota [st]ille bád		M	buᵹan sceolde
303		on	2975		feoll on foldan
		ancre fæst		M	næs he
	M	eoforlic scionon			fæᵹe þa ᵹit
309		þ pæs	2978		brade mece
		foremærost		M	þa his
	M	foldbuendum			broðor læ[ᵹ]
310		receda under roderum	2980		brec[an] ofer bordþeal
	M	on þæm se		M	ða ᵹe
		rica bad·			beah cýninᵹ
311		lixte se leoma	2981		folces hýrd[e] pæs
	M	ofer		M	in
		landa fela·			feorh dropen.
2946		Þæs sio	2983		ricone arærdon
		spatspaðu		M	ða hī ᵹe
	M	spona 7 ᵹeata			rýmed pearð
2961		þær pearð	2984		þ hie
		on[ᵹ]enðioþ			pælstope
	M	ecᵹū speordū		M	pealdan moston
2962		blondenfexa	2995		landes 7 locenra beaᵹa
	M	on		M	ne ðorfte hī ða
		bid þrecen			lean oðþitan
2963		þ se	2996		mon on middanᵹearde
		þeodcýninᵹ		M	sýðða hie ða
	M	ðafian sceolde			mærða ᵹesloᵹon.
2964		eafores anne dom	2997		7 ða
	M	hýne			iofore forᵹeaf
		ýrrinᵹa		M	anᵹan dohtor

3006		folcred fremede.	3028		spa se
	M	oðÐe			secʒ hpata
		furður ʒen		M	secʒʒende pæs
3007		eorlscipe efnde	3029		laðra spella
	M	me is		M	he ne
		ofost betost			leaʒ fel[a]
3008		Þ pe	3033		fundon ða on
		ðeodcÿninʒ			sande
	M	þær sceapian		M	sapulleasne
3011		meltan mid þā modiʒan	3034		hlimbed healdan
	M	ac þær is		M	þone þe hī
		[m]aðma hord			hrinʒas ʒeaf
3013		7 nu æt	3035		ærran mælū
		siðestan		M	þa pæs
	M	sÿlfes feore			endedæʒ
3016		maðÐū to ʒemÿndum	3036		ʒodū ʒeʒonʒen
	M	ne		M	Þ se
		mæʒð scÿne			ʒuðcÿninʒ
3018		ac sceal	3040		laðn.. licʒean
		ʒeomormod		M	pæs se
	M	ʒolde bereaf[od]			leʒdraca
3020		nu se	3046		hæfde
		herepisa			eorðscrafa
	M	hleahtor aleʒde		M	ende ʒenÿttod
3023		hæfen on handa	3047		him
	M	nalles			biʒ stodan
		hearpan speʒ		M	bunan 7 orcas
3024		piʒend peccean	3048		discas laʒon
	M	ac se		M	7
		ponna hrefn			dÿre spÿrd
3026		earne secʒan	3049		omiʒe þurhetone
	M	hu hī æt		M	spa hie pið
		æte speop			eorðan fæðm
3027		þende[n] he pið	3053		Þ ðam
		pulf			hrinʒsele
	M	pæl reafode		M	hrinan ne moste

Subcorpus III: Matched Four-Segment Lines

C1		HPÆT PE		M	þara
		GARDEna·			ÿmbsittendra
	M	in	26		him ða
		ʒeardaʒum·			scÿld ʒepat
9		oð Þ him		M	to ʒe
		æʒhpÿlc			scæphpile

28	hi hỳne [þ]a æt bæron		M	to ʒe fremmanne·
	M	to brimes faroðe	178	pið þeodþreaum
84	þ se secʒhete		M	spýlc pæs þeap hýra.
	M	aþum sperian	257	to ʒe cýðanne
106	siþðan him scýppend		M	[h]panan eopre cýme sýndon·
	M	for scrifen hæfde	264	ʒebad pintra porn
107	in caines cýnne		M	ær he on peʒ hpurfe·
	M	þone cpealm ʒepræc	304	[o]fer hleorberan
109	Ne ʒe feah he þære fæhðe		M	ʒe hroden ʒolde
	M	ac he hine feor forpræc	2954	þ he sæmannū
113	spýlce ʒi[ʒantas]		M	on sacan mihte
	M	þa [pi]ð ʒode punnon	2960	sýððan hreðlinʒas
115	[Ge]pat ða neosian		M	to haʒan þrunʒon
	M	sýþðan niht becom	2982	ða pæron moniʒe
117	æfter [be]orþeʒe		M	þe h.. mæʒ priðon
	M	ʒe bun hæfdon.	2989	h.... frætpū fenʒ
126	ða pæs on uhtan		M	7 hī fæʒre ʒehet
	M	mid ærdæʒe	2999	þ ýs sio fæhðo
138	þ[a] pæs eaðfýnde		M	7 se feondscipe
	M	þe him elles hpær	3009	7 þone ʒe brinʒan
144	Spa rixode		M	þe us beaʒas ʒeaf
	M	7 pið rihte pan	3010	on adfære
174	pið færʒrýrū		M	ne scel anes hpæt

Chapter 6

The Challenge
Halfline Constituents of Synthetic Halflines as the Key to Beowulfian Prosody

INTRODUCTION

The lineator—editor or machine—has synthesized 230 of the 580 halflines in the Matched Corpus.[1] That amounts to 39.6 percent, or two-fifths of the Corpus. Lineation has constructed each of these half-lines from two segments of the text: an interior (or *inner*) segment that begins with the first alliterating syllable and a preceding (*outer*) seg-ment that does not begin with an alliterating syllable but contains syl-lables or words that belong with the word containing the alliterating syllable. The synthesized halflines present a challenge to the proso-dist: is it possible to construct a prosody based on these two kinds of constituent?

It is of course possible that two-fifths of the halflines of the Corpus represent one kind of halfline and the intact halflines that make up the other three-fifths of the Corpus represent another. It is also pos-sible that the synthetic halflines are anomalous. The high percentage of these halflines argues against the latter interpretation, however. A better interpretation seems to be this: the synthetic halflines are nei-ther totally different from the intact halflines nor anomalous. Instead, their clearly defined constituents suggest the exciting possibility that every halfline in the Corpus consists of two constituents.

In this and the chapters that follow I shall argue that the key to the prosody of *Beowulf* is to be found in the segmentation of synthetic halflines. In the present chapter I shall argue that, at the level of the halfline, the synthetic halflines usually consist of these two constitu-ents and no others. I shall then try to show that the constituents of synthetic halflines offer a means of determining the constituents of

---

1. There are 290 verse lines in the Matched Corpus (I: 86; II: 178; III: 26), divided into 580 halflines.

those halflines elicited intact by the procedures of lineation and half-lining.

The procedures of lineation have made it clear that every synthetic halfline is composed of at least two constituents ("HCs" for halfline constituents). But is every synthetic halfline made up of exactly two constituents? If the synthetic halflines are to serve as a guide to the segmentation of the intact halflines, it is necessary to determine whether or not each constituent of these halflines is itself *single*. By single I mean that there is no motivation to split either HC into two HCs at the level of the halfline. Both of the constituents synthesized to form halfline 53a, for example, *ĐA pæs on* + *burʒum*, seem to be single in this sense. But the second HC of 107a, *in caines cýnne*, that is, *caines cýnne*, is not so clearly single.

Since it will prove easier to determine the singleness of HCs that begin with nonalliterating syllables, I begin with these.

NONALLITERATING HCS AS SINGLE HCS

Forty-seven nonalliterating HCs consist of a single monosyllable. I list these HCs toward the beginning of the next section, when I discuss them in connection with monosyllabic alliterating HCs. One HC now consists of only a single letter, *h*. The rest of this word and possibly another have been torn away from the lower right-hand corner of 198R. I count this *h....* in 2989a here. Since they offer no point of division, these forty-eight segments are obviously single HCs. Twenty-five nonalliterating HCs consist of a disyllabic word that does not contain a stressed syllable, for example, *æfter* (85a, 117a), *oððe* (283a, 3006b), and *þara* (9b). It seems likely that these segments, too, consist of single HCs.

Eighty-one nonalliterating HCs consist of two words neither of which is stressed, for example, *him on* (40b, 67b, 76b), *næs he* (2967b, 2975b), and *þa pæs* (138a, 223b, 3035b). Thus there is no motivation to separate one of these unstressed words from the other. These segments, too, must be treated as single HCs.

The same argument applies to the thirty-three trisyllabic nonalliterating HCs that contain no stressed syllable. Dividing the proclitic segment to 3011b, for example, would simply make the conjunction *ac* one HC and the phrase *þær is* another. One can then extend this argument to the eight four-syllable proclitic segments that contain no stressed syllable. The proclitic segment 109b, for example, *ac he hine*, might be divided between *ac* and *he* or between *he* and *hine*, but there seems to be little reason to make either choice. The one five-syllable proclitic HC that contains no stressed syllable, 28a—*hi hȳne [þ]a æt-—* presents three possible points of division but, again, no motivation for beginning a new HC at any of the four words.

These 196 proclitic HCs that contain no stressed syllable make up 85 percent of the 230 proclitic segments. None seems to motivate splitting into smaller segments. All 196 HCs can then be regarded as *single*.

Each of the remaining thirty-four nonalliterating HCs, on the other hand, contains one stressed syllable, a point of possible division. But five of the six single-word disyllabic HCs begin with the stressed syllable, thus providing no interior point of division. Only one, *ȝebad* (264a), might be divided between the unstressed and stressed syllables. I put this HC aside for a moment. Six of the eight two-word disyllabic HCs also begin with the stressed syllable. Only *ac sceal* (3018a) and *ne scel* (3010b) might be split into two HCs between the unstressed conjunction or particle and the stressed verb. I shall consider these two HCs also in the following paragraphs.

Four of the eight trisyllabic nonalliterating HCs that contain a stressed syllable begin with that syllable and thus offer no point of interior division. Only three of the seven four-syllable nonalliterating segments begin with a stressed syllable, and only two of the five five-syllable nonalliterating HCs begin in this way. Thus, of the 230 non-alliterating HCs, only the following offer an interior point of possible division into two HCs:

ȝebad	264a
ac sceal	3018a
ne scel	3010b
7 nu æt	3013a
[Ge]þat ða	115a
ne mihte	190b
ne sceal þær	271b
Ne hȳrde ic	38a
Ne meahte se	2971a
ne þær næniȝ	157a
ne þiston hie	181b
ȝepiton him þa	301a
ne ðorfte hī ða	2995b
þa ȝȳt hie him a-	47a

Thus, only fourteen nonalliterating HCs seem to offer any interior point of division. In all but one instance—157a—splitting at the stressed syllable would have the effect of turning a single unstressed syllable before a nonalliterating syllable into an HC.

As we have seen, an unstressed monosyllable, such as *in* in 107a (*in caines cÿnne*), can indeed function as an HC. But *in* in that halfline occurs before the first *alliterating* syllable, *cai-* in *caines*. It seems, then, that an unstressed monosyllable can function as an HC only if it comes immediately before the first alliterating syllable.

All of the 230 nonalliterating HCs of the Matched Corpus can be regarded as single constituents, partly because there seem to be no compelling reasons for splitting even the longest and heaviest of them into two HCs. More positive reasons for treating these outer or proclitic HCs as single proclitics will, I believe, emerge in the next chapter.

At this point, then, it is possible to state tentatively that all nonalliterating HCs in synthetic halflines can be treated as single constituents of their halflines. I shall henceforth refer to these nonalliterating proclitic HCs as HCs of Type ε (epsilon) and number them 1 through 5 simply according to the number of syllables.[2]

SIMPLE ALLITERATING HCS AS SINGLE HCS

I turn from outer nonalliterating HCs to inner alliterating segments. A few inner segments that begin with an alliterating syllable seem to admit no further division. Any constituent that consists of a single syllable or several syllables of the same word seems to resist any further attempt at splitting. At this point only a few types of segment can be characterized as single, that is, offering no point of segmentation.

The most obvious such HC is the stressed and alliterating monosyllable set off in verse line 3027a:

þende[n] he þið *pulf*   pæl reafode.   3027/199R10–11

The monosyllable *pulf* is the first indicator that a verse line alliterating on *W* is forming. The very next syllable is the last instance of *W*-alliteration in range. Clearly *pulf* is a constituent of the first halfline of verse line 3027. It is also clearly single.

In 262a, *fæder* seems to be a single HC:

pæs min *fæder*   folcum ȝecÿþed   262/137V10

---

2. See my "A New Approach to the Rhythm of *Beowulf*," *PMLA* 81 (March 1966): 23–33.

The two syllables of *fæder* can be split into *fæ-* and *-der*. But the splitter would have to demonstrate that some purpose is served relative to the building of the halfline by such a division.

It is true that a single unstressed syllable is, as we have seen, occasionally isolated as a proclitic HC at the beginning of a halfline. There are, as I noted at the beginning of the previous section, forty-seven such occurrences in the Matched Corpus. I list them here in alphabetic order: *a-* (34a), 7 (39b, 261a, 3048b), *æt* (175a), *for-* (106b), *ʒe-* (94a, 117b, 141a, 220b, 234a, 304b), *He* (80a), *him* (3047a), *hpæt* (173a), *in* (1b, 60a, 107a, 2981b), *mid* (126a, 243a), *ne* (3016b), *on* (27b, 35b, 42a, 212a, 225b, 253b, 285a, 303a, 2962b, 3010a), *on-* (2954b), *Spa* (144a, 164a), *to* (28b, 124b, 158b, 298b, 2960b), *ðæm* (12a, 59a), *þ* (68a), *þurh* (278a), *þið* (155a, 174a, 178a). The difference between the unstressed second syllable of *fæder*, for example, and unstressed proclitic syllables such as *a-*, *ʒe-*, or *on-* lies precisely in the fact that the latter are constituents of their halflines. Each has been added as the first constituent to the alliterating syllable that forms the base around which the halfline has been constructed and that also marks the beginning of the second constituent. That is decidedly not the case with the unstressed second syllable of *fæder*.

The same reasoning applies to *-on* (or *-ron*) in *-bæron*, an HC of 28a:

hi hẏne [þ]a ætbæron   to brimes faroðe   28/132Vo5–6

It also applies to *-tena* in *pitena* and *-sian* in *neosian* in 157a and 115a, respectively:

ne þær næniʒ *pitena*   penan þorfte   157a/135R19–20
[Ge]pat ða *neosian*   sẏþðan niht becom   115a/134Vo4

These HCs—*-bæron*, *pitena*, and *neosian*—function as tightly knit units in each of the contexts quoted.

Is it possible to generalize that every synthetic HC that begins with an alliterating syllable and contains no other stressed syllable forms one and only one constituent of its halfline, that is, is *single*? Since there are no segments of more than four syllables that do not also contain a second stressed syllable, the question focuses on five segments that consist of three syllables beginning with a long alliterating syllable and three segments that consist of four syllables beginning with a short syllable:

bed æfter burum   ða hi[m] ʒebeacnod *pæs*   140/135Ro5–6
on adfære   ne scel *anes hpæt*   3010/198V17–18

aledon þa	leofne þeoden	34/132V10–11
ricone arærdon	þa hī ȝerȳmed pearð	2983/198R16–17
modȝehȳȝdum	hpæt þa *men pæron·*	233/137R04–5
to ȝecȳðanne	[h]panan eopre *cȳme sȳndon·*	257/137V04–5
ðæm *eafera pæs*	æfter cenned	12/132R11–12
ȝodfremmendra	[sp]ȳlcum *ȝifeþe bið*	299/138V02–3

To argue that a new HC begins at the final word—that is, at *pæs, hpæt, þa, pearð, pæron, sȳndon, pæs, bið*—one would have to justify creating an HC out of these categorically unstressed words. One might try, perhaps, by arguing that these words have acquired stress by virtue of their final position in their respective HCs, a reasonable notion. But it carries the correlate that, in order to maintain stress, each of these words must remain where it is—in the final position of its HC. It would lose its stress if it became part of a different HC.

Every synthetic alliterating HC that contains no additional stressed syllable, then, can be characterized as a *single* constituent of its halfline. It will be useful to designate such HCs that contain only one stressed syllable—the first (alliterating) syllable—as *simple*.

SIMPLE ALLITERATING HCS AS TEMPLATES

There are 34 simple HCs in the 230 synthetic halflines of the Matched Corpus. I list them according to the number of syllables in each. I list a word that begins with a *short* syllable before a word containing the same number of syllables that begins with a long syllable:

Monosyllabic

pulf	3027a

Disyllabic, First Syllable Short

fæder	262a

Disyllabic, First Syllable Long

-bæron	28a
læssan	43a
-setton	47a
burȝum	53a
[i]nne	118a
uhtan	126a
piste	128a
laðan	132a
mæran	270a
feran	301a
spenȝe	2966a
snella	2971a
fæhðo	2999a

-bringan	3009a
sande	3033a

Trisyllabic, First Syllable Short

pitena	157a
monige	2982a
sperian	84b(?)

Trisyllabic, First Syllable Long

-ledon þa	34a
-frætpade	96a
neosian	115a
-beacnod pæs	140b
rixode	144a
-fremmanne	174b
þeap hýra	178b
-cýðanne	257a
-rýmed pearð	2983b
gi[gantas]	113a(?)

Four Syllables, First Syllable Short

eafera pæs	12a
cýme sýndon	257b
gifeþe bið	299b

Four Syllables, First Syllable Long

manna hpone	155a

One or another of these thirty-four simple HCs of synthetic halflines matches at least one marked segment in nearly all of the intact halflines of the Matched Corpus. For example, *monige* (2982a) and *burgum* (53a), respectively, match in the number of syllables and length of the first syllable *monegū* and *mægþum* of 5a. The HCs *pulf* (3027a) and *monige* match the two segments of *þeodcýninga* of the intact halfline 2a.

I think that it has been demonstrated that the thirty-four simple HCs can serve as patterns or templates for detecting the segments of the intact halflines of the Matched Corpus. But in order to simplify the process of matching HC with segment it will be useful to refine the catalog of HC types. Before such refining is possible, it will be necessary to discuss the resolution of short stressed syllables.

THE RESOLUTION OF SHORT STRESSED SYLLABLES

There is a discernible difference between the second HCs of halflines 262a and 53a:

HC	HC	
pæs min	fæder	262a
ÐA pæs on	burgum	53a

The two syllables of *burȝum*, properly spoken, should seem longer than the two syllables of *fæder*. At any rate, an Anglo-Saxon speaker was very likely aware that *burȝum* represents a long stressed syllable followed by a short, unstressed syllable, while *fæder* represents a short stressed syllable followed by a short unstressed syllable. Anglo-Saxon poets were aware of the difference between *burȝ-* and *fæ-* and exploited that difference in their poetry. A comparison of two entire verse lines will make this point more clearly.

There is an exact match between *burȝum* in 53a on the one hand and *ȝeatum* in 195a and *bolcan* in 231a. The first syllables of these three words are long, stressed, and alliterating; the second syllables are short and unstressed. I argue that this match makes it possible to claim that *ȝeatum* in 195 and *bolcan* in 231 are HCs of their respective halflines. If that is so, then each of these HCs sets off a rather different first segment:

HC	HC	HC	HC		
ȝod mid	ȝeatum	ȝrendles	dæda	195	
beran ofer	bolcan	beorhte	randas	231	

The four syllables of *beran ofer* match the two syllables of *ȝod mid*. More precisely, the two syllables of *beran* seem nicely designed to match the single long syllable of *ȝod*. Partly because of the match between the rest of the syllables of 195 and 231, it seems likely that a speaker of line 231 would attempt to say *beran ofer* in the same time as it takes to say *ȝod mid*. Thus the speaker would *resolve* the short stressed syllable *be-* with the next syllable in the same word.

Almost every prosodist admits the necessity of resolving two syllables. It is only in this way that the distinction between long and short stressed syllables can be conveyed. On the other hand, few prosodists have asked whether resolution extends to three syllables. This issue amounts to whether or not there is a real distinction between *neosian* on the one hand and *pitena* on the other.

Verse line 12 provides an argument for extending resolution to certain clusters of three syllables. Again, I compare this verse line with 195:

HC	HC	HC	HC		
ȝod mid	ȝeatum	ȝrendles	dæda	195	
ðæm	eafera pæs	æfter	cenned	12	

The second HC of 12a consists of four short syllables, the first three in the same word. How does one read this HC? The first HC of 231 suggests resolving the first two syllables of *eafera pæs*, but not the third:

HC	HC		HC	
	$\underset{\text{beran}}{\diagup}\ \underset{\text{ofer}}{\text{x x}}$		bolcan	231a
ðæm	$\underset{\text{eafera}}{\diagup}\ \underset{\text{pæs}}{\text{x x}}$			12a

On the other hand, the grouping of the four syllables of halfline 12a into two *words* suggests the following division of the second HC of this halfline:

$$\text{HC}$$
$$\underset{\text{eafera pæs}}{\diagup\ \ \ \ \text{x}}$$

Another halfline in the Matched Corpus supports the latter analysis:

HC	HC	
[sp]ȳlcum	$\underset{\text{ȝifeþe bið}}{\diagup\ \ \ \text{x}}$	299b

On the basis of these two examples I propose the following. The resolution of three syllables takes place whenever the following conditions co-exist: (1) the first of the three syllables is stressed; (2) at least the first two syllables are short; and (3) all three syllables belong to the same word.

Certain trisyllabic words that begin with a short stressed syllable continue with a long syllable. A case in point is *moneȝū* in 5a, in which the long syllable, *-eȝ-* (or *-neȝ-*), seems to block trisyllabic resolution. But the fact that the first syllable is short seems crucial. If trisyllabic resolution is blocked, disyllabic resolution does not appear to be. I take the first two syllables of such inflected forms (and indeed the two syllables of uninflected forms of such words) to be resolved:

HC	HC	
ða pæron	$\underset{\text{moniȝe}}{\diagup\ \ \text{x}}$	2982a

The possibility of resolving *four* syllables is suggested only once in the halflines of the Matched Corpus. That possibility occurs in an intact halfline, 286a. But the first segment of this halfline, *peard*, matches the simplest template, *pulf* (3027a), in every way. Hence it is possible to regard *peard* as the first HC of 286a and *maþelode* as the second:

HC	HC	
peard	maþelode	286

If *eafera* in 12a argues for three-syllable resolution, does *maþelode* here argue for four-syllable resolution? Probably not. Apart from the fact that even four very short syllables make a tongue twister, there is a stronger argument in this halfline against quadruple resolution: if even a single short unstressed monosyllabic word were to follow *maþelode* in this HC, the case for four-syllable resolution would be indicated. But no syllable follows in this or any other HC made up of *maþelode*.

Is *maþelode*, then, to be divided into three-syllable resolution followed by a single short syllable in the second part of the HC?

HC

maþelo   de

Both *eafera* in line 12 and *ȝifeþe* in line 299 seem to countenance this division. A better course, however, seems to be to divide the four short syllables equally, more on the analogy of *fæder* than *faroðe*:

HC

maþe   lode

The resolution of four syllables seems to be neither indicated nor necessary. The resolution of three syllables, when all are short and belong to the same word, will, I think, turn out to be necessary whenever the first syllable of the word is stressed.

One point remains. The *Beowulf*-poet does not seem to have given much concern to the length of unstressed syllables. As I have already shown in the section on HCs, he will pile up as many as three long syllables in an HC (47a) that contains five syllables. In other words, although the poet pays close attention to the length of stressed syllables and is careful to resolve a short stressed syllable whenever that is possible, he simply uses just about whatever unstressed syllables he needs. As I shall demonstrate, unstressed syllables count, but they count the same whatever their length.

SIMPLE TEMPLATES

Resolution makes it possible to sort the seven different categories of simple alliterating HCs listed in the section headed "Simple Alliterating HCs as Templates," above, into two types, each with a number of subtypes. I designate one type α (alpha) and the other δ (delta). The members of the largest group of HCs in the list in that section, *Disyllabic, First Syllable Long*, become subtype $\alpha1$ (alpha 1). The next largest group, *Trisyllabic, First Syllable Long*, becomes subtype $\alpha2$.

The three members of the group called *Trisyllabic, First Syllable Short* lack cohesion. I set aside for the moment the first two members of this group and use the third, *monize* in 2982a, as the sole representative of a subtype of α in which the single long stressed syllable is replaced by a short syllable resolved with the next syllable. This $\alpha4$ pattern is then completed by the unresolved final unstressed syllable.

The fact that there are instances of a long syllable followed by one, or two, or three unstressed syllables suggests that there may be three corresponding α subtypes headed by a *resolved* disyllable. The second subtype in this second series, $\alpha5$, occurs in the Matched Corpus under the first four-syllable rubric *Four Syllables, First Syllable Short*. I set out this subtype, *cýme sýndon* (257b); then, finding no instance of a disyllabic resolution followed by three unstressed syllables, leave a place and move on to $\alpha7$. This subtype shows triple resolution followed by a single unstressed syllable. Subtypes $\alpha8$ and $\alpha9$ should consist of a triple resolution followed by two and three unstressed syllables, respectively. Subtypes $\alpha8$ and $\alpha9$ are at this point predicted but unrepresented.

Thirty of the thirty-four simple HCs have been resorted into Type α HCs. The four remaining simple HCs can be sorted as Type δ (delta). HCs of this type consist of either a single stressed syllable, long or short, forming subtype $\delta1$; two resolved syllables the first of which is stressed ($\delta2$); or three resolved syllables the first of which is stressed ($\delta3$). In Tables 6.1 and 6.2 I list all twelve possible subtypes of these two types with one example of each subtype whenever one occurs in the Matched Corpus.[3]

The halfline constituents that are the basis of these templates have not, like Sievers's "feet," been determined arbitrarily. Nor are they,

---

3. I use Greek nonfinal σ to indicate a syllable.

Table 6.1. α Subtypes

α1
/ x
burʒum   53a

α2
/ x x
frætpade   96a

α3
/ x   x x
manna hþone   155a

α4
‿/ x
moniʒe   2982a

α5
‿/ x   x
cȳme sȳndon   257b

α6
‿/ x x x
σ σ σ σ σ

α7
‿‿/ x
eafera pæs   12a

α8
‿/ x x
σ σ σ σ σ

α9
‿‿/ x x x
σ σ σ σ σ σ

Table 6.2. δ Subtypes

δ1
/
þulf   3027a

δ2
‿/
fæder   262a

δ3
‿‿/
þitena   157a

like Pope's "measures," simply the result of intuition. They are the halfline constituents that the lineator has assembled in order to construct 40 percent of the halflines of the Corpus. If a particular template matches a particular segment of a halfline elicited from the text intact, it seems likely that the template is measuring a genuine constituent of that halfline.

SIMPLE CONSTITUENTS OF INTACT HALFLINES

In this section I begin to explore the hypothesis that every halfline is made up of at least two constituents, even halflines that the processes of lineation and half-lining have left intact. I begin by using the templates based on simple alliterating HCs, those I have called α and δ. The matching of template to segment must begin with an already identified boundary, that is, with the beginning or end of the halfline. If the template is, so to speak, placed over the first part of an intact halfline, it must reach exactly as far as some identifiable and significant feature of the intact halfline. The most easily identifiable feature is an alliterating syllable; the next most easily identifiable feature is a stressed syllable. The α1 template *burʒum* does not match the first segment of 6a, *eʒsode eorl*, for example. On the other hand, the α2 template *frætpade* reaches just up to *eorl*, the second alliterating syllable in 6a. The pattern of one long stressed syllable followed by two unstressed syllables exactly matches the first segment of the intact halfline. At the same time it sets off a segment that exactly matches the first δ template listed above, the single long stressed and alliterating segment *pulf*.

A systematic use of simple HC templates begins with the shortest and simplest type, that is, the monosyllable of subtype δ1. There are thirteen expressions of a single long monosyllable like the HC *pulf* (3027a) in halflines that contain a second alliterating syllable. That syllable serves as a readily identifiable boundary:

	δ1		C Halfline
eʒsode	eorl		6a (II)
	leof	(landfruma)	31a
(murnende)	mod		50a
	leo[f]	(leodcýninʒ)	54a
	[h]ean	huses	116a (II)
(·xii· pintra)	tid		147a
	[de]orc	([deaþscua])	160a
	þiʒ	(þeorþunʒa)	176a

(sinȝala)	seað		190a (II)
	fȳrst	(forð ȝepát)	210a
	frod	(felaȝeomor)	2950a
	eorl	(onȝenþio)	2951a
	pulf	(ponr[e]d[inȝ])	2965a

Only two of these brief and simple HCs, 6a and 116a, create a half-line with another simple HC. The poet seems to have a definite preference for combining a monosyllabic HC with a segment that contains more than one stressed syllable—which I shall call an "augmented" segment. The monosyllabic HC template serves to isolate such augmented segments as *landfruma*, *murnende*, and so on, which I discuss in a later section of this chapter.

A short form of δ1, that is, a short stressed monosyllable, adds only one halfline to this group:

	δ1	C
(ponsæli)	per	105a

The δ1 template makes it possible to locate two identifiable segments—and thus probably two HCs—in 14 of the 350 intact halflines of the Matched Corpus.

There are eleven expressions of a disyllable like *fæder*, subtype δ2, in halflines that contain a second alliterating syllable:

	δ2		C
(maȝodriht)	micel		67a (II)
([medoæ]rn)	micel		69a
(ponsceaft)	pera		120a
	micel	(morȝenspeȝ)	129a
(healðeȝnes)	hete		142a
(sinȝale)	sæce		154a
	hpȳder	(helrunan)	163a
	atol	(anȝenȝea)	165a
(þreanȳd)	þolað		284a (II)
	pudu	(punden[hals])	298a (II)
(pælræs)	peora		2947a

HCs of this group show an even stronger preference for combining with augmented segments.

There are thirteen expressions consisting of a short stressed syllable followed by two unstressed syllables in halflines containing a second alliterating syllable. These segments match the HC *pitena* in 157a, the subtype specimen of δ3:

	δ3		C
hæleð under	heofen[ū]		52a (II)
þraȝe ȝe	þolode		87a
	fýrene	fr[e]man	101a
	þolode	(ðrýðspýð)	131a
seomade 7	sýrede		161a
[ce]mpan ȝe	corone		206a
	þerodes	þisa	259a
	æþele	(ordfruma)	263a
	þitena	(þelhþýlc)	266a
receda under	roderum		310a (II)
	eafores	(anne dom)	2964a (II)
(folcred)	fremede		3006a (II)
(omiȝe þurh)	etone		3049a (II)

Expressions of this sort tend to combine with either augmented segments (131a, 263a, 266a, 2964a, 3006a, 3049a) or polysyllabic simple segments: 52a, 161a, 310a are extreme examples, but 87a and 206a might well be included here. Only two, 101a and 259a, combine with expressions of the subtype α1. The three δ templates together make it possible to locate two HCs in thirty-eight intact halflines that contain another alliterating syllable.

There are 106 expressions of the first α subtype—a long stressed syllable followed by an unstressed syllable—in halflines that contain a second alliterating syllable. I list here only representative examples:

	α1		C
(moneȝū)	mæȝþum		5a
þeox under	þolcnum		8a
folce to	frofre		14a
	þuldres	(þealdend)	17a
(beoþulf þæs)	breme		18a
spæse ȝe	siþas		29a (II)
ænne ofer	ýðe		46a
secȝan t[o]	soðe		51a
leomum 7	leafum		97a
fýrene	fr[e]man		101a
fen 7	fæsten		104a
metod for þý	mane		110a
	ȝrim 7	(ȝrædiȝ)	121a
(þritiȝ)	[þ]eȝna		123a
fýrene 7	fæhðe		153a
(feorhbealo)	feorran		156a
(mistiȝe)	moras		162a
	[h]eardra	hýnða	166a
ȝod mid	ȝeatum		195a
	deaȝol	(dædhata)	275a

	picʒ ʒe	pende	315a
	mon on	(middanʒearde)	2996a (II)
(oft nalles)	æne		3019a

It seems, indeed, that expressions of this configuration can combine with almost any kind of HC. The frequency of this subtype indicates that it is the most important kind of HC in the Corpus.

A somewhat rare variant of this subtype, consisting of a two-word phrase the first word of which is stressed and short, should be discussed here. The halfline of 143a, *fȳr 7 fæstor*, poses an interesting question: how did the poet take account of juncture? The solution may lie in the following formulation: a stressed monosyllable, even if short, cannot be resolved with a syllable in a following word and thus functions like a long syllable in this situation. Conversely, a long stressed syllable cannot be resolved with a following syllable even if that syllable is in the same word. Halfline 143a brings the total of halflines divided by α1 templates into two HCs to 107.

The subtype α2, consisting of a long stressed syllable followed by two unstressed syllables, is expressed thirty times in halflines that contain two alliterating syllables. I quote only representative examples:

	α2		C
	eʒsode	eorl (δ1)	6a (II)
	peox under	polcnum (α1)	8a
	folce to	frofre (α1)	14a
	billum 7	bȳrnum (α1)	40a (II)
	ʒeafon on	(ʒarsecʒ)	49a (II)
	þraʒe ʒe	þolode (δ3)	87a (II)
ʒȳddū (α1)	ʒeomore		151a (II)
	ʒodne ʒe	ʒȳrpan (α1)	199a (II)
	lixte se	leoma (α1)	311a (II)
	ʒeald þone	(ʒuðræs)	2991a
	landes 7	(locenra beaʒa)	2995a (II)
	habban on	healse (α1)	3017a

Some comment is probably in order about the three varieties of this single subtype. There is first of all the variety that consists of a single word, like *eʒsode* (6a). Second, there is the variety that consists of two words divided between the first and second syllables, like *peox under* (8a). Third, there is the variety in which the two words are divided between the second and third syllables, like *folce to* (14a). It would be possible, of course, to devise a prosody in which each of these varieties was classed as a separate subtype, but that does not seem necessary. The main point is this: because of its stress and length, the syllable *eʒ-* in *eʒsode* is set off in relation to the two following syllables in the same way as *peox* is set off in relation to *under*.

Four halflines express the α3 pattern—one long stressed syllable followed by three unstressed syllables. Three of the halflines containing α3 HCs have previously been counted, since they combine with α1 HCs.

α3	HC	
ænne ofer	ẏðe	46a
Hƿilum hie ʒe	heton	175a
meltan mid þā	modiʒan	3011a
maðõū to ʒe	mẏndum	3016a

Six halflines express the α4 pattern—two resolved syllables followed by a single unstressed syllable.

HC	α4	HC	
	moneʒū	mæʒþum	5a
madma	mæniʒo		41a
	maniʒre	[m]æʒþe	75a
	leomum 7	leafum	97a
	ʒamol of	ʒeardum	265a
	hæfen on	handa	3023a

In every case, the α4 HC is combined with an α1 HC.

There are five expressions of the subtype α5 consisting of a short stressed syllable resolved with one following syllable, which word is, in turn, followed by two unstressed syllables. These segments match the HC *cẏme sẏndon* of 257b.

α5	HC	C
⟋ x x hǣleð under	heofen[ū]	52a (II)
⟋ x x metod for þẏ	mane	110a
⟋ x x spefan æfter	[sẏ]mble	119a
⟋ x x beran ofer	bolcan	231a
⟋ x x brec[an] ofer	(bordþeal)	2980a (II)

No instances of the predicted subtype α6 occur in halflines of the Matched Corpus that contain a second alliterating syllable. Six instances of subtype α7, however, occur. In this subtype triple resolution is followed by a single unstressed syllable:

α7	HC	C
fȳrene 7	fæhðe	153a
seomode 7	sȳrede	161a
æþele 7	eacen	198a
eoletes æt	ende	224a
seomode on	sole	302a
ricone a	rærdon	2983a

One predicted subtype, α8, actually turns up among halflines of the Matched Corpus that contain a second alliterating syllable.

α8	HC	C
x x ⌐╱⁀ receda under	roderum	310a

No instance of this subtype occurs in the synthetic halflines of the Corpus.

With the help of nine different simple templates from synthetic halflines, and three predicted templates, a total of 206 simple (α or δ) HCs have been located in the 138 halflines that contain a second alliterating syllable. The simple HCs have thrown into relief 70 segments that contain more than one stressed syllable. I shall discuss such "augmented segments" in the next section.

"AUGMENTED SEGMENTS"

The constituents of many halflines that contain two alliterating syllables are distinctively marked by those very syllables. But in many halflines the constituents so marked do not appear to be comparable. For example, three syllables, two of which are long and stressed, are paired with an initial δ2 HC in 129a: *micel morʒenspeʒ*. Four syllables grouped into two resolved clusters are paired with the two syllables of an α1 HC in 236a: *mæʒe[n]þudu mundum*. Such augmented segments raise the question whether they represent single or double constituents of their halflines. Before taking up that question, however, it will be useful to identify the patterns formed by augmented segments marked by alliterating syllables.

These patterns fall into three types, which I have named α' (alpha prime), β (beta), and γ (gamma). In each type the two or more stressed syllables are grouped differently: in the first type, α', there are either no unstressed syllables or the unstressed syllable or syllables are part of a word that begins with a stressed syllable; in the β type, the unstressed syllable or syllables fall between the two stressed syllables (or groups of resolved stressed syllables); in the γ type, the unstressed syllable or syllables follow the two stressed syllables (or groups of resolved stressed syllables):

$$
\begin{array}{lll}
\alpha'\ 1 & \overset{/\ \ /}{\sigma\ \sigma} \\[4pt]
\beta\ 1 & \overset{/\ x\ /}{\sigma\ \sigma\ \sigma} \\[4pt]
\gamma\ 1 & \overset{/\ /\ x}{\sigma\ \sigma\ \sigma} \\[4pt]
\alpha'\ 2 & \overset{/\ \ \overline{/}}{\sigma\ \sigma\ \sigma} \\[4pt]
\beta\ 2 & \overset{/\ x\ x\ /}{\sigma\ \sigma\ \sigma\ \sigma} \\[4pt]
\gamma\ 2 & \overset{/\ /\ x\ x}{\sigma\ \sigma\ \sigma\ \sigma}
\end{array}
$$

Nine subtypes of α' are possible; twenty-four subtypes of both β and γ are possible.

Four subtypes of α' turn up as augmented segments in intact half-lines of the Matched Corpus that contain two alliterating syllables:

$\alpha'1$	C
feasceaft	7a . . .
peorðmýnd	65a, etc.: 27 examples of this subtype

$\alpha'2$

landfruma	31a, etc.: 11 examples

$\alpha'4$

[fe]lahror	27a, etc.: 3 examples

$\alpha'5$

mæʒe[n]pudu	236a: 1 example

Only one of the twenty-four possible β subtypes turns up as an augmented segment in intact halflines of the Matched Corpus that contain two alliterating syllables:

β*1*　　　　　　C

/　x　/
morȝenspeȝ　　129a
/　x　/
forð ȝepát　　210a
/　x　/
anne dom　　2964a, etc.: 5 examples of this subtype

Three of the γ subtypes turn up:

γ*1*　　　　　　C

/　/　x
beopulf pæs　　18a
/　/　x
murnende　　50a
/　/　x
healðeȝnes　　142a
/　/　x
xii pintra　　147a
/　/ x
mistiȝe　　162a, etc.: 14 examples

γ2

/　/ x　x
omiȝe þurh-　　3049a: 1 example

γ7

⏜/　/　x
felaȝeomor　　2950a
⏜/　/ x
hiȝelaces　　2952a: 2 examples

Most of the ε HCs of the synthetic halflines combine with augmented segments. The augmented segments in these halflines can be compared with the augmented segments just listed. In 9a, for example, the ε HC *oð þ him* has been added to the α'1 augmented segment *æȝhpýlc*. There are two more α'1 segments combined with ε HCs in synthetic halflines. In 1a, the ε HC *HPÆT PE* has been added to the α'2 segment *GARDEna*. There are forty more α'2 segments in synthetic halflines. The overlap continues with two examples of α'5 segments. Then, two α'6 segments, a subtype predicted but not exemplified in intact halflines, turn up in synthetic halflines:

$\alpha'6$ C

brimes faroðe   28b

fela fýrena   164a

With these examples, five of the predicted nine α' subtypes have put in their appearance.

Something even more interesting happens with β subtypes. To the single subtype exemplified in intact halflines four subtypes can be added from synthetic halflines. There are fifty-five $\beta1$ segments and fifteen $\beta2$ segments in synthetic halflines. I quote a few examples of the latter:

$\beta2$ C

/ x x /
frofre ȝeba[d]   7b
/   x x /
beot ne aleh   80a
/ x x /
larena ȝod   269b, etc.

There are three instances of the subtype $\beta4$:

$\beta4$ C

/   x /
ȝeomor sefa   49b
/   x /
rumne sefan   278a
/   x /
landa fela   311b

One instance of $\beta7$ turns up:

$\beta7$ C

/   x /
ȝeoȝoð ȝepeox   66b

Even one instance of subtype $\beta13$ appears:

$\beta13$ C

/   x /
iofore forȝeaf   2997a

No γ subtype not already attested in intact halflines turns up in synthetic halflines. Among synthetic halflines there are thirty-six examples of γ1 and seventeen examples of γ7. One possible instance of subtype γ2 turns up:

	γ2?	C
	/ / / x	
	ẏmbsittendra	9b

Sievers found 9b anomalous as it stands in the manuscript and, in Klaeber's word, "cancel[ed]" the *þara* that must be added to it to construct the synthetic halfline.[4] In one sense, Sievers seems to be justified: there are simply too many long stressed syllables in a row in this segment. In another sense, Sievers's "cancellation" hides an interesting problem for the prosodist. It is problems posed by such halfline "constituents" that I turn to next.

ARE "AUGMENTED" SEGMENTS SINGLE HCS?

The fact that every augmented segment contains at least two stressed syllables raises the possibility that some—perhaps all—of these segments are not single. I begin with augmented segments in synthetic halflines that contain two alliterating syllables, quoting the entire halfline:

ε	β1	C
	/ x /	
þenden	þordum þeold	30a
	/ x /	
ʒebad	þintra þorn	264a
	/ x /	
h....	frætpū fenʒ	2989a
	β2	
	/ x x /	
se þe his	þordes ʒeþeald	79a
	γ1	
	/ / x	
þið	þeodþreaum	178a (?)
	/ / x	
[H]im se	ẏldesta	258a (?)

---

4. Fr. Klaeber, ed., *Beowulf and the Fight at Finnsburg*, 3d ed. (Boston: D. C. Heath, 1950), p. 1, textual note 9b.

γ7

	/ / x	
in	þorold pocun	60a
7 to	/ / x fæder fæþmum	188a

Each of these halflines can be divided into three segments. Each second constituent, that is to say, can be subdivided into two segments at an identifiable point, the second alliterating syllable:

/ x þordum	(α1)	/ peold (δ1)	
/ x pintra	(α1)	/ porn (δ1)	
/ x frætpū	(α1)	/ fenȝ (δ1)	
/ x x þordes ȝe	(α2)	/ peald (δ1)	
/ þeod	(δ1)	/ x þreaum	(α1)
/ ẏld	(δ1)	/ x esta	(α1)
/ þorold	(δ2)	/ x pocun	(α1)
/ fæder	(δ2)	/ x fæþmum	(α1)

What is perhaps even more telling, each segment corresponds to one of the simple HCs that have been used as templates. Seven match α1 HCs; one matches the α2 HC; six match δ1 HCs; and two match δ2 HCs. The three "constituents" of the first group of halflines, then, might be said to be ε + α1 + δ1; the three constituents of the single member of the second group, ε + α2 + δ1; the three of the third group, ε + δ1 + α1; and the three of the fourth group, ε + δ2 + α1.

It is possible to analyze α' segments in a similar way. The first subtype, represented by *æȝhpẏlc* (9a), can be characterized as a pair of δ1s; the second as δ1 + δ2; and so on, up to α'9, which can be characterized as δ3 + δ3. It is possible to argue, then, that every augmented segment represents two constituents of its halfline.

That interpretation will, I think, turn out to be unnecessary so long as the augmented segments consist of a combination of α + δ (δ + α) subtypes. Segments that consist of two α subtypes, on the other hand, do not seem to be single; they divide at the first syllable of the second α.

Statistical analysis indicates that an HC-headed segment that can be analyzed as two αs consists of two HCs. A clearly marked α HC occurs repeatedly in the 100 halflines analyzed in this section—152 times out of 200 possible, in fact. Fifty-two of the 100 halflines consist of exactly two α HCs. By contrast, only 9 halflines consist of one α HC and one δ HC.

Halflines that consist of exactly two α HCs are the rule. Halflines that consist of only one α HC and one δ HC are not only uncommon, they are the exceptions. Several have been suspected to be mistakes, for example 6a and 116a. Prosodists have felt uneasy with such "short" or "light" halflines. No one has felt uneasy with such pairs as *ȝomban ȝyldan* (11a).

It seems, then, that a clearly marked HC-headed segment that can be analyzed as consisting of exactly one α + one δ segment or vice versa functions as a single HC. An HC-headed segment that consists of two α segments functions as a double HC, that is, it consists of *two* HCs.

INNER STRESSED (NONALLITERATING) SYLLABLES AS MARKERS OF HCS

At this point it is possible to determine whether there are two or three HCs in 368 of the 580 halflines of the Matched Corpus, the 230 synthetic halflines plus the 138 intact halflines that contain two alliterating syllables. The use of templates made from simple HCs in synthetic halflines has isolated a second HC in intact halflines. The beginning of the other HC—which is sometimes simple, sometimes augmented and single, sometimes augmented and double—is always marked by an alliterating syllable. But 212 intact halflines in the Matched Corpus contain only one alliterating syllable. The single alliterating syllable always heads the halfline. If these halflines are made up of more than one constituent, the second constituent is not marked by an alliterating syllable.

The time-honored practice is to assume that every metrically significant segment must contain a stressed syllable, and that every inner segment will therefore contain—in some cases begin with—a stressed syllable. Sievers—and just about every other scholar—has approached the problem in this way. It is not the only way. On the contrary, it seems wiser to compare segments with already elicited HCs and to look for parallels with what has already been established.

So far only two kinds of HC have emerged, alliterating and nonal-literating. It is the peculiarity of the latter that they are always outer HCs, the nonalliterating HCs that begin the halfline. The processes that elicit each outer nonalliterating HC depend upon an alliterating HC, however. Alliterating HCs, then, can be either inner or outer. The last sections have made a case for locating HCs in halflines that both begin with and contain another alliterating syllable. It seems possible to carry this line of reasoning a step further.

Every inner HC that has been elicited by lineation and half-lining (that is, the synthetic halflines), or has been located with the aid of the templates, begins with an alliterating syllable. But every alliterat-ing syllable is first and most basically a stressed syllable. Any parallel between halflines that contain two alliterating syllables and halflines that contain only one alliterating syllable has to be based on stress and stress alone. That is to say, the second segment in intact halflines that contain only one alliterating syllable can only be marked by a stressed syllable.

Most of the 212 halflines that begin with the only alliterating syl-lable in the halfline contain only one other stressed syllable. It is easy to match the segment set off by this inner stressed syllable with the simple templates discussed earlier in this chapter. The second HC of 2b, *-frunon*, for example, exactly equals the simple template α1. The second HC of 60b, *ræspa*, is also an α1. This matching of this template serves to set off the δ3 template with which this halfline begins, *peo-roda*. The combination of δ3 + α1 is, as I have shown above, unusual. Still, halflines that contain only one inner stressed syllable can be eas-ily dissected into their HCs at that syllable.

It is not so easy to dissect halflines that contain two or more stressed syllables after the initial alliterating syllable. Many of these halflines consist of a compound plus a simplex, for example 8b:

$$/\quad/\quad x\quad/$$
peorðmýndum þah

The compound exactly matches the γ1 template; the simplex, the δ1 template. This division is so obvious that any other seems arbitrary. When the compound follows the simplex, as it does in 30b, for ex-ample, the division into two HCs seems equally obvious:

$$\underline{/}\quad/\quad/\quad x$$
[p]íne scýldinʒa

In this case the simplex matches the δ2 template, the compound the γ1.

The situation is a little more complex in halflines that consist of a compound and a simplex with a prefix, as is the case of 5b:

$$\underbrace{\quad/\quad}\ \ /\ \text{x x}\ \ /$$
meodosetla ofteah

Again, the templates provide help. The compound plus the prefix equals the predicted subtype γ8, while *-teah* exactly equals the familiar δ1. The stressed stem of the simplex, then, marks the beginning of the second HC of this halfline.

These examples point to what might be called "the short compound rule": a compound shorter than a halfline will be split between two HCs only if the compound itself equals two αs. This formulation applies to compounds in halflines that contain two alliterating syllables as well as halflines that do not. It keeps together in a single HC the four syllables of *meodosetla* but divides the four syllables of *middan-ӡearde* (2996a) between two HCs:

$$/\ \ \ \text{x}\ \ \ /\ \ \text{x}\ \ \ /\ \ \ \text{x}$$
mon on middanӡearde

Since in this halfline all three stressed syllables are long, and since each is followed by an unstressed syllable, the HC consists of three α1 HCs. The short compound rule does not apply in such rare cases.

A few halflines consist of two compounds. These rare halflines usually mark the second compound with an alliterating syllable, as in 193a:

$$/\ \ \ \underbrace{\ \ /\ \ }\ \ /\ \ \ /$$
nỹdpracu niþӡrim

The short compound rule clearly applies to both compounds, although the HCs are also marked by the alliterating syllables.

Halflines that contain short compounds are easy to match with templates derived from synthetic halflines. But halflines that consist of three stressed simplexes pose a problem. I quote 18b:

$$/\ \ \ /\ \text{x}\ \ \ /$$
blæd pide spranӡ

The problem here is that *blæd* + *pide* exactly matches the γ1 template, while *pide* + *spranӡ* exactly matches the β1 template. How does one choose between these two alternatives? A simple solution, and one that I shall generally apply, divides the three simplexes at the second stressed syllable: that is, I arbitrarily take the second stressed syllable as heading the second HC. One could just as easily take the third stressed syllable as marking the beginning of the second HC. In such cases one can also be guided by the subtle differences in sense the two alternatives suggest.

STRESS RECONSIDERED

The argument that two—and even, at times, three—stressed syllables belong in the same HC is likely to have consequences for the degree of stress given to each stressed syllable in the HC. If three stressed syllables—to take the extreme case—wind up in the same HC, only a four-stress scale can signal the differences among these syllables. In 232b, for example, the alliterating syllable *fyr-* clearly heads the second HC:

$$\begin{array}{ccccc} x & x & / & / & / \\ \end{array}$$
hine fýrpýt bræc

In the first section of Chapter 3, I argued for a simple binary division into stressed and unstressed syllables. That binary division has served well for eliciting verse lines and then halflines. But one can question whether it is possible for a speaker to give equal, or even roughly equal, stress to all three stressed syllables in a single HC.

We have at last reached the point at which we can make discriminations among degrees of stress. It is only when the prosodist has determined that the syllables *fyr*, *pyt*, and *bræc* belong together in a single HC that one can really begin to apply a subtler analysis of stress. Any attempt to do so earlier is both unnecessary and inelegant. The compound *fyrpýt*, if it alone occupied the HC, would equal an α'1. So would *pyt bræc* or even *fyr bræc*. But no template quite fits the three syllables together. It is clear that *fyr-*, because of its position in the HC, bears the heaviest stress. Because it is the second element of the compound, *-pyt* is probably lighter than the simplex *bræc*, which in turn is somewhat lighter than *fyr-*. Even *-pyt*, however, is heavier than either syllable of *hine* in the adjacent HC.

The three syllables of *fyrpýt bræc* provide a somewhat heavier version of a familiar template, β1:

HC	HC (β1)	C
him þa	/ x / scýld ʒepat	26a
hine	/ / / fýrpýt bræc	232b

Degrees of heavy stress can, then, be treated as functions of the position of the stressed syllable in its HC. Halfline 232b presents an extreme case of the situation in which the performer moves from the heaviest heavy stress through less heavy stresses in order to signal the beginning, continuation, and ending of a single augmented HC.

CONCLUSION

Alliteration-headed HCs of the synthetic halflines can be used to locate analogous constituents in halflines that have been elicited intact. The first part of the hypothesis that I proposed at the beginning of this chapter, that it is possible to construct a prosody based on the synthetic halflines, has been partly verified. At this point it is possible to identify analogous HCs of every halfline in the Matched Corpus. The secondary hypothesis, on the other hand, that every halfline consists of only two HCs, has been falsified by a few cases in which a halfline consists of three HCs. Most halflines, however, consist of only two constituents.

The first step in constructing a prosody based on the procedures of lineating and half-lining is complete. Using the constituents of synthetic halflines, we have assembled a set of templates that match marked segments of the halflines elicited intact by the procedures of lineation. In this way we have determined acceptable constituents of all the halflines in the Matched Corpus. Two different kinds of constituent, αs and δs, match Sievers's "feet." But three—βs, γs, and most εs—do not. Instead, they match Pope's division of most so-called "B" or "C" type verses. Far from being unacceptable, these unbalanced segments have been shown to contribute to the basis for the prosody of all the verses in the Matched Corpus. The next step is to compare the verse lines and halflines at the boundaries indicated by all of these procedures. That is the work of the next chapter.

Chapter 7

Comparing Prosodic Constituents

INTRODUCTION

The prosody of *Beowulf* appears to be complete with the development in Chapter 6 of a method for determining the constituents—the HCs—of every halfline of the poem. That appearance will turn out to be illusory. A thoughtful probing of John Pope's analysis of verses of "Types B and C" offers a glimpse of a level of constituent *below* the HC. In analyzing such verses as C42a, *on flodes æht*, Pope departed from Eduard Sievers's analysis in two ways.[1] First, he correctly began the second HC (which he called a "measure") with the first syllable of *flodes*; second, he added a *rest* before the single syllable of the first HC, *on*. In hypothesizing a rest to complete this short "measure," Pope took a bold step in the direction of constituent analysis of measures, that is, of HCs. But he went no further, leaving for others the task of determining whether every HC might be composed of discernible constituents. That is the task of the present chapter.

So far we have been able to divide the manuscript text into verse lines and then to divide the verse line into its two constituent halflines. Almost every halfline is made up of exactly two constituents, the HCs. The higher levels of the prosody thus display a strong tendency to binary division. I hypothesize that this binary splitting continues on downward. In this chapter I shall test the hypothesis that every HC consists of two parts.

To begin testing this hypothesis I take a very simple verse line, C195. This verse line is made up of eight syllables arranged in four

---

1. John Collins Pope, *The Rhythm of Beowulf* . . . (New Haven: Yale University Press, 1942), 274–75.

HCs. Each HC begins with a long stressed syllable and ends with an unstressed syllable:

F   M

| ⟋ x | ⟋ x | ⟋ x | ⟋ x
ʒod mid |ʒeatum   ʒrendles | dæda

If each of these HCs is made up of two parts, the first part will be heavy (in each HC that part is a long stressed syllable) and the second part will be light:

F   M

| ⟋   x | ⟋   x | ⟋   x | ⟋   x
ʒod : mid |ʒea : tum   ʒrend : les | dæ : da

The preposition *mid* is unstressed and short. The case endings *-um*, *-es*, and *-a* (here morphophonemically divided so as to begin with the final stem consonant) are also unstressed and short.

Is the second part of every HC light? I try splitting the first three HCs of an unusually heavy verse line, C193, into their parts:

F   M

| ⟋   ⟋ | ⟋   ⟋ | ⟋   ⟋ x
nyd : pracu | niþ : ʒrim   niht : bealpa . . .

Unlike *mid* in C195, *-pracu* in C193 is stressed. But its two syllables are short and thus resolved. On the other hand, *-ʒrim* is not only stressed but also long. And the first syllable of *-bealpa* is long, stressed, and crowded between *niht*—also long and stressed—and the short unstressed syllable *-a*. The second parts of the first three HCs of C193 become progressively heavier. Can they be said, nevertheless, to be somehow comparable to the unstressed short syllables that complete the first three HCs of C195, *mid*, *-tum*, and *-les*?

First of all, each of the heavy second parts of the HCs of C193 is the second element of a compound. In Chapter 3, I argued that the second element of a compound does not participate in dominant alliteration. Second, in the penultimate section of the last chapter, "Stress Reconsidered," I argued that "Degrees of heavy stress can . . . be treated as functions of the position of the stressed syllable in its HC."[2] Each of the second elements occurs in the same HC as the first element of the compound. If we apply the logic of "Stress Reconsidered" to the second parts of each of the first three HCs of C193, the three

---

2. See the section in Chapter 6 titled "Stress Reconsidered."

second elements, while retaining some stress, become more lightly stressed than the alliterating syllable of the first part of the HC. In other words, *-bealpa* is heavier than *-les*, which occupies the same position in its halfline two lines below, but lighter than *niht-*, with which it shares the HC. We can go a step farther. In its HC *-bealpa* serves the same function that *-les* serves in its HC: it completes the HC with a stress that is perceived to be somewhat lighter than the stress of the syllable that marks the beginning of the HC.

Finding a basis of comparison between *-bealpa* in C193 and *-les* in C195 suggests a way of dealing with the monosyllabic final HC of C193, *mæst*. The superlative is stressed and long. It shares its HC with no other syllable. The poet might have held on to it long enough to suggest the time it takes to speak the whole HC, as Pope suggests.[3] Or he might have taken no more time to speak *mæst* than he took to say the long stressed syllable *niht-* in the preceding HC. In that case, we would have to show an empty part at the end of the HC:

F   M

| nȳd : pracu | niþ : ȝrim | niht : bealpa | mæst : (x)

This solution to the problem of *mæst* summons into existence an eight-part grid. Yet as soon as one thinks of such a grid the specter of such verse lines as C28 comes to mind:

                    Base 1   Base 2
F   M

| hi hȳne [þ]a æt | bæron | to | brimes faroðe

The second and fourth HCs cause only small problems. The long stressed syllable that marks base 1 is followed by an unstressed syllable exactly like *ȝeatum* in C195. Each of the two words of the last HC fits neatly into one of the two parts of the HC. The problem is *to*. Unlike *mæst* in C193, *to* is unstressed.

But C195 has indicated a place for *to*:

C195	ȝōd : mid	ȝea : tum	ȝrend : les	dæ	da
C28	...	bæ : ron	to	brimes	faroðe

3. Pope, *The Rhythm of Beowulf*, 367.

The unstressed syllable *to* belongs in the same column or "stack" as *-les* in C195.

Finding a place for *to* in the stack created by *-les* opens up exciting possibilities. The empty part in the stack under *ʒrend-* neatly indicates that a rest equivalent to a stressed syllable precedes *to*. The empty part in the stack after *mæst* in C193 neatly indicates that a rest equivalent to an unstressed syllable follows *mæst*. In each case the empty part makes it possible to maintain the integrity of the systematically lineated verse line, its two halflines, and the two HCs that make up each of these halflines.

In 1942, John Pope posited that some verses begin with a rest and some end with one. But apparently he saw no way to demonstrate that rests must exist. The grid provides that demonstration.

In order to begin building the grid, I have had to posit one more level below the three levels indicated in the following diagram:

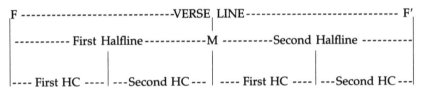

The fourth level of constituents from the top consists of what I shall call the *Fine Parts* (often "Parts" for short) of the HCs. Earlier in the chapter I hypothesized that every HC consists of two Fine Parts. Now it is apparent that the first Fine Part marks a heavy stress, the second a lighter stress. It is time to test that hypothesis by attempting to fit into this grid every one of the 290 whole verse lines of the Matched Corpus.

The grid is not a Procrustean bed. But it will help to understand how each verse line fits into it—indeed, *creates* it—if we approach the grid with some rules for distributing syllables into Fine Parts. It will be useful to test these rules first in shorter examples of the grid and also to remind ourselves how empty Parts in the grid come about. These matters I deal with in the next two sections.

RULES OF DISTRIBUTION

The first set of rules I propose applies to all HCs that begin with a stressed syllable. These are HCs of every type except ε. I remind the reader that the first syllable of HCs of types α, δ, α′, β, and γ always indicates the beginning of the first Part of the HC.

Rule 1a: If the first syllable is long, or the syllable is a monosyllabic word, and there is no other stressed syllable in the HC, the first syllable will occupy the first Part by itself.

Rule 1b: If it is short, the first syllable of the HC will share the first Part with one or two following syllables in accordance with the procedures of resolution discussed in Chapter 6.

The second set of rules concerns augmented HCs.

Rule 2a: If there are two stressed syllables in the HC, the second stressed syllable will normally head the second Part.

Rule 2b: The second stressed syllable will share the first Part with the first stressed syllable if the first syllable is short and both syllables belong to the same word, or if there are three stressed syllables in the HC and the first two belong to the same word or compound.

The location of the unstressed syllables depends upon the stressed syllables. Rule 1a, for example, assigns all accompanying unstressed syllables to the second Part. Rule 2a puts any unstressed syllables that fall between the two stressed syllables in the first Part.

Using these rules, we can distribute the syllables of each HC into two Parts. For example, Rule 1a neatly distributes the two syllables of each HC of both halflines of verse line 195 in this way:

HC		HC		HC		HC	
1	2	1	2	1	2	1	2
ʒod	mid	ʒeat	um	ʒrend	les	dæ	da

The same rule distributes the nine syllables of 211 into packets almost as neat. The first of the ten syllables of 231 requires Rule 1b:

	HC		HC		HC		HC	
	1	2	1	2	1	2	1	2
211	bát	under	beor	ʒe	beor	nas	ʒear	þe
231	beran	ofer	bol	can	beorh	te	ran	das

Rule 1a also applies to the first—and only—syllable of the first HC of verse line 2, where it creates an empty Part. The first part of Rule

2b assigns both stressed syllables of the second HC to the first Part of that HC:

HC		HC		HC		HC	
1	2	1	2	1	2	1	2
þeod		cýninʒ	a	þrým	ʒe	fru	non

There must be a set of rules of distribution that apply especially to ɛ HCs.

Rule 3a: The first syllable of an ɛ HC that contains no more than three syllables and no stressed syllable will occupy the second Part of the HC.

Rule 3b: Four, five, or six syllables of longer ɛ HCs that contain no stressed syllable will be distributed between Parts in accordance with word junctures and in such a way that neither Part will contain more than three syllables.

Rule 3c: If an ɛ HC contains a stressed syllable that is followed by no more than two unstressed syllables, the stressed syllable will head the second Part of the HC.

Rule 3a distributes the nine syllables of verse line 10 as follows:

HC		HC		HC		HC	
1	2	1˙	2	1	2	1	2
	ofer	hron	rade	hý	ran	scol	de

Rule 3c distributes the four syllables of the first HC of verse line 38 so that the stressed syllable, *hýr-*, heads the second Part. Rule 2a distributes the three syllables of the second HC so that the second stressed syllable heads the second Part of that HC:

HC		HC		HC		HC	
1	2	1	2	1	2	1	2
Ne	hýrde ic	cým	licor	ceol	ʒe	ʒýr	pan

The operation of Rule 3a in 10, like the operation of Rule 1a in 2, has left one Part empty in the first HC. The operation of Rule 3c has filled the first Part of the first HC of 38 with an unstressed syllable. I deal with the former problem first.

EMPTY PARTS

The emptying of one Part of a particular HC occurs whenever an HC consists of a single monosyllable. I illustrate with verse line 3027:

HC		HC		HC		HC	
1	2	1	2	1	2	1	2
þende[n]	he þið	pulf		pæl		rea	fode

The HC *pulf* is isolated by the fact that it is the first alliterating syllable of the line and is immediately followed by the last alliterating syllable, *pæl*. Rule 1a empties the second of the two Parts. The second Part of the second HC of verse line 50 is also empty:

HC		HC		HC		HC	
1	2	1	2	1	2	1	2
murn	ende	mod		men	ne	cun	non

An alliterating syllable marks the beginning—heads the first Part—of an HC unless, as sometimes happens, two alliterating syllables fall together into a single HC.[4] Clearly, *pulf* and *mod* mark the beginning of their respective HCs. Just as clearly, *pæl* and *men* mark the beginning of the next HC—and the second halfline.

Both *pulf* and *mod* are long syllables. The option of stretching them is certainly open to the performer of these lines. But is the same option open to the performer of the short isolated syllable *pæl* in line 3027? This monosyllable, too, occupies an entire HC. But stretching,

---

4. Two alliterating syllables occur in the same HC only if the following conditions are met: (1) the halfline does not begin with an alliterating syllable, and (2) both of the segments that begin with the alliterating syllables do not consist of the archetypal stress pattern, $\alpha + \alpha$. In verse line C107, *in caines cýnne*, the first but not the second condition is met.

if applied to any monosyllable isolated in an HC, would break down the distinction between long and short stressed syllables.

There are more examples of either a single monosyllable or two short syllables belonging to the same word occupying the entire second HC of a line:

No.	FHC		HC		MHC		HC	
	Part 1	Part 2	Part 1	Part 2	Part 1	Part 2	Part 1	Part 2
69	[medo	æ]rn	micel		men	ȝe	pȳrce	an
105	þon	sǽli	þer		þear	dode	hþi	le
120	þon	sceaft	þera		[þ]iht		un	hǽlo
142	heal	ðeȝnes	hete		heold	[hȳ]ne	sȳð	þan
147	·xii·	þintra	tid		torn	ȝe	þolode	

Nor is emptiness confined to the second Part of the second HC of a line. The first HC of a line may, as we have already seen, consist of a monosyllable or resolved di- or trisyllable isolated by its own alliteration as outer base 1 and by the alliteration that marks the beginning of the next HC. In these instances, represented by the first set of three examples below, the second Part of the first HC will be empty. The third HC of a line may consist of similar configurations isolated by the alliteration of outer base 2 and a following stressed syllable, as in the second set of three examples. Finally, the last stressed syllable of a verse line may be isolated by the fact that it is the single stressed syllable or the resolved disyllable of a simplex that follows a short compound, as in the final set of examples. In all these cases the second Part will be empty.

No.	FHC		HC		MHC		HC	
	Part 1	Part 2	Part 1	Part 2	Part 1	Part 2	Part 1	Part 2
31	leof		land	fruma	lan	ȝe	ah	te
54	leo[f]		leod	cýninȝ	lon	ȝe	þra	ȝe
129	micel		morȝen	speȝ	mæ	re	þeo	den

No.	FHC		HC		MHC		HC	
	Part 1	Part 2	Part 1	Part 2	Part 1	Part 2	Part 1	Part 2
51	secȝ	an t[o]	so	ðe	sele		ræ	denne
95	leo	man to	leoh	te	land		b[u	en]dum
127	ȝrend	les	ȝuð	cræft	ȝumum		un	dÿrne
5	mone	ȝū	mæȝ	þum	meodo	setla of	teah	
8	peox	under	polc	num	peorð	mÿndum	þah	
17	puld	res	peal	dend	porold	are for	ȝeaf	

As these sets of examples show, an empty Part is not exceptional. The idea of an empty Part is most useful, however, in dealing with outer nonalliterating HCs. A single unstressed monosyllable sometimes introduces a verse line:

> ðæm eafera þæs   æfter cenned   C12/P12

All that is evident in the manuscript of the first HC of line 12 is the long monosyllable *ðæm*. Rule 3a places it unequivocally in the second Part. What happens, however, when we try to move it into the first Part?

HC	
1	2
* ðæm	

So far, I have insisted that the first Part of an HC be reserved for a stressed syllable, which *ðæm* is not. If we move *ðæm* to the second Part, however, the verse line will begin with an empty Part:

HC	
1	2
	ðæm

This situation exactly reverses that of *pulf* in verse line 3027 or, for the sake of easier comparison, of *leof* in 31. I stack the latter line and line 12 under the control line 195:

No.	FHC		HC		MHC		HC	
	1	2	1	2	1	2	1	2
195	ʒod	mid	ʒea	tum	ʒrend	les	dæ	da
31	leof		land	fruma	lan	ʒe	ah	te
12		ðæm	eafera	pæs	æf	ter	cen	ned

In line 31, *leof* stacks with *ʒod*, *land* with *ʒea*, thus leaving empty the second Part of the first HC. In line 12, *eafera* stacks with *ʒea* and with *land*; *ðæm* stacks with *mid* in 195, thus leaving empty the first Part of the first HC.

A number of matched halflines begin with more than one nonalliterating syllable, as we have already seen. Both halflines of line 26, for example, begin with two unstressed syllables. Both of these halflines stack with 119, in which the second Part of both the first and third HCs similarly contains two syllables:

No.	FHC		HC		MHC		HC	
	Part 1	Part 2	Part 1	Part 2	Part 1	Part 2	Part 1	Part 2
119	spefan	æfter	[sẏ]m	ble	sor	ʒe ne	cu	ðon
26		him ða	scẏld ʒe	pat		to ʒe	scæp	hpile

The first halfline of line 53 begins with three nonalliterating syllables. The second HC of this line stacks with the second HC of 46, while the second Parts of the first HCs in each line match:

No.	FHC		HC		MHC		HC	
	Part 1	Part 2	Part 1	Part 2	Part 1	Part 2	Part 1	Part 2
46	æn	ne ofer	ẏ	ðe	um	bor	pe[s]en	de
53		ÐA pæs on	bur	ʒum	beo	pulf	scẏl	dinʒa

Although line C128 begins with four unstressed syllables and line C28 begins with five unstressed syllables, it appears that only a very few Parts of any line in the Matched Corpus contain more than three syllables. I discuss these rare occurrences later in this chapter, early in the section titled "Stacking: In General." At this point I repeat my earlier statement that the four, five, or six syllables of ε HCs may well have been divided between the two Parts, even though such a division appears to stack nonalliterating with alliterating syllables. I illustrate, using verse line 119 as a control:

No.	FHC		HC		MHC		HC	
	Part 1	Part 2	Part 1	Part 2	Part 1	Part 2	Part 1	Part 2
119	spefan	æfter	[sẏ]m	ble	sor	ʒe ne	cu	ðon
128	þa pæs	æfter	pis	te	póp		up a	hafen
28	hi hẏne	[þ]a æt	bæ	ron		to	brimes	faroðe

BUILDING THE GRID

The rules of distribution can be used to distribute in orderly and explicable ways just about every syllable of the Matched Corpus into the grid or "great net" of Table 7.1 The rules, operating within the conceptual scheme of the grid, thus make it possible to compare every one of the remarkably varied verse lines, halflines, and HCs of the Matched Corpus.[5]

5. For reasons related to the computer lineation program, Table 7.1, the grid or "net," unlike the examples in the preceding section of this chapter, divides polysyllabic words between the stem and a formative, where there is one, and between a stem or formative and a case-, verb-ending, or "marker." In other words, the division is not morphophonemic. For example, in line 5, *moneʒū* is divided into *moneʒ-* and *-ū*, not *mone-* and *-ʒū*; in line 17, *pealdend* is divided at the formative *-end*: *peald-* and *-end*, rather than morphophonemically into *peal-* and *-dend*.

Table 7.1. A Part Analysis of the Lines of the Matched Corpus

Line	SC	-HC- 1	-HC- 2	-HC- 1	-HC- 2	-HC- 1	-HC- 2	-HC- 1	-HC- 2
1	III		HPÆT ÞE	GAR	DEna·		in	ʒear	daʒum·
2	I	þeod		cyninʒ	a	þrym	ʒe	frun	on
5	I	moneʒ	ū	mæʒþ	um	meodo	*setla of^*	teah	
6	II	eʒs	ode	eorl			syððan	ær	*est pearl[ð]*
7	II	fea	sceaft	fund	en		he þæs	*frofre ʒe*	ba[d]
8	I	peox	under	polcn	um	peorð	*myndum*	þah	
9	III		oð þ him	æʒ	hpylc		para	ymb	*sittendra*
10	II		ofer	hron	*rade*	hyr	an	scold	e
11	II	ʒomb	an	ʒyld	an		þ þæs	ʒod	cyninʒ·
12	II		ðæm	eafera	þæs	æf	ter	cenn	ed
13	II	ʒeonʒ	in	ʒeard	um		þone	ʒod	*sende*
14	I	folc	e to	frofr	e	fyren	*ðearfe on*	ʒeat	
15	II	lanʒ	þ hie	ær	druʒon	ald	or	..as	e.
16	II		e	hpil	e		him þæs	lif	frea
17	I	puldr	es	peald	end	porold	*are for*	ʒeaf·	

164

Line	SC	-HC- 1	-HC- 2	-HC- 1	-HC- 2	-HC- 1	-HC- 2	-HC- 1	-HC- 2
18	I	beo	*pulf pæs*	brem	e	blæd		*pide*	spranʒ
26	III		him ða	*scyld ʒe*	þat		to ʒe	scæp	*hpile*
27	II	[fe]la	hror	fer	an		on	frean	*pære*
28	III	hi hyne	[þ]a æt	bær	on		to	brimes	faroðe
29	II	spæs	e ʒe	siþ	as		[Sp]a he	*selfa*	bæd
30	II		þenden	*pordum*	peold	[p]ine		scyld	*inʒa*
31	I	leof		land	fruma	lanʒ	e	aht	e
32	II		þær æt	*hyðe*	stod	hrinʒ	ed	stefn	a
33	I	is	*iʒ 7*	út	fus	æþel	*inʒes*	fær·	
34	II		a	*ledon*	þa	leof	ne	þeod	en
35	II	beaʒ	a	brytt	an		on	bearm	scipes
38	II	Ne	hyrde ic	cym	*licor*	ceol	ʒe	ʒyrp	an
39	II	hild	e	pæpn	um		7	heaðo	*pædum*
40	II	bill	um 7	byrn	um		him on	*bearme*	læʒ
41	II	madm	a	mæniʒ	o		þa him	mid	*scoldon*
42	II		on	*flodes*	æht	feor	ʒe	pit	an·

continued next page

Line	SC	-HC-		-HC-		-HC-		-HC-	
		1	2	1	2	1	2	1	2
43	II	Nalæs	hi hine	læss	an	lac	um	teod	an
46	I	æn	ne ofer	ýð	e	um	bor	pe[s]end	e
47	II	þa	ʒýt hie him a	sett	on	seʒen		[ʒe.]d	enne
48	II	heah	ofer	hea	fod		*leton*	holm	ber[an]
49	II	ʒeaf	on on	ʒar	secʒ		him þæs	*ʒeomor*	sefa
50	I	murn	*ende*	mod		men	ne	cunn	on·
51	I	secʒ	an t[o]	soð	e	sele		ræd	enne
52	II	haleð	under	heofen[ū]			hpa þæm	*hlæste on*	fenʒ·
53	III	leo[f]	ÐA pæs on	burʒ	um	beo	pulf	scyld	*inʒa*
54	I			leod	cýninʒ	lonʒ	e	þraʒ	e
59	II		ðæm	*feoper*	bearn	forð	ʒe	rim	ed
60	II		in	porold	*pocun*	peoroda		ræsp	a
65	II	piʒ	es	peorð	mýnd		þ him his	pine	*maʒas*
66	II	ʒeorn	e	hýrd	on		oðð þ seo	*ʒeoʒoð ʒe*	peox
67	II	maʒo	driht	micel			hi on	*mod be*	arn
68	II		þ	heal	reced	hat	an	pold	e·

Line	SC	-HC-		-HC-		-HC-		-HC-	
		1	2	1	2	1	2	1	2
69	I	[medo	æ]rn	micel	e	men	ȝe	þẏrce	an
75	II	maniȝ	re	[m]æȝþ			ȝeond þisne	*middan*	ȝeard
76	II	folc	ste[de]	fræþp	an		him on	*fyrste ȝe*	lomp
77	II	æd	re [m]id	ẏld	um·		þ hit þearð	eal	ȝearo
78	II	heal	*ærna*	mæst	peald		scop him	heort	naman
79	II		se þe his	*pordes ȝe*	leh	pid	e	hæfd	e·
80	II	lað	He	*beot ne a*	es	beaȝ	as	dæld	e
83	II		an	liȝ	hete		ne þæs hit	*lenȝe þa*	ȝen
84	III		þ se	secȝ	*niðe*	pæcn	aþum	sperian	
85	II		æfter	pæl	ȝæst	ear	an	scold	e·
86	II		ða se	*ellen*			foð	lic	e
87	II	þraȝ	e ȝe	þolode	e	siȝe	se þe in	*þẏstrū*	bad
94	II		ȝe	sett			*hreþiȝ*	sunn	[an] 7
								mon	an
95	I	leom	an to	leoht	e	land		b[u	*en]dum*
96	II		7 ȝe	fræþp	ade	fold	an	sceat	a[s]

continued next page

Line	SC	-HC-		-HC-		-HC-		-HC-	
		1	2	1	2	1	2	1	2
97	I	leomum	7	leaf	um	lif		*eac ȝe*	sceop
98	II	cý[n]n	a ȝe	hpýlc	um		þara ðe	cpice	*hpýrf[laþ.]*
99	II	ead	Spa ða	driht	ȝuman	dream	um	liif[d	on]
100	II		iȝ	lic	e		oððæt	*án on*	ȝan
101	I	fýrene	þæs se	fr[e]m	an	feond	on	hell	e
102	II		e	*ȝrimma*	ȝæ[st]	ȝren	del	hat	en
103	II	mær	7	mearc	stapa		se þe	*moras*	heold
104	I	fen	*sæli*	fæst	en	fif	el	cýn	nes
								eard	
105	I	pon	*siþðan him*	per		peard	ode	hpil	e
106	III		in	scýpp	end		for	scrifen	*hæfde*
107	III		e	cain	es	cýnn	e		þone
								cpealm ȝe	præc
108	II	ec	Ne ȝe	driht	en		þæs þe he	*abel*	*sloȝ·*
109	III			feah	he þære	fæhð	e	ac	he hine
								feor for	præc

Line	SC	-HC- 1	-HC- 2	-HC- 1	-HC- 2	-HC- 1	-HC- 2	-HC- 1	-HC- 2
110	I	metod	for þý	man	e	mann	*cýnne*	fram	*pumon*
113	III		spýlce	ʒi	*[ʒantas]*		þa [þi]ð	ʒode	*ʒeald.*
114	II	lanʒ	[e	þraʒ	e		he] him ðæs	*lean for*	
115	III	[Ge]	pat ða	neos	ian		sýþðan	*niht be*	com
116	II	[h]ean		hus	es		hu hit	hrinʒ	dene
117	III		æfter	[be]or	þeʒe	æþel	ʒe	bun	*hæfdon.*
118	II		Fand þa ðær	[i]nn	e		*inʒa ʒe*	driht	
119	I	spefan	æfter	[sý]mb	le	sorʒ	e ne	cuð	on
120	I	pon	sceaft	pera		[þ]iht		un	*hælo*
121	I	ʒrim	7	ʒræd	iʒ	ʒearo		*sona*	pæs
122	II	reoc	7	reþ	e		7 on	*ræste ʒe*	nam
123	I	þri	tiʒ	[þ]eʒn	a	þanon	to	*eft ʒe*	pát
124	II	huð	e	hrem	iʒ		a	ham	faran
125	II		mid þære	pæl	*fylle*	pic		neos	an·
126	II		ða pæs on	uht	an		mid	ær	dæʒe
127	I	ʒrend	les	ʒuð	craeft	ʒumum		un	*dyrne*

continued next page

169

Line	SC	-HC- 1	-HC- 2	-HC- 1	-HC- 2	-HC- 1	-HC- 2	-HC- 1	-HC- 2
128	II	þa þæs	æfter	pist	e	þóp		*up a*	hafen
129	I	micel		*morʒen*	speʒ	mær	e	þeo	den
130	I	æþel	inʒ	ær	ʒod	un		sæt	
131	I	þolode		ðrýð	spýð	þeʒn	*bliðe*	dreah	
132	II	sýðþan	hie þæs	lað	an	last	*sorʒe*	sceap	edon
133	II	perʒ	an	ʒast	es			*pin to*	stranʒ
134	II	lað	7	lonʒ	sum		þæs þ ʒe	*lenʒra*	[fyrs]t
135	II		ac ým[b]	*ane*	niht	e[ft]	næs hit	fremede]	
138	III		þ[a] þæs	eað	*fynde*		ʒe	*elles*	hþær
140	II	bed	æfter	bur	um		þe him	*beacnod*	þæs
141	II	an	ʒe	sæʒd		soð	ða hi[m] ʒe	spe[oto]lan	
							lice	tac	ne
142	I	heal	*ðeʒnes*	hete		heold	[hý]ne	*sýð*	þan
143	II	fýr	7	fæst	or		se þæm	*feo[nde] æt*	pand·
144	III	an	Spa	rix	ode		7 pið	*rihte*	pan
145	II	an	a þið	eall	um		oð þ	*idel*	stod

Line	SC	-HC-		-HC-		-HC-		-HC-	
		1	2	1	2	1	2	1	2
146	II	hus	a	sel	es[t]		pæs seo	hpil	micel
147	I	·xii·	*pintra*	tid		torn	ȝe	þolode	
148	I	pine		scýld	*enda*	pean	a ȝe	hpelc	ne
151	I	ȝýdd	ū	ȝeo	more		þætte	*ȝrendel*	pan
152	I	hpil	e pið	hroþ	ȝar	hete	*niðas*	pæȝ	
153	I	fýrene	7	fæhð	e	fela		miss	*era*
154	I	sin	*ȝale*	sæce		sibb	e ne	pold	e
155	II		pið	*manna*	hpone	mæȝenes		deniȝ	a
156	I	feorh	bealo	feorr	an	fea		þinȝ	ian
157	II	ne þær	næniȝ	pitena		pen	an	þorft	e
158	II	beorht	re	bot	e		to	banū	*folmū.*
160	I	[de]orc		[deaþ	scua	du[ȝu]þe	7]	ȝeoȝoþe	
161	I	seomade	7	sýrede		[sin]	*nihte*	heold	
162	I	mist	*iȝe*	mor	as	men	ne	[cu]nn	on
163	I	hpýder		hel	*runan*	hpýrft	um	[sc]riþ	að
164	II		spa	fela	fýrena	feond		man	cýn[ne]s

continued next page

Line	SC	-HC-		-HC-		-HC-		-HC-	
		1	2	1	2	1	2	1	2
165	I	atol		an	*ʒenʒea*	oft	ʒe	fremede·	
166	I	[h]eard	ra	hýnð	a	heorot		eard	ode
171	I	mod	es	brecð	a	moniʒ		*oft ʒe*	sæt
172	I	ric	e to	run	e	ræd		eaht	edon
173	II		hpæt	spið	*ferhðum*	sel	est	þær	e
174	III	Hpil	pið	fær	ʒrýrū		to ʒe	fremm	anne·
175	II	piʒ	um hie ʒe	het	on		æt	hrærʒ	trafum
176	I		þ him	peorþ	*unʒa*	[p]lord	um	bæd	on
177	II	dæd	pið	ʒæst	bona	ʒeoc	e ʒe	*fremede·*	
178	III		a	þeod	*þreaum*		spýlc pæs	þeap	hyra.
181	II		[ne hie]	dem	end	ne	piston hie	*drihten*	ʒod·
182	II			h]u	ru	[h]eof[ena]	h]elm	herian	[ne]
			7 to			freoðo		cuð	on
188	II		Spa ða	fæder	*faþmum*	maʒa		piln	ian·
189	II	sin	*ʒala*	mæl	ceare	ne		healf	denes
190	II			seað			mihte	snotor	hæleð

172

Line	SC	-HC-		-HC-		-HC-		-HC-	
		1	2	1	2	1	2	1	2
191	II	þean	on	þend	an		pæs þ ʒe	*þin to*	spyð
192	II	lað	7	lonʒ	sum		þe on ða	*leode be*	com
193	I	nŷd	pracu	niþ	ʒrim	niht	*bealþa*	mæst	
194	II		þ fram	*ham ʒe*	fræʒn	hiʒe	*laces*	þeʒn	a
195	I	ʒod	mid	ʒeat	um	ʒrend	les	dæd	lidan
198	II	æþele	7	eac	en		het him	yð	cyninʒ
199	II	ʒod	ne ʒe	ðŷrp	an		cpæð he	ʒuð	e
200	II		ofer	span	*rade*	sece	an	þold	þearf
201	II	mær	ne	þeo	den		þa him pæs	*manna*	as
202	II	lŷt	ðone	sið	*fæt him*	snotere		ceorl	
203	II	[ce]m	hpon	loʒ	on·		[þeah h]e him	[l]eof	*[þære]*
206	II	*laʒu*	þan ʒe	corone		þara	þe he	cen	*oste*
209	I		*cræftiʒ*	mon		land	ʒe	mŷr	cu
210	I	fŷrst		*forð ʒe*	þæt	flota	pæs on	yð	um·
211	I	bát	under	beorʒ	e	beorn	as	ʒearp	e
212	II		on	stefn	stiʒon	stream	as	pund	on

continued next page

Line	SC	-HC-		-HC-		-HC-		-HC-	
		1	2	1	2	1	2	1	2
215	I	ʒuð	searo	ʒeato	lic	ʒuman		ut	scufon
219	II	pund	oð Þ ymb	an	tid	oþ	res	do	ʒores
220	II		en	stefn	a	land	ʒe	paden	*hæfde*
221	II	brim	Þ ða	lið	*ende*	beorʒ	ʒe	sap	on
222	I	sid	clifu	blic	an		as	steap	e.
223	II	eoletes	e	sæ	*næssas*		þa þæs	sund	liden
224	II	pedera	æt	end	e		þanon	up	hraðe
225	II	sæ	pudu	leod	e		on	panʒ	stiʒon·
226	I	ʒuð	ʒe	sæld	on	syrc	an	hrýsedon·	
227	I			pæd	o	ʒode		þanc	edon
228	II		Þæs Þe him	ýþ	*lade*	eað	e	þurd*	on·
229	II		[þa] of	*pealle ʒe*	sea[h]	peard		scild	*inʒa*
230	II		se [þe]	holm]	clifu	heald	an	scold	e
231	I	beran	ofer	bol	can	beorht	e	rand	as
232	II	fyrd	searu	fus	licu		hine	*fyrþýt*	bræc
233	II	mod	ʒe	hyʒd	um		hpæt þa	men	þæron·

174

Line	SC	-HC-		-HC-		-HC-		-HC-	
		1	2	1	2	1	2	1	2
234	II		Ge	þat him þa to	paroðe	picз	e	ri[d	an]
235	I	þeзn		hroð	зares	þrymm	um	cpeht	e
236	I	mæзe[n]	pudu	mund	um	meþel	*pordum*	fræзn·	
242	II		þe on	land	dena	lað	ra	naen	iз
243	II		mid	scip	*herзe*	sceðþ	an ne	meaht	e
246	I	зuð		fremm	*endra*	зearp	e ne	þiss	on
247	II	ma	зa зe	med	u		næfre ic	*maran зe*	seah
250	II	þæpn	um зe	peorð	ad	næfre	him his	plite	*leoзe*
253	II	leas		sceap	eras		on	land	[dena]
254	II	[fu]r	þur	fer	an		nu зe	feor	*buend*
255	I	mere		lið	*ende*	min	e зe	hýr	að
256	I	an	*fealdne зe*	[þ]oht		ofost	is	sel	est
257	III		to зe	cýð	anne	[h]panan	eopre	cýme	sýndon·
258	II		[H]jim se	ýld	*esta*	7		sparode	
259	I	perodes		þis	a	pord	*hord on*	leac	
260	II		þe sýnt	зum	*cýnnes*	зeat	a	leod	e

continued next page

175

Line	SC	-HC-		-HC-		-HC-		-HC-	
		1	2	1	2	1	2	1	2
261	II		7	hiȝe	*laces*	heorð	ȝe	neat	as·
262	II		þæs min	fæder		folc	um ȝe	cýþ	ed
263	I	æþele		ord	fruma	ecȝ	þeop	hat	en·
264	III	ȝe	bad	*pintra*	porn		ær he on	þeȝ	*hpurfe·*
265	II	ȝamol	of	ȝeard	um		hine	*ȝearpe ȝe*	man
266	I	pitena		pel	hpylc	pid	e ȝeond	eorþ	an·
269	II	leod	ȝe	byrȝe	an		þes þu us	*larena*	ȝod·
270	II	habbað	þe to þæm	mær	an	micel		ær	*ende*
271	II	deniȝ	a	frean·		ne	sceal þær	*dýrne*	sum
274	II		þ mid	scyld	*inȝum*	sc[eaðona]	ic	nat	hpylc
275	I	deo	ȝol	dæd	hata	deorc	u[m]	niht	um
276	I	eap	eð þurh	eȝs	an	un	*cuðne*	ni[ð]	
277	II	hýnð	u 7	hra	fýl		ic þæs	*hroðȝar*	mæȝ
278	II		þur[h]	*rumne*	sefan	ræd	ȝe	lær	an·
279	II		hu he	*fro[d. 7]*	ȝod	feond	ofer	spýð	eþ
280	II		ȝyf him	ed	*pend[an]*	æf	re	scold	e.

Line	SC	-HC-		-HC-		-HC-		-HC-	
		1	2	1	2	1	2	1	2
283	II	brea	oððe	ear	foð	a	sýþðan	þraʒ	e
284	II	peard	nýd	hus	þenden	þolað	stede	þær	punað
285	II	nip	on	nacan	a	heah	ode	sel	est·
286	II	ar	um	lleof	þær on	maþel	pýdne	picʒe	sæt
295	I	pudu	ofer	[hál]	on	týr	an	sand	e
296	II	god	þ þone	flota	opðæt	heald	strealmas	eft	býreð
297	II	ʒe	piton him þa	sid	ne	laʒu	[hals	mann	an
298	II	seomode	on	eofor	to]	punden	endra	peder	mearce
299	II		on	ferh	[splylcum	fremm	ræs	ʒifeðe	bið
300	II	fah	[o]fer	ʒuman	ʒe	hilde	an	diʒ	eð·
301	II	ʒuþ	[7]		færmed	fer	e	[stille	bád
302	I		mod		lic	sol	fæst	[scilp	
303	II				ʒe	ancre	beran	scionon	golde
304	III				pearde	hleor	heard	hroden	etton
305	I					fýr		heold	
306	I					ʒrumm	on	on	

continued next page

177

		-HC-		-HC-		-HC-		-HC-	
Line	SC	1	2	1	2	1	2	1	2
309	II	receda	þ pæs	fore	*mærost*	fold		bu	*endum*
310	II	lixt	under	roderum			on þæm se	*rica*	*bad·*
311	II	ʒeʒn	e se	leom	a		ofer	*landa*	*fela·*
314	I	picʒ	um	ʒanʒ	an	ʒuð	*beorna*	sum	
315	I	pæl	ʒe	pend	e	pord		æfter	*cpæð·*
2946	II	frod	Þæs sio	spat	spaðu	spon	a 7	ʒeat	a
2947	I	eorl	ræs	peora		pid	e ʒe	sȳn	e
2950	I	hæfd		fela	*ʒeomor*	fæst	en	sece	an
2951	I	plonc		onʒen	þio	ufor	on	cird	e
2952	I		e	hiʒe	*laces*	[hild]	e ʒe	frun	en
2953	I		es	piʒ	cræft	piðr	es [ne]	trupode	
2954	III	[h]leaðo	Þ he	sæ	*mannū*		on	sacan	*mihte*
2955	I	speon	a	lið	*endū*	hord	for	stand	an
2958	I			leod	ū	seʒn		hiʒe	*lace.*
2959	I	freoðo	ponʒ	þone		ford	ofer	eod	on
2960	III		*sȳððan*	hreðl	*inʒas*		to	haʒan	*þrunʒon*

178

Line	SC	-HC-		-HC-		-HC-		-HC-	
		1	2	1	2	1	2	1	2
2961	II	blond	þær pearð	on[ʒ]en	ðioþ	ecʒ	ū	speord	ū
2962	II		en	fex	a		on	bid	precen
2963	II	eafores	þ se	þeod	cýninʒ	ðafian		sceold	e
2964	II			*anne*	dom		hýne	ýrr	*inʒa*
2965	I	pulf	þ hi for	pon	*r[e]d[inʒ]*	þæp	ne ʒe	ræht	e
2966	II			spenʒ	e	spat		ædr[ū]	spronʒ
2967	II	forð	under	fex	e		næs he	*forht spa*	ðeh
2968	II	ʒomela		scilf	inʒ		ac for	ʒeald	hr[aðe]
2969	I	þýrs	an	prixl	e	pæl	hlem	þone	
2970	II		sýððan	ðe[od]	cýninʒ	þýder	on	cir	de.
2971	II	Ne	meahte se	snell	a	sunu		pon	*redes*
2974	II		þ he	*blode*	fah	buʒ	an	sceold	e
2975	II	feoll	on	fold	an		næs he	*fæʒe þa*	ʒit
2978	II	brad	e	mec	e		*þa his*	*broðor*	læ[ʒ]
2979	I	eald	speord	eoten	isc	ent	*iscne*	helm	
2980	II	brec[an]	ofer	bord	peal		ða ʒe	beah	cýninʒ

continued next page

Line	SC	-HC-		-HC-		-HC-		-HC-	
		1	2	1	2	1	2	1	2
2981	II	folc	es	hýrd	[e] pæs		in	feorh	dropen.
2982	III		ða pæron	moniʒ	e		þe h..	mæʒ	priðon
2983	II	ricone	a	rærd	on		ða hi ʒe	rĳmed	pearð
2984	III		þ hie	pæl	stope	peald	an	most	on
2989	III		h.....	frætpú	fenʒ		7 hi	fæʒre ʒe	het
2991	I	ʒeald	þone	ʒuð	ræs	ʒeat	[a	dry]ht	en
2995	II	land	es 7	locen	ra	beaʒ	a	ne	ðorfte hī ða
						lean	oð	pit	an
2996	II	mon	on	midd	an	ʒeard	e	sýðða	hie ða
						mærð	a ʒe	sloʒ	on.
2997	II	ham	7 ða	iofore for	ʒeaf	anʒ	an	doh	tor
2998	I		þ ýs sio	peorð	unʒe	hýld	o to	pedd	e
2999	III	folc	red	fæhð	o		7 se	feond	scipe
3006	II		scipe	fremede.			oððe	furður	ʒen
3007	II	eorl		efnd	e		me is	ofost	betost
3008	II		þ pe	ðeod	cýninʒ	þær		sceap	ian

Line	SC	-HC-		-HC-		-HC-		-HC-	
		1	2	1	2	1	2	1	2
3009	III	7	þone ȝe	brinȝ	an		þe us	beaȝas	ȝeaf
3010	III		on	ad	fære	ne	scel	anes	hþæt
3011	II	melt	an mid þā	mod	iȝan		ac þær is	[m]aðma	hord
3013	II	7	nu æt	sið	estan	sýlf	es	feor	e
3016	II	maðð	ū to ȝe	mýnd	um		ne	mæȝð	scýne
3017	I	habb	an on	heals	e	hrinȝ		peorð	unȝe
3018	II	ac	sceal	ȝeomor	mod	ȝold	e be	reaf	[od]
3019	I	oft		æn	e	el	land	tredan	
3020	II		nu se	here	þisa	hleah	tor a	leȝd	e
3023	II	hæfen	on	hand	a		nalles	hearpan	speȝ
3024	II	piȝ	end	þecce	an		ac se	þonna	hrefn
3025	I	fús	ofer	fæ	ȝū	fela		reord	ian
3026	II	earn	e	secȝ	an		hu hī æt	æte	speop
3027	II	þende[n]	he pið	pulf		þæl		reaf	ode.
3028	II		spa se	secȝ	hpata	secȝȝ	ende	þæs*	
3029	II	lað	ra	spell	a		he ne	leaȝ	fel[a]

continued next page

181

Line	SC	-HC- 1	-HC- 2	-HC- 1	-HC- 2	-HC- 1	-HC- 2	-HC- 1	-HC- 2
3032	I	poll	en	tear	e	pund	u.	sceap	ian
3033	II	fundon	ða on	sand	e	sa	pul	leas	ne
3034	II	hlim	bed	heald	an	þone	*þe hī*	*hrinȝas*	ȝeaf
3035	II	ærr	an	mæl	ū		*þa pæs*	*ende*	dæȝ
3036	II	ȝod	ū ȝe	ȝonȝ	ean		Þ se	ȝuð	cýninȝ
3040	II	lað	n..	licȝ	ean		pæs se	leȝ	draca
3046	II		hæfde	eorð	scrafa	end	e ȝe	nýtt	od
3047	II		him	biȝ	*stodan*	bunan	7	orc	as
3048	II	disc	as	laȝ	on		7	*dýre*	spýrd
3049	II	om	*iȝe þurh*	etone			spa hie pið	*eorðan*	faeðm
3053	II		þ ðam	hrinȝ	sele	hrin	an ne	most	e

*Line 5, third HC: *setla of* is the first of many instances of a *crowded Part*, that is, a long stressed syllable followed by at least one unstressed syllable *crowded* into a single Part. The contents of every crowded Part are set off by the use of italics.

*Line 228, fourth HC: The fact that *purdon* fills this HC guarantees it unusual (Rhetorical) stress.

*Line 3028, third and fourth HCs: Since the stressed second syllable of *secȝende* is not the second element of a compound but the marker of the present participle, that syllable should probably not be separated from the stem. *pæs* is thus left to fill the fourth HC of the line and thereby acquires unusual (Rhetorical) stress.

STACKING: IN GENERAL

It may at first appear that there are many empty Parts—which, for the sake of brevity, I shall call "holes"—in the great "net" created in Table 7.1. The impression is misleading. There are indeed 337 holes in 333 different halflines in the net. But the net consists of a total of 2,340 Parts, holes included. In other words, 2,003 filled Parts enclose the 337 empty Parts. Surrounding and containing the 14.4 percent empty Parts are the Parts containing one syllable or more—85.6 percent of the fabric of the net. The net is more tightly woven than it may at first seem to be.

It is true that one has to look hard to find completely filled verse lines. There are actually only eleven in the Matched Corpus: verse lines 46, 119, 162, 195, 211, 222, 231, 275, 2952, 2991, and 3032.

The percentage increases tenfold if we count by halflines. Of the 580 halflines of the Matched Corpus, 221 are both properly filled and contain no holes. Twenty-six halflines are not counted here, even though each Part in each of these halflines contains at least one syllable. The reason is that the outermost Part in these halflines is "improperly" filled with a nonalliterating syllable either because the HC consists of four or more unstressed syllables or because it contains a stressed nonalliterating syllable. Even if we put aside these twenty-six halflines, 38 percent of the net consists of halflines each Part of which is properly filled.

The weave of the net is most simply indicated by a pattern that occurs only once as an entire verse line in the 290 verse lines that form the net, at verse line 195:

FHC		HC		MHC		HC	
1	2	1	2	1	2	1	2
ʒod	mid	ʒea	tum	ʒrend	les	dæ	da

If the halfline pattern doubles only once to build a whole verse line, the basic halfline α + α (α1 + α1)—which I have called the doubled "archetype"—nevertheless occurs 96 times. Thus, 16.5 percent of the halflines exactly express this archetypal pattern.

The 221 completely filled halflines express variations on the archetype exemplified in verse line 195. So, indeed, does every halfline in the Corpus, whether or not the halfline contains a hole. The function of these holes is, in fact, to make it possible to express the archetype in some form even when a syllable would be inappropriate. Before I pursue this matter farther, however, I shall look more closely at some of the verse lines, halflines, HCs, and Parts of the grid.

Detailed Commentary on Some Results of Stacking

The second Part of the fourth HC of line 28 sets the limits to *resolution*: three short syllables, all of which belong to the same word and the first of which is stressed, can be accommodated in a single Part, *faroðe*. The second Part of the third HC of line 17 sets the limits to what I shall call *crowding*: three syllables the first of which is stressed and long will on occasion be crowded into a single Part, *are for*. The first Part of the last HC of line 66, *ʒeoʒoð ʒe*, seems to indicate that, very rarely, a hybrid of these two accommodations can occur to create a *resolved-crowded Part*.

Although two *resolved* Parts can occur in the same HC, as in the last HC of line 28, *brimes faroðe*, and both a crowded and a resolved Part can occur in the same HC, as in the third HC of line 5, *meodosetla of*, two crowded Parts cannot occur in one HC. In line 107, *caines* and *cýnne*, as I argued in Chapter 6, are not successive crowded Parts but successive HCs of the halfline.

The second Part of the first HC of line 3049, *iʒe þurh*, seems to establish limits for syllables that occupy the second Part of an HC that begins with an alliterating syllable: three syllables, two of which may be long.

The longest series of stressed and unresolved syllables other than the three of the fourth HC of line 9 (*ýmbsittendra*) occurs in the fourth HC of line 232: *fýrpÿt bræc*. All three of these syllables are short, whereas all three stressed syllables in the last HC of line 9 are long. More important, the last long stressed syllable of 9b is followed by an unstressed syllable. The second Part of the fourth HC of line 9 as it stands in the manuscript seems unusual according to Part analysis as well as HC analysis.

The "Rule of Three"

The clearest generalization that emerges from this analysis might be called the "rule of three." Either Part of an HC accommodates more than three syllables only very rarely. Only 5 Parts of the 2,340 into which I have analyzed these 290 verse lines seem to violate the rule of three. These are: the second Part of the first HC of lines 47 and 301, the first Part of the second HC of lines 234 and 2997, and the second Part of the fourth HC of line 2995, a six-HC line. These 5 Parts make up 0.2 percent of the total number of Parts.

These four-syllable Parts call for further comment. Part analysis of line 234 suggests that the segment *pat him þa to paroðe* might not be a single HC. Since the alliterating syllable *pat* clearly marks the beginning of the second HC, *paroðe* would then mark the beginning of the third HC. The three unstressed syllables between these two alliterating syllables belong not in the same Part with *pat* but in the now emptied second Part of the second HC. The first two of the last four syllables of this line, *picȝe*, mark the midpoint of a *five*-HC line:

FHC		HC		HC		MHC		HC	
Part 1	Part 2	Part 1	Part 2	Part 1	Part 2	Part 1	Part 2	Part 1	Part 2
	Ge	pat	him þa to	paroðe		picȝ	e	ri	[dan]

The four-syllable second Part of the first HC of both lines 47 (top) and 301 (bottom) might be dealt with similarly:

FHC		HC		HC		MHC		HC	
Part 1	Part 2	Part 1	Part 2	Part 1	Part 2	Part 1	Part 2	Part 1	Part 2
	þa	ȝẏt	hie him a	set	ton	seȝen		[ȝe.]d	enne
	ȝe	piton	him þa	fe	ran	flota		[st]ille	bàd

But the problem in these two lines is different from that in line 234 because, unlike *pat*, neither *ȝẏt* nor *piton* alliterates in its line.

The four-syllable first Part of the second HC of line 2997 is particularly interesting. It is tempting to move *ȝeaf* into the first Part of the third HC of the line. The context of line 2997 provides some argument for this solution since the line follows two six-HC lines, or rather four three-HC halflines. On the other hand, it is intriguing to speculate on the possibility that the virtuoso composer of the poem violated the limits within which he usually worked in order to produce on this occasion a tongue-twisting hybrid, a resolved-crowded four-syllable Part: *iofore for*.

The four-syllable second Part of the fourth HC of line 2995—a verse line consisting of two three-HC halflines—is harder to deal with. Both the first and fourth syllables are long, and the first syllable, *ðorf*, is stressed. I leave this four-syllable Part to stand as a particularly intractable exception to the rule of three. The three examples just discussed are probably also exceptions.

VERSE LINES AND HALFLINES AS PROSODIC UNITS

Most of the halflines of the Matched Corpus readily divide into two HCs each of which consists always of two Parts. But not all halflines stack into only two HCs. A few, like *in caines cynne*, seem to contain one more HC and thus one more pair of Parts. What happens, then, to the notion that halflines are prosodic units and therefore in some sense comparable to each other? The answer requires a brief review of the steps taken to arrive at this point.

The halfline is one of the two segments of the verse line, which is itself a passage of the poem that can be isolated from its immediate context on the basis of alliteration. The first halfline of a pair is built around the first alliterating syllable; the second halfline of a pair is built around the last alliterating syllable. The determination of alliteration and therefore of the verse line has been made without regard to any other prosodic or "metrical" considerations.

The attempt to identify verse lines purely on the basis of alliteration has yielded 290 verse lines in the sample passages that exactly match 290 sets of paired verses in Kemble's text. Stacking has then shown that 97 percent of the verse lines consist of four HCs. If we count by halflines, stacking has shown that 569, or 98 percent, consist of two HCs. The two-HC halfline thus establishes the norm.

The norms can then be expressed hierarchically: every verse line consists of two halflines. *Almost* all halflines consist of two HCs. Every HC consists of two Parts. Nearly every halfline in the Matched Corpus is indeed exactly comparable to every other halfline, even though halflines have not been elicited on the basis of a predetermined metrical feature such as a "foot." The HC has emerged in the present study from the "top-down" procedures of progressive identification of constituents. Like verse lines and halflines, HCs can be characterized as semi-independent prosodic units.

The two-HC halflines establish a norm against which the rare three-HC halflines in *Beowulf* can be heard as variations. Both the two-HC halfline and the three-HC halfline are prosodic units, but the latter always equals the normal halfline plus exactly one additional HC.

The so-called "hypermetric lines," like lines C2995 and 2996, simply consist of two three-HC halflines. They are best considered, then, not as exotic hybrids or unfathomable constructions but as multi-HC half-lines.

Replotting Halflines: Two HCs or Three?

Restacking—which might also be called *replotting*—verse lines C47, 234, and 301 in order to redistribute syllables so as to avoid placing more than three syllables in a single Fine Part has brought the first halflines of these verse lines into conflict with what may be a higher principle. Briefly stated, that principle runs something like this: since the normal halfline consists of two HCs, any variation from this norm in either direction should be regarded as exceptional. Single-HC half-lines at one extreme and three-HC halflines at the other should be carefully scrutinized and, if possible, redistributed.

I have plotted—or replotted—as three-HC halflines a total of thirteen halflines in the two sample passages studied in this book. The verse numbers of these thirteen halflines are as follows: C94a, 104b, 107a, 109a, 141a, 182a, 2995a, 2995b, 2996a, 2996b, and the replotted 47a, 234a, and 301a.[6]

Only three of the thirteen halflines begin with an alliterating syllable. One halfline of this small group, *fifelcỹnnes eard* (104b), may be affected by the reduction of the second syllable to near 0, as in Old Norse *fifl*. The two other halflines that begin with an alliterating syllable, 2995a and 2996a, cannot be reduced or condensed. They are genuine variations.

Are the remaining ten halflines also genuine variations? If one looks closely at the replotted halflines—47a, 234a, and 301a—one observes that an entire HC has been generated by a single unstressed and nonalliterating syllable, specifically the syllables *þa*, and *Gelȝe*. These syllables, and certain others, might have been relegated to anacrusis—brief passages that do not "count" metrically—if the computer had not shown that the composition of the poem can be considered to have been a continuous process. It is certainly possible

6. John Miles Foley neatly solves the problem raised by some of these halflines, as well as the problem of anacrusis, with his η (*eta*) measure, sketched in his "Formula and Theme in Old English Poetry," in *Oral Literature and the Formula*, ed. Benjamin A. Stolz and Richard S. Shannon, III (Ann Arbor: Center for Coordination of Ancient and Modern Studies, the University of Michigan, 1976), 207–32. The η-measure (or η-HC) offers an alternative and possibly better solution than the one presented here.

that the poet was guilty of bad economy in constructing an empty Fine Part followed by a nearly empty one. On the other hand, it is also possible that he violated the rule of three syllables per Fine Part in order to compose these halflines within the confines of a normal two-HC halfline.

Verse line 234a is crucial to this question. It is one thing to suggest the possibility that *þa* in 47a or *ʒe* in 301a may have been performed as the first Part of the first HC of its line. The stressed syllable that begins the second Part according to this reading does not participate in the dominant alliteration of these lines. The stressed syllable *þat* in 234a, on the other hand, does alliterate.

So, too, do *sett* in 94a, *feah* in 109a, *sæʒd* in 141a, and *hu* in 182a, although only one of these halflines (109a) also contains three syllables after the first alliterating syllable. In these five halflines alliteration and the principle of the two-HC norm appear to be in conflict.

Which is the higher principle? By attending to alliteration, I have been able to develop a systematic lineation. But systematic lineation establishes as the norm a halfline consisting of two HCs. Only 13 of 580 halflines have been plotted as three HCs. Four of the thirteen can be reduced to two-HC halflines by ignoring the rule (or custom) established by more than 2,000 Fine Parts that no Part should contain more than three syllables. Two of these same halflines along with three more can be reduced to two-HC halflines by distributing the first alliterating syllable into the second Fine Part of the halfline. One halfline may contain a syllable reduced to near o in speaking. One more, *in caines cýnne* (107a), resists redistribution but belongs with the group that begins with a nonalliterating syllable.

In all, nine of the thirteen halflines can be treated as variations that might have occurred because of the demands of performance. Only the four three-HC halflines grouped together in lines C2995 and 2996 seem to have been deliberate exceptions to the two-HC rule.

In the next chapter I deal in detail with conflicts between principles operating at various levels. It will, I think, become clear that the two-HC principle only rarely conflicts with that other high-order principle, namely, that alliterating syllables within range of each other belong to the same line. When these two principles conflict, the first—the two-HC principle—seems to me to outweigh the second, even though it is alliteration that builds the verse line. Mediating between these two principles are the twin principles of economy and balance. Operating at a still lower level is the custom that permits only three syllables per Fine Part. The final chapter will introduce the device that holds all of these forces in balance.

CONCLUSION

The attempt to stack the syllables of the text of *Beowulf* seems to have fulfilled Mrs. Beeton's household saying, "A place for everything, and everything in its place." All but a very few Fine Parts of the Matched Corpus fall easily into place in relation to Fine Parts in other verse lines to form the great net or grid. As each syllable establishes its appropriate position in relation to other verse lines, its positioning also works to empty certain Parts and thus create the holes in the net. The net or grid thus makes it possible to compare every verse line with every other verse line of the poem. But it is only the fact that every HC can be divided into exactly two Fine Parts that has made possible the building of the grid. The significance of this two-part division of every HC will become clear in Chapter 9. In the meantime Chapter 8 demonstrates that the grid makes it possible to reexamine P verse lines that do not match C lines and to attempt to fit these verse lines into the scheme of Fine Parts.

Chapter 8

Kemble's Additional Principles of Lineation
Replotting Mismatches

KEMBLE'S TWO-HC NORM

John Mitchell Kemble constructed in accordance with his general method—here rigorously reconstructed as P-Lineation—nearly four-fifths of the verses in the two sample passages studied in the present work. We shall probably never know the extent to which he consciously formulated the basic principle that guides his—and P—lineation, namely, that each verse must be built forward or back from the first syllable that alliterates with at least one syllable in the following or preceding verse. Kemble's prefaces suggest that he saw himself as a careful empiricist putting into good order what his predecessors— Thorkelin, Sharon Turner, and Conybeare, in particular—had all too often miscopied, misunderstood, or mislineated.

The 78.4 percent match between the halflines of P-Lineation and Kemble's verses shows that the image of Kemble as no more than a careful empiricist is inadequate. The mismatched portion of the sample might, on the other hand, suggest that he constructed at least some of his verses according to no discernible principles.

That hypothesis—or rather, its contrary—can be tested. It is clear that Kemble seems to have ignored alliteration when it occurs inconveniently. He completed verse 44, as Thorkelin had before him, with a word that alliterates with his verses 45 and 46. P-Lineation appropriately places that word, ʒepuniʒen, at the beginning of a long W line, P22. Why, then, did Kemble construct his verse 44 as he did? It is not because he was simply following Thorkelin, since it is possible to show in even more detail than I have done that Kemble never simply followed Thorkelin—or Conybeare either. On the contrary, Kemble knew what would happen if he placed the first word containing the W-alliteration in the first of the two verses linked by W. A monosyllabic halfline, *eft*, would be followed by the eight-syllable halfline of P-Lineation: *ʒepuniʒen [pilʒ]esiþas*. It is possible to argue, then, that Kemble was not so much ignoring the early *W*-alliteration in these verses as distributing words according to a sense of balance—and economy.

Kemble probably did not think in terms of economy, at least as I am using the term here. Yet many of the verses he accepted or constructed display an economical avoidance of unnecessary constituents, particularly empty Fine Parts. When one stacks halfline P21b, *eft*, for example, the monosyllable in its context not only generates an entire HC which is followed by an empty second Part, it also becomes an entire halfline:

	MHC	
	Part 1	Part 2
P21b	eft	

At the head of the next halfline, *ʒepuniʒen* generates two HCs: *ʒe* forms the second Part of the first HC, *puniʒ* the resolved first Part of the second, and *en* the second Part of the second HC:

	FHC		HC	
	Part 1	Part 2	Part 1	Part 2
P22a		ʒe	puniʒ	en

By accepting Thorkelin's verse, *eft ʒepuniʒen*, Kemble accepted an economical distribution of the syllables: *ʒe* forms the second Part of the HC that begins with *eft*. His verses 44 and 45 eliminate two empty Fine Parts and collapse two HCs into one:

	F/MHC		HC	
	Part 1	Part 2	Part 1	Part 2
K44	eft	ge	wunig	en
K45	wi[l]	ge	siþ	as

I do not intend to suggest that Kemble plotted each—or even any—verse in this way. It is more likely that he went about his work in a simpler way, possibly by first attending to the stress pattern of his verse 45 and realizing that it needs not a single additional syllable. Verse 45—only one segment of P22a—sounds the stress pattern (1/ o 1/ o)[1] that underlies every verse in Kemble's text. Kemble cannot have been totally unaware of the importance of what I have called the double archetypal stress pattern, α + α.

Kemble's ear for that pattern may have led him to arrange the syllables of the text so that all but the very few "hypermetric" verses are made up of just two HCs. Thorkelin, on the other hand, failed again and again to understand the operation of this norm. His "verse" 85, for example, consists of a single nonalliterating HC: *Nalæs he hine.*[2] With no help from Conybeare, who does not include this passage in his *Illustrations*, Kemble completed his verse 85 with the second HC:

	FHC		HC	
	Part 1	Part 2	Part 1	Part 2
K85	Nalæs	hi hine	læss	an

Again and again Kemble improved on Thorkelin's "verses" by constructing a verse that can be shown to consist of two HCs rather than one or three. On a few occasions he improved on Conybeare as well.

It appears that the two-HC norm was an extremely important consideration in Kemble's lineation. That norm seems to have guided his lineation even where the verses he accepted or constructed—apparently at the expense of alliteration—show either no gain or even a loss of economy. In order to prove the hypothesis that Kemble always reconstructed the verses of the poem according to principles—to prove, that is, the strong form of the first major hypothesis—it will be necessary to analyze several more of the mismatches between Kemble's verses and P-Lineation halflines.

PLOTTING MISMATCHES ONTO THE GRID

At the end of Chapter 4 I set aside approximately 18 percent of the two sample passages for later consideration. The verse lines of this

---

1. Here, as elsewhere, "1" indicates that the syllable is stressed, "o" that it is unstressed, and "/" indicates that the syllable is long.
2. G. J. Thorkelin, *De Danorum rebus gestis secul. III & IV. poema danicum anglosaxonica* (Copenhagen, 1815), 6.

group of passages from the sample do not match the verse pairs in Kemble. In many cases one halfline, usually the second of the verse line, matches one of Kemble's verses. In a few instances both halflines are mismatched.

It is important to bear in mind that every verse line produced by the computer from the indications of the syllables of the manuscript text is, in an important sense, well formed. A verse line contains at least two alliterating syllables from the last of which the beginning of the second halfline is determined. This means that all the alliterating syllables except the last always appear in the first halfline. When there are only two—and usually when there are no more than three—alliterating syllables making up an alliteration, the two halflines are likely to match Kemble's verses. But, whenever the alliteration either begins "early," as it does with *ʒepuniʒen* at 132Vo1, or continues on four or more syllables, mismatches of the first halfline/first verse of the pair are bound to occur.

For Kemble, and for other careful lineators, what I am calling "early alliteration" or "continuing alliteration" presents no problem. That is probably because Kemble developed a sense that no verse should exceed certain limits. Each verse had to contain at least one alliterating syllable and might contain two. But, since none of Kemble's verses contains three alliterating syllables, it is clear that Kemble at times constructed two successive pairs of verses around the syllables of the same alliteration.

Kemble's verses 221–24 provide a good example of continuing alliteration. I quote them from the 1835 edition:

> þanon untydras
> ealle on-wocon,
> Eotenas and Ylfe
> and Orcneas:

P-Lineation builds, as it should, a single verse around the first four alliterating syllables:

> þanon untýdras ealle onpocon eotenas 7 ýlfe   7 orcneas (P103)

Since Kemble's verse 224 exactly matches P103b, no more need be said about this match.

Kemble turned P103a into three verses. On what basis did he do so? There is a rough approximation in the number of syllables Kemble assigned to each of his verses 221–23: five, five, and six. It is possible, then, that Kemble simply counted syllables. He did not simply count stressed syllables, if he assigned stress to the first syllable of *þanon*, as I do, since that verse then contains three stressed syllables while 222 and 223 each contain only two.

Kemble's handling of his verse 512, *hwanon eowre cyme syndon*, suggests, however, that he never simply counted syllables.[3] It is impossible to know whether he assigned full stress to adverbs such as *hþanan* and *þanon*. What is clear from his verses 221–23 is that the first verse is constructed from the alliterating segment *untydras* and the nonalliterating segment *þanon*. The first syllable of this verse marks the beginning of the clause that contains all the alliterating syllables of this alliteration. Verse 222 begins with the second alliterating syllable and verse 223 with the third. Verse 222 continues with the nonalliterating stressed syllable -*wo*- and verse 223 with the alliterating syllable *yl*-.

Each verse thus contains at least one alliterating syllable and at least two stressed syllables. Whenever possible, Kemble elicited verses according to both requirements. When it appeared difficult to fill both requirements, as may have been the case in verse 521, *wæs mín fæder*, Kemble made sure that the verse contained at least the alliterating syllable.[4] As far as possible, then, Kemble seems to have tried to maintain the twin requirements that every verse contain at least one alliterating syllable and at least one more stressed syllable. But it is clear that he found alliteration a more important guide than stressed syllables.

It is alliteration that, from the point of view of the human lineator, misguides the computer here. In such passages Kemble's principle of balance comes into play and produces verses that fit the grid constructed in the last chapter. The systematic lineator cannot, however, simply abandon the P halflines and fit Kemble's verses into the grid. There must be some systematic way of mediating between mismatched halflines/verses.

The grid itself suggests the way. The grid, which demonstrates Kemble's principle of balance for the halflines/verses of matched verse lines/verse pairs, can be turned into a plotting sheet for mismatched

---

3. See Chapter 1 for a discussion of verse 512.
4. It is possible that Kemble's acute accent over *min* in verse 521 is intended to mark a stress.

halflines/verses. Thus, I try to plot P103a, *þanon untÿdras ealle onpocon eotenas 7 ÿlfe*, as a single halfline. I assign *þanon*, because it does not alliterate, to the second Fine Part of the first HC:

HALFLINE					
HC 1		HC 2		HC 3	
Part 1	Part 2	Part 1	Part 2	Part 1	Part 2
	þanon				

All three syllables of *untÿdras* might be crammed into the first Part of the second HC, where at least the first, the alliterating syllable *un-*, belongs:

FHC		HC	
Part 1	Part 2	Part 1	Part 2
	þanon	untÿdras	

I have tried to cram all of *untÿdras* into the first Part of the second HC in order to fit *ealle on-* into the second Part in accordance with this principle: if the halfline does not begin with an alliterating syllable, the second alliterating syllable may be plotted onto the second Part of the second HC, as in the case of *þordum þeold* (P29a). So I plot *ealle* as the second Part of the same HC:

FHC		HC	
Part 1	Part 2	Part 1	Part 2
	þanon	untÿdras	ealle

The plot shows that something is wrong. The second HC as plotted thus far contains three stressed syllables, *un-*, *tÿ-*, and *eal-*. Nothing would appear amiss if two of these stressed syllables were short or if the passage consisted of only these three syllables. But all three are long, and both the second and third are followed by an unstressed syllable. The two Parts together violate the constraint that no pair of

Fine Parts in the same HC can equal the archetypal halfline, that is, a sequence of two αs. The attempt to plot *untȳdras* and *ealle* in the same HC is thwarted. The second word must be moved into the next HC. The two stressed syllables of *untȳdras* can now be properly distributed between the two Parts of the second HC.

It turns out that *ealle on-* and *-pocon*, too, must be split between the two HCs, since to place them in the same HC would violate the same constraint against re-creating the archetypal halfline in a single HC. So, just as *þanon untȳdras* must be plotted as the two HCs of one halfline, *ealle onpocon* must be plotted as two HCs of the next halfline.

But is the next halfline a three-HC halfline?

HALFLINE					
HC 1		HC 2		HC 3	
Part 1	Part 2	Part 1	Part 2	Part 1	Part 2
eal	le on	po	con	eotenas 7	ȳlfe

Kemble rejected such a distribution, probably because it is possible to pair *eotenas 7 ȳlfe* with *7 orcneas* to end the series of four halflines. I reject the distribution into a three-HC halfline on the grounds that the three-syllable resolution of *eotenas* together with the unstressed syllable 7 approximates the long stressed syllable followed by an unstressed syllable, the α-pattern. Thus, *eotenas 7 ȳlfe* suggests a pattern that has to be spread between two HCs.

One long-standing piece of unfinished business remains. Neither halfline of line P3 matches Kemble's verses 5 and 6. Instead, P3a equals both these verses together, while P3b equals only the first word of Kemble's verse 7. Again plotting sorts out the relationships. The first segment, *hu ða*, fits the second Part of the first HC. Since *æþelinȝas* and *elle[n]* violate the rule that says that the two Parts of the same HC cannot equal the archetypal halfline, *elle[n]* moves into the third HC and *-inȝas* moves into the second Part of the second HC. Together, *elle[n]* and *fremedon* might be accommodated as Part 1 and Part 2 of a third HC. But, since they are not forced into the same HC by what follows, *elle[n]* can occupy one HC and *fremedon* another.

If *elle[n]* thus constitutes the third HC and *fremedon* the fourth, then *Oft* begins the fifth. Since the first halfline of the next verse line contains only three syllables, it is one short of the usual—though not guaranteed—minimum number of syllables per halfline. By moving *Oft* to the beginning of verse 7, the early lineators including Kemble restored the balance between the third and fourth verse pairs. The alliteration of *Oft* with *el-* and *æ-* now creates a subdominant effect.

Whenever the manuscript is both complete and legible, all of the mismatched halflines/verses can be plotted onto the grid in this way. Lines P19 and 20, on the other hand, point up the fact that one of two syllables alliterating on *G* seems to have been lost.

P23 points up another kind of problem that leads to mismatches. I have marked a clause boundary before *sceal*, which thus places that boundary after the end of the last word—a compound, in this case— alliterating on *L*. The computer finds a clause boundary before the first alliterating syllable of the next alliteration, *mæჳ-*, and after the end of the word that contains the last alliterating syllable of the previous alliteration. By moving the word that heads the clause, *sceal*, to the beginning of the next halfline, the computer creates a three-syllable halfline, *[l]ofdædū*. If *sceal* is restored to P23, where Kemble placed it, a more balanced halfline results.

It is now possible to discuss the one instance in the sample passages in which Kemble's lineation shows a small loss of economy. I quote Kemble's verses 71–74:

> mærne be mæste;
> þær wæs madma fela,
> of feor-wegum,
> frætwa ge-læded.

I plot the P lines and then Kemble's verses.

FHC		HC		MHC		HC	
Part 1	Part 2	Part 1	Part 2	Part 1	Part 2	Part 1	Part 2
P35	mær	ne be	mæs	te		þær pæs	mad	ma
P36	fela	of	feor	peჳum	fræt	pa ჳe	læ	ded
K71–72	mær	ne be	mæs	te		þær wæs	madma	fela
K73–74		of	feor-	wegum	fræt	wa ge-	læ	ded

Plotting Kemble's verses produces two empty Parts, one achieved at the expense of alliteration. The two P lines, on the other hand, alliterate correctly and leave only one empty Part. Since both lineations achieve the two-HC norm for each verse or halfline, Kemble did not have to sacrifice alliteration. To the argument in support of Kemble's lineation that *fela* belongs with its dependent noun, *madma*, I counter that *fela* not only alliterates with the *F* line but also bears the same syntactic relationship to *frætpa* later in that line.

Such ambiguous passages are rare. More often, close attention to alliteration produces a disyllabic, one-HC halfline, even if there is no question of a gain or loss of empty Parts; somewhat more often, attending only to alliteration produces both a one-HC halfline and a loss in the economy of Fine Parts, as is the case with *eft* at P21b.

It is important to bear in mind that all variations caused by attention to alliteration and to no other principle of lineation amount to less than 15 percent of the total number of halflines studied. A small percentage of variations between P- and C-Lineation such as at P295/C307–8 result from imperfections in the manuscript. Another small percentage result from the fact that P-Lineation does not take into account rhetorical stress. The long P line 238, which equals C248b plus 249, illustrates the effect of rhetorical stress.

However many variations there are between C- and P-Lineation, the latter is the basis of the former. Nearly every one of Kemble's verses begins with either an alliterating syllable or a proclitic segment to that syllable. The simple principle of P-Lineation, that alliteration is the key to lineation and half-lining, explains and justifies Kemble's versification. Like P-Lineation, Kemble's lineation is principled. Whenever the two lineations diverge, the divergence is caused not so much by Kemble's ignoring alliteration but by his application of additional principles.

Kemble probably intuited the most important of the additional principles, the two-HC norm, from passages in which alliteration provides an unambiguous guide to lineation. In these verses alliteration does not continue beyond a third syllable—sometimes it is completed with a second syllable—nor does the new alliteration begin early. The 674 matches between Kemble's verses and the corresponding P halflines are of this sort. All but a handful of these verses can be construed into exactly two HCs.

Most of the mismatches between Kemble's verses and the computer's halflines have been caused by either early or continuing alliteration. When Kemble encountered these phenomena, he simply divided verses in such a way that every verse contained at least one alliterating syllable and no verse contained more than two. Thus, whenever his general method seemed in danger of reconstructing unusually long verses, he applied the principles derived from his intuition of the two-HC norm.

Early alliteration accounts for the mismatching of 68 verses/halflines. Continuing alliteration accounts for the mismatching of 44 verses/halflines. A third pattern, in which a stressed syllable at the end of one of Kemble's verses shares the same initial sound with a stressed syllable at the beginning of the next verse, causes a total of four mismatches.[5] Thus, unusual patterns of alliteration cause the mismatching of 116 verses/halflines, or 13.4 percent of the total. When the P halflines are replotted and "balanced" in accord with Kemble's principles, the match between Kemble's verses and P halflines increases to 92 percent. A clause boundary that occurs early, that is, after the end of the word that contains the last alliterating syllable but before the syllable with which Kemble begins the following verse, accounts for twenty-two mismatches. The replotted halflines of this type increase the match to 94.4 percent. Sixteen halflines mismatched because Kemble has selected for stress a word that normally is unstressed, when replotted, increase the match to 96.3 percent. The remaining mismatches are caused by the state of the manuscript.

P halflines can, then, be plotted according to Kemble's principle of the two-HC norm to match 828 of Kemble's 860 verses in the two samples. The thirty-two mismatches that remain are largely caused by defects in the manuscript that led Kemble to emend certain verses. The 96.3 percent match between P halflines plus replotted P halflines and Kemble's verses verifies the strong form of the first major hypothesis: Kemble elicited all of the verses of the consensus by the application of a method to the indications of the syllables in the manuscript text. Kemble's method includes not only eliciting verses on the basis of alliteration but also the principled breaking up of long alliterations.

---

5. I quote the two examples of this unusual pattern of alliteration: first, *nihtum* (135V08), since it alliterates with the adverb *no* that follows immediately, joins with the latter to create verse line P159. Second, *topehtan* and *ʒepat* (197V10) create verse line PA4.

Kemble's intuition of the two-HC norm, as I have demonstrated, is firmly based on the poet's usual practice as shown by the grid in Table 7.1. The grid indicates something else as well, that the poet was very likely guided in composing his verses by a simple but powerful rhythm. That rhythm is the subject of the next chapter.

Chapter 9

The Rhythm of Beowulf

Every syllable in the two-part sample analyzed in this study either has been or can be distributed in accordance with specified procedures and principles. Some groups of syllables have fallen into place early and thus have helped determine the places of others. Some, like *Oft* in verse line 4, have had to be fitted into place after much trial and error. The result is the "great net" or grid of Chapter 7, into which, as I showed in Chapter 8, the remaining passages of the two samples can also be plotted. There is a strong presumption that the syllables of the unsampled remainder of the poem (approximately 87 percent of the total number in the poem) can be distributed in the same way.

The procedures for distributing syllables into an eight-part grid work from the "top down." That is, the prosodist begins by eliciting verse lines from the representations of the syllables in the manuscript. The verse line is thus an asymmetrical constituent of the text as a whole. The two halflines into which every verse line can then be divided are the symmetrical constituents of that verse line.

Many of the halflines are synthetic. The demonstration of the strong form of the second major hypothesis of this study, that Kemble's method of verse lineation provides the key to the constituents of every halfline, begins to emerge during the process of determining verse lines and halflines. A tentative verification of that hypothesis consists of the fact that one can construct the grid of Chapter 7.

In that chapter an even more interesting fact emerges. Every halfline constituent—HC—can be divided into two Parts. Indeed, the HCs must be divided into two Parts in order to construct the grid. The Parts of the HCs have become evident in the process of comparing those HCs that have emerged from Kemble's versification.

It is clear that prosodists have missed something about the way the verses have been extracted from the manuscript text. Even John Pope, who might have justified his analysis of "B" and "C" verses on the basis of the synthesized halflines of the lineator, seems unaware of the support he would have found for his theory had he examined the process of verse lineation.

Pope has identified the constituents of the halfline, the HCs, as *measures*. In *The Rhythm of Beowulf* he has attempted to determine every measure of the poem and to work out the precise time for speaking each syllable according to an analogy with music. Although a few of Pope's "measures" cannot be justified according to the procedures of constituent analysis, and although his quasi-musical notation is unnecessarily precise, he has found the proper term for what I have been calling HCs.[1] The HCs are the *measures* of the halflines. In the remaining pages of this study and elsewhere I shall refer to HCs as measures.

The use of the term *measure* for the two (or, rarely, three) constituents of the Beowulfian halfline indicates important features of these constituents. A musical measure is a clearly marked segment. The onset of 80 percent of the measures of *Beowulf* is marked by the occurrence of the most heavily stressed syllable. A musical measure can contain a varying number of notes. A measure of *Beowulf* can consist of as few as one or as many as six syllables.[2]

There is another way in which the musical analogy works. It accounts for the "missing" heavy initial stresses in the 230 halflines of the sample passages that do not begin with a stressed syllable. Pope hypothesized that these apparently "headless verses" begin with a stress that does not fall on a *syllable*. It falls, instead, he conjectured, on a *rest* that might have been filled in by an accompaniment played on an instrument.

The present study supports Pope's conjecture. The first Fine Part in such measures is very often "empty." Yet such empty Fine Parts "stack" with the 60 percent in this position that begin with an alliter-

---

1. All of Pope's so-called examples of "Types B, C, and D with *anacrusis*" (my emphasis) show confusion between *measure* division, which can only be determined by the procedures discussed above in Chapter 6, and *Part* division, for which see Chapter 7.

2. In his Types A, D, and E, Sievers (usually correctly) isolated *measures* (which can consist of a variable number of syllables) apparently without realizing he had done so. Conybeare is more accurate in dividing the "feet" of what Sievers was later to call "Type A verses" into trochees and dactyls. (See William D. Conybeare, ed., *Illustrations of Anglo-Saxon Poetry* . . . [London, 1826], ix–xi, in particular.)

ating stressed syllable. Pope's brilliant hypothesis has remained untested for more than forty-five years because neither Pope nor anyone else has pointed out that a careful analysis of the relationships among the syllables represented in the manuscript text makes it possible to construct a grid in which an empty Fine Part can be precisely located. The present study has, then, developed a way of turning Pope's conjecture into a hypothesis and testing it.

Despite the careful way in which Pope notated every syllable, he did not carry his analysis far enough. The present study goes beyond verifying Pope's measure hypothesis and identifies the constituents of the measure. Eighty percent of the measures consist of a more heavily stressed syllable followed by a more lightly stressed syllable. These measures begin with what is perceived to be the heaviest stress in that measure. Stacking in the grid aligns such heavily stressed syllables with a Fine Part that is empty of syllables. The first Fine Part of the first measure of a halfline, then, always begins either with a stressed syllable or with something that seems to "stand in" for that stressed syllable. Similarly, an empty second Fine Part in either measure of the halfline can be supplied by something that stands in for an unstressed syllable. Pope conjectured that that "something" in either Part may have been either a rest, or a note or passage played on an accompanying instrument.

Pope's most interesting conjecture is contained in the title of his book, *The Rhythm of Beowulf*. The present study provides support for the theory that the poet was guided by a rhythm as he performed the verses of his poem. I summarize in the following section the evidence for what I shall state now as a hypothesis: a simple two-part rhythm controls the distribution of every syllable in the poem.

SUMMARY OF THE EVIDENCE FOR INTERPRETING THE DATA AS INDICATING A RHYTHM

1. The fact that the syllables of the "third-level-down" constituents (measures) can always be divided into just two Fine Parts.
   This fact suggests a two-part rhythm.

2. The irreversibility of bottom-level constituents (Fine Parts).
   The constituents of two higher levels (2: halflines; 3: measures) can at times be reversed. A verse line (top level) can also take the place of another verse line. At the lowest level, however, reversibility or re-

placeability is no longer possible: the first Fine Part appears to be radically different from the second.

In theory—and sometimes in practice—one verse line can replace another. For example, verse line 405, *beopulf maðelode   on him byrne scan*, might replace 529, *beopulf maþelode   bearn ecᵹþeopes*. The two half-lines of a verse line might, at times, trade places, for example at 126 *mid ærdæᵹe   ða pæs on uhtan*. Perhaps even more frequently, the order of the two measures of a halfline might be reversed:

*ᵹyldan ᵹomban	11a
*funden feasceaft	7a
*eafera scyldes	19a
*feran [fe]lahror	27a
*feohᵹiftum fromum	21a
*fær æþelinᵹes	33b
*morᵹenspeᵹ micel	129a

But *-dan*, the second Part of the second measure of 11a, cannot trade places with *ᵹyl-*, nor can *-sceaft*, the second Part of the first measure of 7a, trade places with *fea-*. The two Fine Parts of these—and all—measures are irreversible, thereby suggesting an alternation of heavy and lighter stress.

3. The "emptiness" of either (but not both) of the two Fine Parts of the first measure of a verse and the emptiness of the second Fine Part (never the first) of the second measure of the verse.

Such empty Parts provide the strongest argument for interpreting the data in terms of a rhythm that can be communicated by the use of what are perceived to be precisely timed pauses. In effect, the empty Fine Part transmits the sense of a rhythm even more effectively than the performance of "filled" Parts.

4. The variability in the number of syllables in measures.

The number of syllables in a single measure ranges from one to six. Giving every syllable equal length results in an "irrational" or prose rhythm; giving stressed syllables more length to accentuate their importance also results in an irrational rhythm. Neither of these choices is, however, necessary. On the contrary, the performer can learn to perform so that the syllabic and nonsyllabic material, despite the varying length and weight of the former, create a sense that the time it takes to perform one measure is equal to the time it takes to perform any other measure.

5. The variability in the number of stressed syllables in measures.

A given measure may contain, on the one hand, as many as three or, on the other hand, as few as no stressed syllables. This fact is the strongest argument against analyzing the syllables of the poem into "feet."

6. The fact that the first Fine Part begins with the most heavily stressed syllable in the measure in 80 percent of the measures.

This fact points to the likelihood that the rhythm begins with a (heavy) downbeat and ends with a (light) upbeat.

There is at least one other piece of evidence for a simple, two-part rhythm beginning with a downbeat: it is possible to *perform* the poem effectively according to this rhythm. The performer soon learns to deliver each measure as one complete rhythmic pulse: downbeat/upbeat.

The performer learns to detect the rhythm whether a beat falls on or rises over syllabic or nonsyllabic material. The rhythm can be sustained on or over several syllables at a time. A virtuoso of the poetic tradition might even, on occasion, crowd as many as four syllables under the upbeat or downbeat. But most often the pulse begins on one long stressed syllable marking the downbeat, followed by a single, often short, syllable—or two such syllables—under the upbeat. In this way the performance of the poem depends upon what I called in Chapter 6 the "double archetypal stress pattern," $\alpha + \alpha$ (1/ 0 + 1/ 0).

It is necessary to ask whether there is any way of accounting for the distribution of syllables other than as indications of a rhythm. I do not think there is. The simplest interpretation of the groupings of syllabic and nonsyllabic material appears to be this: the text was produced as a series of rhythmic pulses, each completed by the second Fine Part of the measure.

The concept of a simple rhythmic pulse provides independent verification of the hypothesis that every measure can be divided into two and only two Fine Parts. This concept thus becomes the keystone of the system, locking all of the elements into place. To put it differently, the rhythm indicates a simple way to control great diversity, diversity indicated by the varying numbers of syllables in halflines and the variety of combinations in measures of such syllabic features as stress and length.

The grid thus indicates a way to perform the poem: the performer simply translates the measures (HCs in the grid) into units of time that can be perceived as identical. The most important goal of a prosody has thus been achieved.

DEFINITIONS OF PROSODIC UNITS

It is now possible to refine the definitions of the verse line and the halfline/verse. Tentative definitions of these constituents appear in the section titled "The First Major Hypothesis" in Chapter 1. A more accurate definition of the verse line runs as follows: a verse line is a sequence of measures (usually four, but sometimes five or six) that begins either with the first alliterating syllable of an alliteration or with the rest before (or musical augmentation of) the proclitic passage (beginning with a clause boundary or a proclitic word or syllable) to the first alliterating syllable; the verse line ends just before either the first syllable of the next alliteration or the rest before (or musical augmentation of) the proclitic passage to that syllable. To put it more simply: a verse line is a sequence of measures based on an alliteration. The beginning of the verse line is determined, but not necessarily marked, by the first alliterating syllable of the series. The *second* half-line of the verse line consists of the measure that begins either with the last alliterating syllable of an alliteration or with a rest before (or musical augmentation of) the proclitic passage to the last alliterating syllable and continues with the remaining measure(s) of the verse line. The *first* halfline consists of the first measure of the verse line and the remaining measures up to the beginning of the second half-line.

These definitions bring to an end more than 150 years of uncertainty about the larger prosodic structures of the poem. This study makes it clear that every constituent of Beowulfian prosody represents a passage heard in a continuum of sound.

STRESS AND RHYTHM

The analysis of recoverable features and functions of syllables, Chapter 3, begins with stress, the most basic feature of the prosody. Every syllable of the poem has been distributed into one of the two Fine Parts of its measures largely on the basis of stress. Stress and the alliteration of stressed syllables are the most important keys to the rhythm of the poem. Yet an apparent paradox emerges if we look at the placement of certain syllables in the grid in Chapter 7. I take one example: stress, alliteration, and the fact that it marks a clause boundary assign the unstressed syllable *Ne* of manuscript line 132V13 to the first Fine Part of halfline 38a, to a position occupied by a stressed syllable. The paradox disappears when we realize that it is not necessary to argue that *Ne* acquires more than its usual light stress simply because it has been distributed into the first Part of a measure. Unstressed *Ne* can mark the beginning of its verse line even as it maintains its usual light stress. That is because this study has made it possible to recover the rhythm of the original performance. *Ne* does not need to be stressed because the *rhythm* marks the beginning of a new verse line. This fact suggests that the modern performer can develop a degree of control that permits him or her to play with stress—to raise or lower somewhat the stress of a particular syllable—so long as he or she does so within the constraints of the rhythm. This study offers to the modern performer, then, something like the same degree of freedom that the Anglo-Saxon *scop* exercised during the first performance of the poem.

Appendix A

Procedures for Systematically Eliciting Verse Lines and Halflines from Manuscript Lines

Marking the manuscript text (encoding the syllables of the manuscript for computer analysis)

1. Mark stresses.
    A. Mark for heavy stress the stem syllable of every simplex belonging to the following nine categories:
        Nouns
        Adjectives
        Inflected verbs (*except* finite forms of the copula [*pesan, beon, eom*] and *peorðan*)
        Adverbs
        Infinitives
        Present participles
        Past participles
        Pronouns (*except* personal, interrogative, possessive, and demonstrative)
        Numbers;
        Mark for heavy stress the stem syllable of *both* elements of all compounds *except* compound conjunctions (such as *sippan*);
        Mark for heavy stress the first or only syllable of all formative affixes *except* those derived from case endings or such worn-down (nonsyllabic) forms as -ȝ- from -iȝ-.
    B. Mark all remaining syllables to indicate weak stress.
        (Note on marking/encoding: The acute accent (´) or virgule (/) is useful for marking stressed syllables on reproductions of the manuscript. For computer processing I have marked every stressed syllable 1, every unstressed syllable 0.)
2. Determine dominant alliterations.
    A. Do not mark the stem syllables of second elements of compounds.
    B. Mark all alliterating syllables listed under 1A that are within range.
        Range is measured by the interposition of no more than two syllables of the types listed under 1A plus no more than one subdominant syllable (defined as the stem syllable of the second element of a compound).

(Note on marking/encoding: Underlining the initial letter(s) is useful for marking alliterating syllables on reproductions of the manuscript. For computer processing I have marked every alliterating syllable 2, that is, I have changed from 1 to 2 every stressed syllable within range of another stressed syllable that has the same initial sound.

The maximum range of dominant alliteration as defined above can be illustrated by the following passage:

$$\text{[m]id } \acute{y}\text{ldum· } \text{þ hit pearð } ealʒearo\ heal{\ae}r$$

$$\text{na mæst scop him } heort\ \text{naman se þe his} \qquad (133\text{Vo}8\text{–}9)$$

heort alliterates with *heal* since only two potentially dominant syllables, *mæst* and *scop*, and only one subdominant, *ærn*, are interposed between the two stressed syllables that begin with the same sound.)

3. Determine clause boundaries.
   A. Mark the first syllable of every successive or blended clause.
   (Note on marking/encoding: Triple underlining of the first letter of the first word in a clause may be a useful way of marking the beginning of a clause on reproductions of the manuscript. For computer processing I have marked every syllable that heads a clause 3.)
4. Mark appropriate proclitics.
   A. Mark the first or only proclitic to the first syllable of a dominant alliteration *unless* the proclitic coincides with or is preceded by a clause boundary at an unstressed syllable. A proclitic is an unstressed syllable or syllables—whether bound (such as a prefix) or free—that is or are generally to be associated with a following rather than a preceding stressed syllable.
   B. Mark the first or only proclitic to the last alliterating syllable of a series. (Do not mark proclitics to any intervening alliterating syllable.)
   C. Mark heavy stress on any proclitic shifted from its normal position.
   (Note on marking/encoding: Placing a vertical bar before the first letter of the first or only proclitic to the first alliteration of a series may be a useful way of marking proclitics on reproductions of the manuscript. For computer processing I have marked such syllables with a 4. A shifted proclitic (4C) should be marked 1 or, if it alliterates, 2.)
5. Lineate and Half-Line.
   A. Determine the first syllable of each verse line and place an "F" before that syllable. The "F" will be:
      —either the first alliterating syllable (marked "2" for computer programming);
      —or the first clause boundary ("3") after the end of the word containing the last alliterating syllable of the preceding alliteration;
      —or the first or only proclitic syllable to the first alliterating syllable of the series ("4").

B. Mark the midpoint (the beginning of the second halfline) of the verse line by placing an "M" before that syllable. The "M" will be:
   —either the last alliterating syllable of a series;
   —or the first clause boundary between the next-to-last and last alliterating syllables;
   —or the first or only proclitic syllable to the last alliterating syllable of the series.

Appendix B

How To Scan the Verses of an Edited Text

Begin with simple verses, for example, the two verses of verse line 195 in Klaeber's third edition:[1]

gōd mid Gēatum, Grendles dǽda;

1. Mark every stressed syllable:

gōd mid Gēatum Grendles dǽda

2. Mark every *long* stressed syllable unless it is already marked:

gōd mid Gēatum Grendles dǽda

3. Place a vertical measure bar before the first alliterating syllable in each verse (halfline):

| gōd mid Gēatum | Grendles dǽda

4. If the first verse (halfline) begins with an alliterating syllable and contains a second alliterating syllable, place a measure bar before that syllable. (Otherwise, go to 9, below.)

| gōd mid | Gēatum | Grendles dǽda

5. If either verse contains only one stressed syllable in addition to the alliterating syllable, place a vertical measure bar before that syllable:

1. Fr. Klaeber, ed., *Beowulf and the Fight at Finnsburg,* 3d ed. (Boston: D. C. Heath, 1950).

| gód mid | Géatum | Grendles | dǽda

A simple verse line like 195 is now completely divided into its measures.

6. If the syllable that heads a measure is long and the measure contains no other stressed syllable, place a dotted vertical bar before the first syllable after the long stressed syllable:

| gód : mid | Géa : tum | Grend : les | dǽ : da

Simple measures, like those in the two verses/halflines of verse line 195, are now divided into their two Fine Parts.

These six steps will serve to locate all the Fine Parts of simple verse lines, such as 810 and 211:

> mōdes myrðe   manna cynne,
>
> bāt under beorge.   Beornas gearwe

For a verse line like 231, additional steps are needed to determine the Fine Parts of the first measure. Begin to analyze the verse line by performing steps 1–5.

> beran ofer bolcan   beorhte randas,

Apply step 6 to the last three stressed syllables:

| beran ofer | bol : can | beorh : te | ran : das

Now apply step 7 to the first stressed syllable:

7. If a stressed syllable is short, resolve it with the second syllable in the same word whether that syllable is long or short. If the word consists of three syllables (not four) and the first two are short, resolve all three syllables.

> beran ofer

8. Place a dotted vertical bar after the resolved pair or triplet:

> beran : ofer

Verse line 231 has now been divided into its Fine Parts.

9. If the verse/halfline does not begin with an alliterating syllable, place a measure bar a bit to the left of the first syllable of the measure and then apply steps 2 and 3:

| sē þe | hólmclífu |héaldan scólde,   230

Apply steps 5 and 6 to the verse/halfline that begins with an alliterating syllable. If this is the first verse of the verse line, it may also be necessary to apply step 4:

| héal : dan | scól : de

10. If a measure that begins with a stressed syllable contains a second stressed syllable, place a dotted vertical bar before the second stressed syllable:

| hólm : clífu

11. Divide the syllables of a measure that contains no alliterating syllable as follows:

(a) If the measure begins with a stressed syllable and contains no more than three syllables, place a dotted vertical bar before the stressed syllable, as with *lēton* in the following example (to which all appropriate steps have been applied):

| héah : ofer | héa : fod, | : lēton | hólm : béran   48

(b) If the measure begins with or contains a stressed syllable and contains four or more syllables, place the dotted vertical bar in such a way as to take account of word- or phrase-boundaries as far as possible and so that no more than three syllables will fall in either Part, as in the first measure of the following example:

| Nalǣs : hí hine | lǣs:san | lá : cum | téo : dan,   43

(c) If the measure contains but does not begin with a stressed syllable and the stressed syllable is followed by no more than two syllables, place a dotted vertical bar before the stressed syllable, as in the first measure of the following example:

| ne : hȳrde ic |cȳm : lí cor | céol : ge | gȳ̄r : wan   38

(d) If the measure contains no stressed syllable and no more than three syllables, place a dotted vertical bar before the first syllable, as in the first measure of the following example:

| ⦙ Ðā wæs on | bū̄r : gum | Béo : wū̄lf | Scȳl : dí nga,   53

(e) If the measure contains no stressed syllable but contains four or more syllables, place a dotted vertical bar before one of the syllables in such a way as (1) to avoid as far as possible violating word- and phrase-boundaries and (2) to distribute no more than three syllables into either Part, as in the first measure of the following example:

| hī hyne : þā æt |bǣ ⦙ ron | ⦙ tō | brímes : fároðe,   28

12. Place a stress sign (/ for heavy stress, x for light) in parentheses in an empty (or over an "improperly filled") Part:

| (/) ⦙ sē þe |hólm : clífu . . .   230

| (/) hī   hyne : þā æt | bǣ ⦙ron . . .   28

| wéras : on | wíl : sī́ð | wúdu : (x)| bún : denne.   216

13. If a measure contains a third stressed syllable, place a dotted bar before the stressed syllable of a simplex in preference to the second element of a compound:

| fȳrd : séaru | fū̄s : lícu; | (/) ⦙ híne | fýrwyt : bræc   232

Appendix C

Encoding the Syllables of the Manuscript for Computer

Each group of symbols set off by a space represents one syllable. Each syllable is encoded according to whether or not it begins a clause; if it does, the numeral "3" appears before the 0, 1, or 2. A "0" indicates that the syllable is unstressed, a "1" indicates that it is stressed. If a "1" has the same initial sound as another "1" that is not separated from it by more than three "1s" each of which begins with a different sound, the two "1s" that thus establish an alliteration within verse line range are raised to "2s." The first syllable of a proclitic passage to the first or last "2" of a series will be marked "4" before the "0" indicating the weak stress of the proclitic.

A capital letter indicates the initial sound of the syllable. "B," for example, indicates that the initial sound of the syllable is *b*, "C" that it is *c* or *k*, "D" that it is *d*, and so on. "V" indicates that the initial sound of the syllable is *vocalic*, that is, *a, æ, e, i, o, u*, or *y*, or one of the diphthongs. I use "A" to indicate the sound represented by *sp*, "I" to indicate the sound represented by *st*, "K" to indicate the sound represented by *sc*, and "U" to indicate the sound represented by *þ* or *ð*.

The sign for the initial sound of the syllable is followed by either "/" to indicate that the syllable is long or "-" to indicate that the syllable is short. If the syllable is not the last in the word, it is simply followed by one empty space. If it is the last, it is followed by an "*" that is in turn followed by an empty space. If the syllable is the last in the first element of a compound, it is followed by a " + " and then an empty space. The last syllable in the manuscript line is marked by a "Z" set off both by the space after the last syllable and by a following space.